TiA
2120

CW00541025

10/27

WITHDRAWN

B000 000 027 9180

ABERDEEN LIBRARIES

FINDING YOUR
SCOTTISH
ANCESTORS

Techniques for Solving Genealogy Problems

In memory of my grandmother,
Mary Sneddon McNeil (1919–2001)

FINDING YOUR SCOTTISH ANCESTORS

Techniques for Solving Genealogy Problems

KIRSTY F. WILKINSON

ROBERT HALE

First published in 2020 by
Robert Hale, an imprint of
The Crowood Press Ltd,
Ramsbury, Marlborough,
Wiltshire SN8 2HR

enquiries@crowood.com

www.crowood.com

© Kirsty F. Wilkinson 2020

All rights reserved. No part of this publication may be
reproduced or transmitted in any form or by any means,
electronic or mechanical, including photocopy, recording
or any information storage and retrieval system, without
permission in writing from the publishers.

British Library Cataloguing-in-Publication Data

A catalogue record for this book is available from the
British Library.

ISBN 978 0 7198 3053 2

The right of Kirsty F. Wilkinson to be identified as author
of this work has been asserted by her in accordance with
the Copyright, Designs and Patents Act 1988.

Typeset by Chapter One Book Production, Knebworth
Printed and bound in India by Parksons Graphics

Contents

Acknowledgements

This book is the product of many years spent tracing Scottish ancestors and learning from the work of others. As such, it is not possible to acknowledge everyone who has contributed to it in some way, but my particular thanks go to the following: my clients, past and present, for entrusting me with their family history research and presenting me with many interesting problems to solve. My many friends in genealogy, online and in person, who have generously shared their knowledge and expertise over the years, and in particular Celia Heritage, who provided helpful feedback on an early draft. My publishers for their patience during what turned out to be a somewhat lengthier writing process than anticipated. My parents for gifting me the ancestors, who continue to inspire my family history research. And last but not least, my husband Phil for proof reading and for being an unwavering source of support.

Introduction

This book is aimed primarily at those who have begun the journey of discovering their Scottish ancestors, but who find themselves facing problems that prevent them from progressing their research further, commonly known in family history circles as 'brick walls'.

The term 'brick wall' has become something of a cliché in the world of genealogy. Pick up any family history magazine and you are likely to find an article or two promising to help you break through one. A brick wall is generally considered to be a problem that prevents a particular person or family line from being traced further. However, the term may also be used more broadly to describe any genealogy problem, such as when an individual cannot be found in records in which they are expected to appear (such as in a census taken during their lifetime), even if that doesn't prevent them from being traced further.

This book provides a range of information, advice and techniques to help solve these genealogy problems. The first three chapters describe the main records used to trace Scottish ancestors, and the repositories and websites where those records can be found. The next three chapters discuss good research techniques, and some of the approaches that genealogists worldwide have developed to ensure their research is thorough and accurate. Chapter 7 looks at some of the reasons we may encounter difficulties when tracing our ancestors, and at solutions that may be applicable to many different situations. The final chapter deals with some specific genealogy problems and the sources available to tackle them, as well as looking at ways to take research further.

This arrangement reflects my own belief that many so-called brick walls are of our own making. Genealogy problems may be caused not only by a lack of knowledge of records and an inability to access them, but also by a failure to search effectively, approaching a problem with too narrow a perspective, and an unawareness of how to correctly interpret information found in records and to use that information to advance research.

It is no exaggeration to say that the availability of digitized records online, an area in which Scotland has been well ahead of her neighbours, has revolutionized genealogical research. When I first became interested in family history I would visit my local library after work on one of the evenings it was open late, hope to get a seat at one of the few microfilm readers, spend hours scrolling through census microfilms, and with luck, perhaps find one record of my family before closing time. Today I can access the same records, fully indexed, from home, at three in the morning whilst wearing my pyjamas (if I so choose!) and can quite literally find my ancestors at the click of a button. This has made tracing Scottish family history much easier, and has opened up genealogy to a far wider audience. But it has also created new problems, particularly in terms of searching online databases, and it has certainly not eliminated the need for good research technique.

When I decided I wanted to learn more about my Scottish ancestors, my first trip was to the library to borrow a book on tracing family history. I had little idea what I needed to know in order to get started, but found myself learning about what records were available, why they were created, where they could be found, and how to use them to trace my family tree. Before I began to scroll through those census microfilms, I had to consider where my ancestors were most likely to be living at that time. When I finally found them, I had a good understanding not only of the census records and their arrangement, but also of my ancestors' community.

Today's beginner is most likely to start their research online and with a website that invites them to simply type in an ancestor's name. That is not to say research guidance isn't available online – there is plenty of useful information to be found on websites hosting genealogical records and elsewhere – but it is often up to the individual to seek it out. It is surprisingly easy for the newly fledged family historian to trace several generations of their family, even quite accurately, with little understanding of the records they are using. It may only be when a problem is encountered that any outside guidance is sought.

I am certainly not advocating a return to the old way of tracing family history (if for no other reason than I rather enjoy researching in my pyjamas!), but I would argue that the need for good research practices is greater than ever if we are to get the most out of online records. And if we hope to solve the more challenging research problems, we need to look beyond the records available online to the many treasures to be found in Scotland's archives.

Good genealogical research technique means not only familiarizing ourselves with archival sources, but also changing how we approach a particular problem. Instead of thinking of which website or database we need to search, we should instead think about what records may exist that could solve our problem and how to access those records, whether that be online, in an archive, or by searching an online or published index prior to visiting a physical repository.

It is easy to imagine that the answer to our brick wall lies in a document hidden in some 'dusty' archive, which will unequivocally provide the answer we are seeking (if only someone would digitize it and put it online!). But in many cases the document we imagine will solve our problem may not survive, or may never have been created in the first place. It is by conducting thorough, methodical research, by analysing available records, extracting small clues and comparing information found in different sources that we can begin to piece together a possible solution. Often we don't so much break through a brick wall as find a way round it.

A book of this size cannot hope to cover all possible genealogy problems, or all the sources that may be used to solve them. However, it does give guidance on tackling some of the most commonly encountered issues, and provides details of a wide range of Scottish records, some of which may be unfamiliar to readers. Tips on using particular records or techniques are given in short 'Expert Tip' boxes throughout the text, while in Chapters 7 and 8 a list of 'solutions' at the end of each section summarizes the main points. Suggestions for additional study, and a list of further reading that expands upon the information given in this book, are provided at the end.

Those who have picked up this book in the hope of solving a

specific genealogy problem may be tempted to skip straight to the relevant section. I would recommend instead that you begin by reading the chapters on research techniques (Chapters 4 to 7), or at least that you read them before beginning research. You may well find that the solution to your brick wall is one that applies to many different situations, such as an indexing error or spelling variation, or that by spending time analysing the information you have already gathered and taking a more methodical approach to your problem, the answer becomes readily apparent.

I hope that, whatever your level of experience in tracing your Scottish forebears, this book will provide you with some new suggestions for tackling old family history problems, and that it will inspire you to look at your research afresh. Finally, I wish you good luck in finding your Scottish ancestors, however elusive they may be!

1 Sources for Scottish Family History Research

There are many different kinds of historical record that can be used to trace ancestors who lived in Scotland and to resolve family history problems. This chapter describes the main sources used in Scottish genealogy research as well as some lesser known records.

More information on these sources can be found in the record guides within the 'Help and guidance' section of the ScotlandsPeople website (www.scotlandspeople.gov.uk) and the research guides on the National Records of Scotland website (www.nrscotland.gov. uk) as well as in the publications listed in the 'Further Reading' section of this book.

Statutory Registers of Births, Marriages and Deaths

Civil registration of births, marriages and deaths began in Scotland on 1 January 1855, and the resulting records are known as the statutory registers of births, deaths and marriages. From the start, registration was compulsory and free, and so the statutory registers provide a more or less complete record of every birth, marriage and death that has occurred in Scotland from 1855 until the present day.

Most family historians begin their research in the statutory registers, perhaps with their own birth, or that of a parent or grand-parent. The registers have been digitized and are fully indexed. They can be accessed at the ScotlandsPeople Centre in Edinburgh (part of the National Records of Scotland), at one of the associated Local Family History Centres around Scotland, or online through the ScotlandsPeople website (www.scotlandspeople.gov.uk).

When statutory registration was first introduced, Scotland was divided into registration districts (initially a total of 1,027), mainly based on existing parishes. A separate register of births, marriages and deaths was kept for each registration district, and at the end of each year the register was closed and a copy transmitted to the General Register Office in Edinburgh.

In 1855, the first year of statutory registration, more information was collected than in later years. However, this was found to be impractical, and from 1856 onwards the amount of information was reduced, although the exact details recorded have varied over the years. This means that 1855 is a particularly significant year for family historians, and you can count yourself as very lucky if one of your ancestors was born, married or died in that year. If the birth, marriage or death of an ancestor's sibling was registered in 1855, then it is particularly worth seeking out the record, as the information on birthplace and parents may well assist in tracing your own line.

From 1856, the statutory registers of births provide the following details:

- Name and surname of the child
- Date, time and location of the birth
- Sex of the child

A page from the Statutory Register of Births.
CROWN COPYRIGHT, NATIONAL RECORDS OF SCOTLAND

- Father's name and occupation
- Mother's name, including maiden surname and any former married surnames
- Parents' usual place of residence (if not the same as the place of birth)
- Signature, designation and residence of the informant (often, but not always, one of the parents)
- Date of registration and signature of the registrar

The date of the parents' marriage, a particularly useful piece of information, was added in 1861. The basic format of the birth record remained unchanged until the later twentieth century, and the details recorded remain very similar today.

EXPERT TIP

A peculiarity of the Scottish registration system that can cause confusion is that until 1934 if a birth took place in a different registration district from where the father usually resided (or the mother in the case of an illegitimate birth), a copy of the birth entry was sent to the registrar of the district of residence and the birth was also entered into the register there. This can make it appear as if a birth has been mistakenly registered twice. In fact if both entries are examined, it will be apparent that one is the original (containing the original signature of the informant) and the other is a copy, with a note in the margin cross-referencing to the original registration.

When a couple married in Scotland, details were entered on to a form known as a 'schedule', which was filled in by the person officiating the marriage. This form was then taken to the relevant registrar who entered the details into the marriage register for the district. For this reason, marriage records do not include the original signatures of the bride and groom.

From 1856, marriage records include the following information:

- Date and location of the marriage
- Mode of celebration (for example, by the forms of which church)

- Name, occupation and marital status of each party (although occupations were not always recorded for women, even those who worked)
- Relationship between the bride and groom (if any)
- Age and usual residence of each
- Names of both sets of parents, including father's occupation and mother's maiden surname
- Names of the officiating minister and two witnesses
- Date of registration and the signature of the registrar

EXPERT TIP

In the nineteenth century, most marriages in Scotland did not take place in a church. The most common location was the bride's home, although the manse (the minister's home) and hotels were also popular. In order to determine which church the couple attended, in particular the bride as it was most likely her minister who performed the marriage, note by what forms the marriage was performed (for example, 'according to the forms of the Church of Scotland') and the name and designation of the minister. The designation of the minister may state which church he was attached to (and in rural parishes there may have been only one church of each denomination), but if not, it may be necessary to consult directories and biographical dictionaries of church ministers in order to identify the relevant church. Knowing which church a family attended is particularly important when researching in the pre-1855 period, but as churches kept their own collections of useful records, it may also be helpful after 1855.

Scottish death records are an important genealogical source because they record not only when and where a person died, but also give the names of parents and any spouses. It should be noted, however, that information may only be as reliable as the knowledge of the informant, who was not always a close relative.

The information found on a death record includes:

- Name of the deceased
- Occupation (rarely recorded for married women)
- Marital status, along with the names and occupations of all spouses (current and former)

- Date, time and location of the death
- Usual residence (if not the same as the place of death)
- Sex and age
- Names of parents, including father's occupation and mother's maiden surname, and whether they were deceased
- Cause of death and the name of any attending medical practitioner
- Signature and qualification of the informant
- Date of registration and the signature of the registrar

In the period 1855–1860, the place of burial and the name of the undertaker were recorded, although the name of any spouse was not included in the period 1856–1860. Since 1967, the person's full date of birth has been given as well as their age, but not their place of birth.

EXPERT TIP

Scottish death records are indexed under all surnames by which a person has been, or may have been, known. This means that married women are indexed under both maiden and married surnames, and both surnames can be entered into search fields together (as 'surname' and 'other surname') in order to identify the correct entry. As a result, women's deaths are often easier to locate than men's. When searching for the deaths of a married couple, search for the woman's death first. Her death record will show whether her husband was then living or dead, and so narrows down the time period in which he is likely to have died.

In addition to the above records, from 1860 each registration district maintained a separate register known as the Register of Corrected Entries. This relates to births, marriages and deaths, and records either an alteration or additional information concerning a registered event. The registers of corrected entries and the records they contain are generally referred to as RCEs. Common reasons for an RCE relating to a birth include a change of name, the legitimization of an illegitimate child by the subsequent marriage of its parents, and the addition of a father's name to an illegitimate birth originally recorded without one (often as the result of a court case). RCEs added to a marriage record usually concern a subsequent divorce, or the marriage being identified as bigamous and therefore invalid. An RCE relating to a death frequently reports the result of a precognition by the procurator fiscal into a sudden or suspicious death, and may give additional details regarding the cause of death and circumstances surrounding it.

The registers of corrected entries cannot be searched directly, but digitization and linking means that any RCEs relating to a record of interest can be easily accessed. When an RCE was created, a note was originally written in the left margin of the relevant entry of birth, marriage or death, indicating the volume and page number of the RCE. From the late 1960s, when the format of the registers changed, details were noted instead in the space provided at the bottom of the entry. When you view a record that has an associated RCE, either online or at a ScotlandsPeople centre, a message will appear above the record alerting you to the existence of a correction, which includes a hyperlink to an image of the RCE. Keep an eye out for these, as in many cases the RCE will contain valuable information.

In some cases an RCE may not have been linked to the original record, or it may have been attached to the wrong entry. If you see a note in the margin of an entry indicating an RCE but there is no link, then contact the ScotlandsPeople website or staff at the centre. In most cases the right RCE can be easily identified and a copy supplied. However, be aware that not every margin note relates to an RCE – in some cases it may simply indicate a clerical error that has been corrected on the original entry.

An entry in the Register of Corrected Entries providing details of a divorce.

CROWN COPYRIGHT, NATIONAL RECORDS OF SCOTLAND

EXPERT TIP

An RCE was not always created in circumstances where one would be expected, presumably because information was not passed to the relevant registrar. This includes some marriages that were found to be bigamous, and some illegitimate births where the name of the father was subsequently established by a sheriff court decree. Do not presume that no RCE always means no court case.

In addition to the main series of birth, marriage and death registers, the General Register Office for Scotland (now part of the National Records of Scotland) maintains various other registers, collectively known as the 'minor records'. These concern events relating to Scots that took place outside Scotland, and include the Foreign Register, Marine Register, Air Register, Consular and High Commissioner Returns, and Service and War Registers (including details of those killed whilst serving in the armed forces). These registers have varying covering dates, and a full list can be found on the National Records of Scotland website. The minor records can be searched in the 'Statutory Registers' section of the ScotlandsPeople website and at centres, either by leaving the location as 'All' or by selecting 'minor records' from the dropdown list of places.

EXPERT TIP

Not all events concerning Scots overseas are included in the minor records, as registration was usually voluntary and depended upon the informant making the effort to do so. However, don't presume that because a Scottish ancestor was born, married or died outside Scotland you won't find that event recorded in Scottish records. It is worth checking both the minor records and any local record of the event, as different information may be given in each.

A number of additional statutory registers are maintained by the National Records of Scotland. A register of stillbirths was begun in 1939, although for reasons of sensitivity it is not publicly searchable. Prior to this, details of stillbirths can sometimes be found in burial registers but were not routinely recorded.

An Adopted Children's Register has been kept since 1930

and includes details of some children who were born earlier but were adopted after the introduction of the Adoption of Children (Scotland) Act 1930. An entry in the Adopted Children's Register shows the date of birth of the child, the names, occupations and address of the adoptive parents, the date of the adoption order, and the court that issued it. There is no information given concerning the original name or birth parents of the child. Adoptions cannot be identified via the ScotlandsPeople website, but can be found using the system at the ScotlandsPeople Centre, where they appear in the birth index with the code NRH in place of the registration district. The full entries are not digitized, but can be requested on microfiche with a limit of three record requests per day.

Civil partnership was introduced in Scotland in 2005, and the statutory register of civil partnerships can be searched via the ScotlandsPeople website and at ScotlandsPeople centres. Same-sex marriages have been legal in Scotland since December 2014 and can be found within the statutory register of marriages.

The statutory register of divorces, also searchable via the ScotlandsPeople website and at centres, began on 1 May 1984. Prior to this date, details of divorces were entered into the relevant register of corrected entries, and can be found by viewing the marriage record. Only the index to divorces can be viewed, which provides the name of one spouse, the surname only of the other spouse, the year of the divorce, the full date of marriage and the name of the court. It is possible to order an extract decree of divorce, but in most cases the only additional information this will provide is the addresses of both parties at the time of the divorce. A separate statutory register of dissolutions of civil partnerships began in 2007.

Census Returns

A census has been taken in Scotland every ten years since 1801, with the exception of 1941. In the majority of cases, only statistical information survives prior to 1841, and the 1841 census is the earliest complete census available to family historians. Census returns are closed for one hundred years, and the most recent census currently available is the 1911 census. The 1921 census for Scotland is due to be released in 2021.

The 1841 census (taken on the night of 6 June 1841) provides fewer details than returns from later years. The information

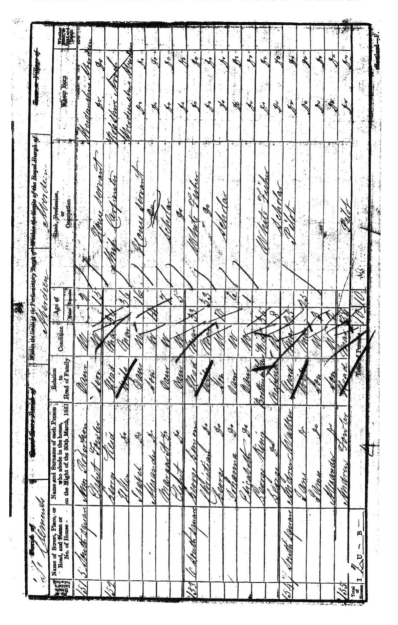

A page from the 1851 census.

CROWN COPYRIGHT, NATIONAL RECORDS OF SCOTLAND

recorded is as follows: address, name and surname, age, occupation, if born in Scotland whether born in the county of residence or not, or whether born in England or Ireland or elsewhere (listed as 'F' for foreign). Individuals are grouped into households, but relationships between household members are not shown. The ages of people over fifteen years of age were generally rounded down to the nearest five years (so someone aged between fifteen and nineteen would be recorded as fifteen), although it is not unusual to find exact ages given. Married and widowed women frequently appear in the 1841 census under their maiden surname. This is helpful for confirming that a particular household is the correct family, but can create issues when searching.

EXPERT TIP

Relationships between members of a household in the 1841 census can often be inferred, but this should be done with caution. A young girl with the same surname as the head of the household may likely be that person's daughter, but could also be a granddaughter, niece or more distant relation.

The 1851–1911 censuses are all in a similar format, although some details varied over the years. They provide address, name and surname, relationship to the head of household, marital condition, age and sex, occupation, where born (usually parish and county for those born in Scotland), and various disabilities. The number of children aged six to thirteen in education was recorded in 1861 and 1871. The number of rooms in the dwelling with one or more windows was included from 1861 (shedding light on living conditions), and whether a person was an employer or employed was noted from 1891. Whether a person spoke Gaelic or Gaelic and English was officially included from 1891 but also noted in 1881.

The 1911 census included a fertility question for married women only (not widows), which records the duration of the marriage in years, the number of children born alive, and the number of those children still living. Other new questions asked which industry or service a person worked in, and their nationality, if born in a foreign country.

Census returns for 1841–1911 have been digitized and fully indexed by name. Digital images can be viewed on the Scotlands-People website or in ScotlandsPeople centres, and many genealogy and local studies libraries have microfilm copies of the 1841–1901 censuses for their area. Indexes to the 1841–1901 censuses are available on several commercial genealogy websites, and partial indexes can be found on a number of free websites. Prior to the censuses being made available online, many family history societies published census indexes for their areas, and these can be found in libraries or purchased cheaply from the society.

There are a few surviving records from the 1801–1831 censuses that include the names of individuals. Other lists of inhabitants of particular parishes or areas were compiled for a variety of reasons at different times, and these are often described as early censuses, although they generally provide less detail than the later nation-wide censuses. Some of these pre-1841 population listings have been indexed and published by family history and historical societies. Details are given on the website of the Scottish Association of Family History Societies (www.safhs.org.uk/populationlists.asp).

A register of everyone living in the UK was compiled in 1939 for the purpose of issuing identity cards and ration books. Records for Scotland from this 1939 register cannot be searched directly, but it is possible to request details of deceased individuals by applying in writing to the National Records of Scotland (*see* www.nrscotland.gov.uk/statistics-and-data/nhs-central-register/about-the-register/1939-national-identity-register-and-how-to-order-an-official-extract). The information provided is address, date of birth, marital status and occupation, but not the names of other people living at the same address.

EXPERT TIP

The census returns we use to trace our Scottish ancestors are not in fact the original records, but rather contemporary copies made by census enumerators, who transcribed details from the original forms into enumeration books. Inevitably some errors and omissions occurred during the copying process and so information may not always be accurate. Unfortunately the original census forms do not survive.

Old Parish Registers (Church of Scotland)

Prior to 1855, when statutory registration was introduced, the main source for locating details of births, marriages and deaths in Scotland was the registers kept by the parish churches of the Church of Scotland. These are collectively known as the old parochial registers or old parish registers, or OPRs for short.

Up until 1929, the Presbyterian Church of Scotland was the established or state church of Scotland, as well as being the largest religious organization. This means that the majority of the population had some connection with the Church of Scotland, although they may have chosen to worship elsewhere.

The parliamentary act that established statutory registration in Scotland also specified that the Church of Scotland parish registers kept prior to 1 January 1855 were to be transferred to the civil authorities. Those registers kept up until 1819 were transmitted directly to the Registrar General's Department, whilst those for 1820–1854 were initially sent to the new registrar in each parish, before later being sent on to the Registrar General. This decision means that pre-1855 Church of Scotland registers now have a special status (they belong to the government rather than to the church), and records that might otherwise have been lost have been preserved. Something family historians can be very grateful for!

EXPERT TIP

The Church of Scotland continued to keep registers of baptisms, marriages and burials after 1855 but they do not form part of the old parish registers (with the exception of a small number of post-1855 events recorded in the OPRs). Later church registers generally contain less detail than the statutory records of the same event, but may still be worth searching.

The old parish registers have been digitized and indexed and can be found on the ScotlandsPeople website and at ScotlandsPeople centres under the heading of 'Church registers'. They are divided into 'Births and baptisms', 'Banns and marriages' and 'Deaths and burials', and can be searched by selecting 'Church of Scotland (old parish registers)' from within each record type.

The earliest surviving Old Parish Register, beginning 27 December 1553.
CROWN COPYRIGHT, NATIONAL RECORDS OF SCOTLAND

Those new to Scottish family history may initially be excited to learn that the old parish registers begin in 1553. In fact there is just one parish that has records dating back to 1553, Errol in Perthshire, and even that register starts on 27 December 1553. The majority of parish registers began far later, some only in the 1800s, and many contain significant gaps.

The research guides found on the website of the National Records of Scotland include a 'List of Old Parish Registers', arranged by county, which note the covering dates of each parish register and provide a useful reference guide for checking the available records for each parish (*see* www.nrscotland.gov.uk/research/guides/old-parish-registers/list-of-old-parish-registers). However, even these dates can conceal large gaps in the registers.

In 1872 the Registrar General produced the 'Detailed List of the Old Parochial Registers', which, as the name suggests, provides a more detailed description of the contents of each register with useful remarks noting missing, damaged or irregular entries. This publication can also be accessed on the National Records of Scotland website using the link above.

EXPERT TIP

The Stamp Duties Act, imposed from 1783 to 1794, placed a tax of three pence on all baptism, marriage and burial entries recorded in parish registers. This was very unpopular, even with those who could afford to pay, and led to an under-recording of events during this period.

Rather than births, marriages and deaths, the old parish registers typically record baptisms, banns of marriage and burials. There was no standard format, and the amount and type of information varies considerably from one register to the next, as well as within each register over time. If we are lucky, a baptism record will give the child's date of birth, a record of the proclamation of banns of marriage will note the date the couple married, and a burial record will provide a date of death. However, this is often not the case, and we then generally have to presume that the child was probably born shortly before the baptism, the couple likely married soon after banns were proclaimed, and that the deceased died a few days prior to burial, unless there is evidence to the contrary.

In general, a baptism register will provide the date of baptism, the child's name, and the names of the parents, including the mother's maiden surname, although earlier registers may omit the mother's name entirely. There will usually be an indication as to whether the parents were married to one another and the child was legitimate, often termed 'lawful', or alternatively whether the parents had been 'guilty of fornication' making the child illegitimate or 'natural'.

Additional details found in a baptism register may include the child's date of birth, the father's occupation, the family's place of residence (not necessarily the same as the child's place of birth), the names of witnesses to the baptism, who were sometimes relatives, and the name of the minister who performed the baptism (not always the parish minister). These are all important details that can help to identify the family and connect generations, as well as suggesting additional sources for research. Other details that may very occasionally be recorded include the birth order of the child (for example, whether it was the couple's first or fifth child), after whom the child was named, and the relationship between the child and the witnesses who were present. Such details are one of the reasons why it is always important to view the original records, rather than relying on an index.

Registers of marriages or banns of marriage will often only provide the names of the couple and a date. This could be one of the days when banns were proclaimed (banns were usually proclaimed on three successive Sundays), when the marriage was arranged or 'contracted', or when the marriage actually took place. Sometimes more than one of these dates will be recorded, although often it is unclear exactly which date is being given. It may be noted that the couple were 'afterwards married', even if the date of the marriage is not specified.

The parish of residence of both bride and groom is often noted (typically 'both of this parish'), and sometimes a specific place of residence within the parish is given. The groom's occupation may be recorded (rarely the bride's), and the name, occupation and place of residence of the bride's father may be given (rarely those of the groom's father). Unlike baptism registers, marriage registers generally do not provide the names of witnesses.

When a bride and groom came from different parishes, banns of marriage had to be proclaimed in both parish churches and two records should have been created, one in each parish. This can sometimes cause confusion, as from indexes it may appear that the couple were married twice, often on slightly different dates. It is always worth looking at both records of the marriage, as one may give details that the other does not. The place of marriage may not be stated, but it was typical for the marriage to take place in the bride's parish, often in her family home.

EXPERT TIP

Pre-1855 Scottish marriage registers almost never state whether the groom was a bachelor or a widower, and only occasionally note if the bride was a widow (the name of her former husband may be given in place of that of her father). It is therefore easy to overlook a previous marriage, particularly as widows usually married under their maiden surnames. Don't presume a marrying couple were necessarily young or on their first marriage!

Scottish burial registers are most notable for their absence. Many parishes kept no records of deaths or burials at all, and where a burial register does exist it will usually cover a far shorter period than the marriage or baptism register. A date of burial and a name may be all that is given, although other details may include date of death, occupation, age, place of residence and cause of death. Children may be identified in terms of their father (for example, 'a child of John Brown'), and the burials of married or widowed women may include their husband's name (ideally 'Mary Robertson, wife of John Brown' but sometimes just 'Mrs Brown').

Many records described as burial registers are in fact accounts kept of the hire of mortcloths. A mortcloth was a cloth used to cover the coffin during a funeral and each parish had its own, sometimes several of different quality and size, which was available for a fee. Mortcloth records are often even less detailed than burial registers and may give only a date, which may be when the fee was paid rather than the date of death or burial, and a name, which could be the name of the relative who paid the fee rather than the name of the deceased.

Poor families may have been unable to afford the hire of the mortcloth and so their burials may not be recorded. Other families may have had their own mortcloth or had access to an alternative one, such as through being the member of a trade incorporation, and so, again, may not be recorded.

Unless our ancestors had an unusual surname, it may be

impossible to identify them from the limited information given in a burial or mortcloth register, but any records are worth examining. Some people were buried in a different parish to the one where they died due to being buried in an existing family burial plot elsewhere, so it is worth extending a search beyond the parish where the person is known to have lived.

EXPERT TIP

Some burial registers include a location of burial within the burial ground, which may be given in terms of distance from the wall of the churchyard or some other feature. These locations may be hard to decipher but are worth noting as they can sometimes be used to determine that two people were buried in the same or neighbouring burial plots and were therefore probably related.

Records of Other Churches

In addition to the Church of Scotland, there are various other churches and religious bodies whose records can be used to trace our ancestors. These can be divided into two groups: first, Presbyterian churches that split from the Church of Scotland at various periods, known as 'secessionist' churches; and second, all other religious groups, including Catholics, Episcopalians, Methodists, Baptists, Quakers, Jews and others.

The history of the Church of Scotland, and of those 'seceders' or 'dissenters' who separated from it, is complex, and there are plenty of reference works available for those with a particular interest. For most family historians it is sufficient to understand that the Church of Scotland parish church may not have been the only church available to our ancestors as a place of worship, and that records of other churches may also need to be searched. Secessionist churches included the Burghers and Anti-Burghers, the Relief Church, the United Secession and the United Presbyterians, amongst others. The most significant break, known as 'The Disruption', came in 1843 when around a third of the Church of Scotland broke away to form the Free Church of Scotland.

The Scottish Episcopal Church began as a distinct church from the Church of Scotland in 1582, and was confirmed as separate from the established Church in 1690, when Presbyterianism was restored in Scotland after the religious upheavals of the preceding century. Episcopalianism was strong in some parts of Scotland, and if an English ancestor was a member of the Church of England, or if an Irish one attended the Church of Ireland, then they may have joined an episcopal congregation after moving to Scotland.

Roman Catholicism remained strong in some Highland areas of Scotland after the Protestant Reformation of 1560, and was boosted in the mid-nineteenth century by the arrival of Irish Catholics fleeing the Great Famine. Later Catholic immigrants to Scotland included Italians and Lithuanians.

Other churches with a presence in Scotland included the Quakers (Society of Friends), Independents or Congregationalists, Baptists and Methodists. Their numbers were generally small, and they were usually found in urban areas. Prior to the twentieth century, the only non-Christians found in Scotland in any number were Jews, many of whom were immigrants from eastern Europe.

From 1855 onwards, a person's religious affiliation can often be identified from that of the minister who married them, although a non-religious form of marriage was also possible. It is particularly important to note any marriages that took place outside the Church of Scotland in the early decades of statutory registration, as these may indicate which church's records need to be examined when research turns to the pre-1855 period.

The old parish registers include some records of baptisms and marriages that took place in other churches, sometimes recording the name and religious affiliation of the minister who performed the ceremony, or noting that a particular event concerned a 'dissenter'. Often, though, it is a family's absence from the parish register that will alert us to a possible secessionist ancestor. For example, if a couple had children regularly baptised in the parish church up until the early 1840s but there are no baptisms found for younger children, it would be a strong indication the family had joined the Free Church of Scotland after the Disruption.

Unfortunately, not all of these other churches have surviving records, and where records do exist they may be very limited in scope – for example, consisting of minute books of church meetings but no registers of births, marriages or deaths. The good news is that many records can be found in archives, and they are increasingly being indexed.

The National Records of Scotland (NRS) holds a substantial collection of other church records as well as some digitized copies of records held elsewhere. Others can be found in local, university and religious archives and some are still held by the relevant church. Searching online archive catalogues, described in the next chapter, will help to identify these. The publication *Registers of the Secession Churches in Scotland* by Diane Baptie (*see* 'Further Reading' at the end of this book) has been somewhat superseded by the availability of online catalogues, but is still a useful guide for identifying these records.

Many baptism, marriage and burial registers taken from church records held by the NRS are now included on the ScotlandsPeople website listed as 'other churches' within the church registers section. By selecting the record type, then 'other churches', it is possible to see a list of churches included, which can be narrowed down by county or city. Additional church records are held by the ScotlandsPeople Centre in the miscellaneous records (MR) series, and a list of these is included on the NRS website (www.nrscotland.gov.uk/research/guides/old-parish-registers/list-of-old-parish-registers).

EXPERT TIP

Don't just look for churches within the parish where an ancestor lived. Those who did not attend the Church of Scotland may have travelled some distance to worship in their chosen congregation. Check for churches in surrounding parishes as well, particularly those containing towns or large settlements.

Between 2007 and 2010, a project was undertaken to gather in, digitize and index Scottish Catholic parish records and the registers of the main Catholic cemeteries in Glasgow and Edinburgh. As a result, all known pre-1855 Catholic registers, and some post-1855 ones, can now be easily accessed, either through the ScotlandsPeople website under 'Roman Catholic Church' within the church registers section, or on the Findmypast website (www.findmypast.co.uk) as four separate collections of 'Scotland Roman Catholic Parish' records. The publication *Scottish Catholic Family History* by Andrew R. Nicoll (see Further Reading) provides a useful guide to these registers. Additional Catholic records are held by the Scottish Catholic Archives, housed within the University of Aberdeen Special Collections Centre.

Various Scottish church registers were microfilmed by the genealogical department of the Church of Jesus Christ of Latter-Day Saints (now FamilySearch), and can be accessed at the Family History Library in Salt Lake City, Utah, USA, and in associated family history centres and affiliated libraries around the world. These records can be identified through the FamilySearch catalogue (www.familysearch.org/catalog/search) or the FamilySearch Research Wiki (www.familysearch.org/wiki/en/scotland_genealogy), which has dedicated pages for each parish in Scotland. A small number have been indexed and can be searched through the main FamilySearch Historical Records site (www.familysearch.org/search).

Some family history societies have indexed and published records of other churches within their areas, including records that are still held by the relevant church. The Scottish Genealogy Society (www.scotsgenealogy.com) has published many indexes to church records, particularly for churches in Edinburgh and the Lothians, and a large number of Free Church records from the Highlands have been indexed by Stuart Farrell and published by the Highland Family History Society (www.highlandfamilyhistorysociety.org). Some records from both societies can be accessed online through Findmypast (www.findmypast.co.uk). Some unpublished or privately published indexes to church records can be found in family history and reference libraries, including several indexes to episcopal registers for Aberdeen and the North East of Scotland produced by A. Strath Maxwell.

Additional indexes to records of other churches can be found online through Old Scottish Genealogy & Family History (www.oldscottish.com/records.html) and Scottish Indexes (www.scottishindexes.com). The non-OPR births/baptisms, banns/marriages and deaths/burials indexes on the Scottish Indexes website include records of Quaker births, marriages and deaths, as well as a variety of records from Church of Scotland and other Presbyterian churches.

The registers of Scotland's synagogues and Jewish cemeteries are held by the Scottish Jewish Archives Centre in Glasgow (www.sjac.org.uk). The centre holds many other records of the

Jews in Scotland, including an extensive database with information taken from over seventy sources.

Wills and Testaments

Scottish wills and testaments can sometimes seem disappointing. Relatively few people left them, and when records are located they often contain less information than expected. However, they are valuable genealogical sources that can help to connect generations. Knowing a little more about the records will assist in understanding what is, and isn't, included.

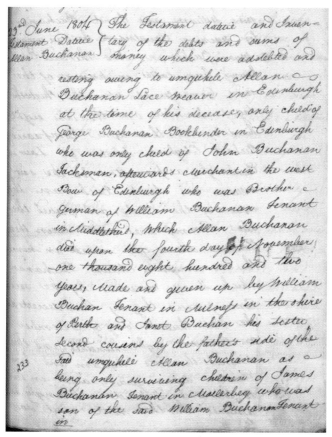

A page from a testament dative from 1804. Even though this man died without writing a will, his testament provides a large amount of family information.

CROWN COPYRIGHT, NATIONAL RECORDS OF SCOTLAND

A testament is a document drawn up after a person dies, which provides details of what property that person owned, specifies who will act as the executor to manage and distribute that property, and may indicate who inherits what. In other countries these types of document are commonly known as probate records, but the term probate is not used in Scots Law.

There were two types of testament: testaments testamentar and testaments dative. A testament testamentar is technically a testament in which the deceased person, prior to their death, nominated their executor. In most cases a will or 'latter will', in which the deceased specified who was to receive their property, is also included. A testament dative was drawn up when the person died intestate: that is, they left no will and did not nominate an executor, and instead the court selected the executor. This was usually a close relative, although it could also be a creditor.

Testaments testamentar include three sections: an inventory of the person's goods or possessions, a copy of their will, and the confirmation or official recognition of the executor. Testaments dative just include the inventory and confirmation of the executor. Depending on the court and the time period, all sections may be found in a single document, or they may be contained in two or three separate documents.

It is important to understand that historically in Scotland property was designated as being one of two types: heritable property or moveable property. Heritable property was mainly land and buildings, but could also include fishing and mineral rights and coats of arms. Moveable property was basically everything else a person owned, including money, furniture, clothes and farm animals. Prior to 1868, the ownership of heritable property could not be transferred through a testament, and therefore any land or buildings a person owned will not be mentioned. To identify any heritable property, a separate series of records needs to be consulted (discussed below). However, it was possible to get round this using a document known as a Trust Disposition and Settlement, and some of these can be found recorded with testaments. From 1868 it was possible to pass on heritable property through a will, and since 1964 most property has been passed on in this way.

Scots Law specified how a deceased person's moveable estate could be distributed. If a man died leaving a wife and children, then his moveable property would be divided into three parts: the widow's part (or *jus relictae*), the bairns' or children's part, and the dead's or deid's part. If he was survived by a wife but no children, or vice versa, the estate would be divided into two. If he had no surviving wife or children, then all the moveable property was designated as the deid's part. Only the deid's part could be bequeathed in a will.

Testaments were recorded in local commissary courts up until 1823, and in sheriff courts from the 1820s, with the estates of those who died outside Scotland or who owned property in more than one part of the country recorded in Edinburgh. The process of identifying in which court a document is likely to be found is greatly simplified by the fact that all records up to 1925 (with the exception of Orkney and Shetland from 1902) have been digitized and indexed and can be accessed through the ScotlandsPeople website. However, particularly when researching a common surname, it may still be helpful to know which courts covered the areas where an ancestor lived.

The index to wills and testaments on the ScotlandsPeople website includes the name of the deceased person, a description (usually specifying occupation, place of residence and sometimes date of death, along with the name of the husband of married or widowed women), the date the testament was recorded, the type of document, the court where it was recorded, and a reference number. Multiple records for the same person will often be due to the will and inventory being recorded separately, but could also be because there was an 'eik' or extra record created when additional property was identified after the testament had been confirmed. Look at all available records, as they will contain different information.

EXPERT TIP

Testaments could be recorded many years after a person died. Don't restrict a search to just the year of death or you may not find the record you are looking for. It is a good idea to search indexes for at least ten years after a known date of death.

To obtain copies of testaments recorded after 1925 you will need to visit or contact the National Records of Scotland (NRS) in

Edinburgh, or the Orkney Archive and Shetland Archives for testaments recorded in those counties. For the period 1926–1959 there are yearly printed calendars of confirmations and inventories that have been digitized and are accessible on computers in the NRS search room. These same calendars for the period 1876–1936 are also available on the Ancestry website (www.ancestry.co.uk). For the period 1960–1983 there was a card catalogue with the cards later put on microfiche, and now digitized and available on NRS computers. For the period 1984–1999 there is a computer database at NRS called the 'Commissary Court Index', which links to digitized images. Finally, wills and testaments from 1999 to the present day can be accessed through the Commissary Department of Edinburgh Sheriff Court.

Valuation Rolls

Valuation rolls are records of property, and property owners and occupiers, compiled for taxation purposes. The Lands Valuation (Scotland) Act 1854 established a standard system for the valuation of property throughout Scotland, with valuation rolls compiled annually from 1855 until 1989. The rolls provided local authorities with accurate information on the ownership, tenancy and occupancy of all properties within their area, allowing them to levy rates to pay for a variety of local services.

Valuation rolls are arranged by county and divided into parishes, with separate rolls compiled for royal burghs, and the rolls for larger towns and cities arranged by electoral ward. They provide the address, type of property (for example, house or shop), the name of the proprietor, the name of the occupier or tenant, occupations, and yearly rent or rateable value. However, in the earlier rolls there is little or no detail given for properties rented at under £4 annually.

The National Records of Scotland (NRS) holds valuation rolls for the whole of Scotland. Valuation rolls for 1855–1957 can be viewed as digital images in the NRS search room. Those from 1958 onwards have mainly not been digitized (with the exception of some that were previously microfilmed), and the original records need to be consulted.

Valuation rolls for every ten years from 1855 up to 1915, and every five years from 1915 to 1955, have been indexed by place and personal name, with digital images linked to the index. These indexes and the accompanying digital images can be accessed in the NRS search room. The ScotlandsPeople website and ScotlandsPeople centres currently have access to indexed valuation rolls for 1855–1940 only.

For years for which no indexes exist it is necessary to search the valuation rolls manually. However, as the rolls were compiled in a similar order each year, if a property has been identified in an indexed year it is fairly straightforward to locate it in a subsequent unindexed roll. There are some street indexes for Edinburgh valuation rolls, and post office directories are useful when searching for properties located in a city, as they often identify the electoral ward in which a street was located.

In addition to those available through ScotlandsPeople, a small number of valuation rolls can be found online through other websites. Valuation rolls for Perth and Perthshire for 1857–1899 can be found in the 'Perthshire, Scotland, Cess, Stent and Valuation Rolls, 1650–1899' collection on Ancestry (www.ancestry.co.uk). Valuation rolls for Glasgow for 1913–1914 only are available on The Glasgow Story website (www.theglasgowstory.com/ valuation-rolls), and valuation rolls for Dumfriesshire for 1896– 1897 are available on the Flickr site of Scottish Indexes (www.flickr. com/photos/maxwellancestry/collections/72157649815538386).

EXPERT TIP

Many local archives hold valuation rolls for their areas. In some cases these are manuscript working copies that record changes that occurred throughout the year, and which may allow changes of address to be tracked more accurately than through the centrally held rolls. These local copies are mainly not indexed and can be time-consuming to search.

Valuation rolls are a useful source for family history research as they identify whether an ancestor was a proprietor (property owner) or a tenant, they record the value or yearly rent of their home, and allow movements to be traced on a yearly basis, including between censuses. However, they record heads of households only, and in the earlier years do not include the occupiers of property of low value, such as many industrial or agricultural workers who lived in homes tied to their jobs.

Street and Post Office Directories

Directories listing individuals and commercial organizations have been compiled in Scotland since the 1700s. The earliest directories were printed by private publishers using information gathered from a variety of sources, but from the early 1800s onwards the Post Office became the major publisher and so these directories are commonly referred to as 'Post Office directories'.

Some directories covered the whole of Scotland and others were produced for particular regions or individual counties. However, the most detailed directories are for Scotland's towns and cities. The earliest directory for Edinburgh was published in 1773, and with the exception of a few gaps in the earlier years, directories were produced annually for the capital for around 200 years up until the 1970s.

The earlier city directories are generally arranged alphabetically by surname, and provide name, occupation and place of residence. The majority of those listed are men, but many women were included when they had an occupation or were the head of the household, although sometimes they were listed as just Mrs or Miss without a forename. By the mid-1800s, the city directories became more extensive, including an increasing amount of information about the city and the services available as well as paid advertisements. Inclusion in directories was voluntary, and information was not always accurate or up to date. The majority of those listed were heads of household, and those in the professions or living in affluent areas are far better represented than the poorer classes.

EXPERT TIP

City directories often include a general directory arranged by name, a street directory listing the residents within each street, and a trade directory arranged by occupation. It is worth searching all three sections for an ancestor as additional details may be given in one section that do not appear in another.

The National Library of Scotland (NLS) has made hundreds of directories available online for free through the Internet Archive. These can be accessed either through the Scottish Post Office Directories website (http://digital.nls.uk/directories), or directly through the Scottish directories section of the Internet Archive (https://archive.org/details/scottishdirectories), which at the time of writing contained over a thousand directories.

A selection of directories covering Scotland can also be found in the Schools, Directories & Church Histories section of the Ancestry website, and the Directories & Social History section of the Findmypast website. Many local studies libraries and archives hold directories for their local areas. Few directories from the mid to late twentieth century are available online due to copyright restrictions. Publications from this period can be accessed in hard copy form at the NLS and in local libraries.

Directories can be useful for identifying an ancestor's address in a particular year, for establishing when an ancestor entered and left a property, and for identifying who or what was located at a particular address. They may also provide information on an ancestor's trade or business, and shed light on the community in which a person lived. Early directories pre-date both the valuation rolls and national censuses, and so are particularly valuable.

Electoral Registers and Voters' Rolls

Prior to 1832, only a tiny minority of men in Scotland, and no women, had the right to vote. In 1831 the electorate consisted of less than 5,000 men out of a population of 2.4 million. Representatives of counties were elected to parliament by the owners of land or other heritable property above a certain value, known as freeholders, while representatives of burghs were elected by the burgh council.

The Scottish Reform Act of 1832 increased the electorate to about 65,000. The right to vote was extended to house owners with property valued over £10, and to tenants of £50 rental value in rural areas. Further reform acts in 1868 and 1884 expanded the electorate to include lodgers and occupiers, and reduced the value of the property needed to qualify. From 1882 women could vote in burgh council elections, and from 1889 in county council elections, provided they were proprietors or tenants and either unmarried or married but not living with their husband.

Following World War I, the Representation of the People Act 1918 granted the right to vote to all men aged over twenty-one and all women over the age of thirty years, regardless of the value of their property. In 1928 women were given the vote on the same terms as men, and in 1969 the voting age for all was reduced to eighteen years. Sixteen- and seventeen-year-olds in Scotland were allowed to vote in the Scottish Independence Referendum of 2014, and the voting age for Scottish parliamentary and local government elections was subsequently reduced to sixteen. The voting age for UK general elections remains eighteen years.

Electoral registers, also known as voters' rolls, were a creation of the 1832 Reform Act, and since that date a voter's name must be on the register in order for them to cast their vote. Prior to 1918, the registers had to show a person's qualification to vote, and the information recorded typically includes their name, occupation, whether proprietor or tenant, and details of the qualifying property.

Electoral registers were produced annually with a specific qualifying date given. Registration was suspended during the two world wars, and there are no registers for Scotland for 1915–1917 or 1940–1944. There were two registers a year (the spring and autumn registers) produced in the period 1919–1926, and also two registers in 1945–1946. From 1951, young voters who came of age during the life of the register have been included, with some indication as to their age.

Early registers were arranged by parish or burgh, with the names of voters listed alphabetically. There may be separate registers for local and parliamentary elections, and women who qualified may be listed in supplementary registers. From the late nineteenth century onwards, most electoral registers were compiled by address, and unless searching a small rural community, it is usually necessary to know an ancestor's place of residence in order to locate them. From 1918 the information recorded was name and address only, and members of a household were grouped together, although no relationships are shown.

Many local archives and libraries hold electoral registers for their areas, although surviving registers may be incomplete, particularly for the nineteenth century. The National Library of Scotland holds a complete run of Scottish electoral registers from

1946 and the British Library in London has a complete set of electoral registers for the whole of the UK from 1947. Some electoral registers can be found among burgh and sheriff court records at the National Records of Scotland, with a few miscellaneous voters' rolls held in collections of 'Gifts & Deposits'.

Over the past few years, Scottish electoral registers have begun to be digitized and put online. Digitization is particularly valuable as, through the use of optical character recognition (OCR) technology, it is possible to search these online registers by name, rather than address, for the first time. The Ancestry website currently has electoral registers for Aberdeenshire, Edinburgh, Fife, Glasgow and Perth & Kinross, while Findmypast has registers for the county of West Lothian.

Details from current and recent electoral registers for the whole of the UK can be accessed online via a number of commercial organizations, some of which allow limited free searches, and local libraries hold printed copies of the current register for their area. Both Ancestry and Findmypast have collections of recent UK electoral registers.

EXPERT TIP

The small number of Scots included in early electoral registers limits their value to family historians, although the details given regarding property ownership or tenancy are useful for ancestors who are included. From 1918 the registers become increasingly valuable, in particular because, unlike the directories and valuation rolls described above, they include details of all adult residents and not just the head of household.

Newspapers

Newspapers are a valuable source for tracing people in the past, as not only can they provide details of births, marriages and deaths, but they also shed light on many aspects of a person's life and reveal previously unknown family stories.

Newspapers began to be regularly printed in Scotland in the 1700s, and were initially published in the cities of Aberdeen, Edinburgh and Glasgow, but as the 1800s progressed an increasing number of local newspapers appeared that were based in smaller towns and circulated in the surrounding areas. Local papers often reported on national and international news, but their value for genealogists is mainly in the reports of local events.

Most local studies' libraries hold copies of newspapers covering their area, either original or on microfilm, and some manually compiled indexes are available. The National Library of Scotland holds an extensive collection of Scottish newspapers, and details are given on their website (www.nls.uk/collections/newspapers) and in their online catalogue.

The largest collection of newspapers from the UK (including Scotland) and overseas is held by The British Library. The British Library's main newspaper collection is held at its Boston Spa site in Wetherby, West Yorkshire, England. Some microfilm and digital newspapers can also be accessed in the newsroom at the library's London St Pancras site. Many of these newspapers are available online through digitization projects.

The largest collection of online UK newspapers can be found on The British Newspaper Archive website (www.britishnewspaper archive.co.uk), a joint project between Findmypast and The British Library, and the same titles are also available through Findmypast's 'British Newspapers' collection. A large number of Scottish newspapers are included, and the collection is regularly updated.

EXPERT TIP

Many libraries within Scotland, including the National Library of Scotland, subscribe to various online newspaper archives, and registered users can access these from home, or by visiting the library, for free. It's worth checking what is available through the local library before signing up for an expensive subscription.

The Edinburgh Gazette, one of the official newspapers of the UK government, is available online for free through The Gazette (www.thegazette.co.uk). *The Edinburgh Gazette* was first published in 1699, but only began continuous publication in 1793. *The Scots Magazine* began in 1739 and claims to be the oldest magazine in the world still in existence, although it has gone through several incarnations, with lengthy periods without publication. Births, marriages and deaths, including of Scots abroad, were regularly published, and digitized copies can be found online through various subscription and free websites. *The Scotsman* newspaper has its own online digital archive (http://archive.scotsman.com), although some editions are also included on other sites.

Burial Records

In addition to the statutory registers of deaths from 1855 and the pre-1855 old parish registers, burial or cemetery registers are a useful source for identifying deaths and places of burial.

Originally the kirkyard attached to the parish church was the only place of burial in many Scottish parishes, but by the Victorian period these were becoming full, and interdenominational burial grounds, such as the Glasgow Necropolis, were created. Many of these cemeteries became the responsibility of the local council, although some are still privately owned. Records are mainly held by the burial and crematoria departments of local councils, although some older records may be deposited in local archives. Councils typically charge a fee to carry out searches of their registers, and may only do so when fairly precise information (such as a date of death and the name of the cemetery) are known.

Some Scottish burial and crematoria registers can be accessed online through DeceasedOnline (www.deceasedonline.com). The site has good coverage of Aberdeenshire and Angus and a small collection from private crematoria and cemeteries in Edinburgh. It also includes headstone collections (gravestone inscriptions) from burial grounds across Scotland.

Some burial registers from the southwest of Scotland (Dumfriesshire, Kirkcudbrightshire and Wigtownshire) can be found in the 'England & Scotland, Select Cemetery Registers, 1800–2016' collection on Ancestry (www.ancestry.co.uk).

EXPERT TIP

In addition to burial registers, arranged chronologically by date of burial, many burial grounds also kept lair registers. These typically record the name and address of the owner of each lair or burial plot and the names of all those buried there, and may reveal previously unknown relatives.

Monumental Inscriptions

Gravestones are particularly valuable in Scotland due to the inadequacies of the old parish registers. They may give details of deaths for which no other records exist, as well as providing evidence to connect several generations of a family. The inscriptions found on gravestones are generally known in Scotland as 'monumental inscriptions' (abbreviated as MIs).

A large number of monumental inscriptions from throughout Scotland have been recorded and published by family history societies. These publications can be purchased from the societies or found in genealogical and local studies libraries. The website of the Scottish Association of Family History Societies (www.safhs.org.uk) includes a list of over 3,500 burial grounds in Scotland with details of published MIs. The library of the Scottish Genealogy Society (www.scotsgenealogy.com) holds the largest collection of Scottish MIs in the world, including some unpublished transcriptions.

The company Scottish Monumental Inscriptions (https://scottish-monumental-inscriptions.com) sells transcriptions and photographs of gravestones on CD and as PDF files. Some of their transcriptions can also be accessed through DeceasedOnline (www.deceasedonline.com) and the 'Scotland Monumental Inscriptions Index' collection on Findmypast (www.findmypast.co.uk).

Photographs and transcriptions of Scottish gravestones can be found online through international websites such as BillionGraves (https://billiongraves.com) and FindAGrave (www.findagrave.com), although in many cases only a few inscriptions from each burial ground are included. There are also many smaller websites containing inscriptions from particular burial grounds or areas, such as for the County of Sutherland (http://public.fotki.com/rhemusaig/burial_grounds).

EXPERT TIP

Some burial grounds have been surveyed more than once, and it is worth checking all available transcriptions. Older publications may include inscriptions that are no longer legible, while newer ones may include additional gravestones, or further details added to stones after the original survey.

Tax Records

Tax records provide useful lists of residents in an area prior to the national censuses, as well as giving details of the property they owned, but mostly include only a small percentage of Scots.

A number of mostly seventeenth- to eighteenth-century Scottish tax records can be found online on the free ScotlandsPlaces website (https://scotlandsplaces.gov.uk). Records are available as digital images with associated transcriptions, but search options are limited. It is usually necessary to first identify the records of the parish where an ancestor lived, and then to browse through them to locate the person of interest.

ScotlandsPlaces' online tax records include land tax rolls 1645–1831, hearth tax 1691–1695, window tax 1748–1798, and male and female servant tax 1777–1798 (some of which include names of servants as well as of the masters and mistresses who paid the tax). The most useful tax records for most family historians are the farm horse tax rolls 1797–1798, which include a large number of tenant farmers.

Additional tax records are held by the National Records of Scotland and in local archives. Some early land or stent records from Perth & Kinross Council Archive can be found in the 'Perthshire, Scotland, Cess, Stent and Valuation Rolls, 1650–1899' collection on Ancestry (www.ancestry.co.uk). Indexes to stent rolls for the Burgh of Dumfries are available on the historical indexes section of the Dumfries & Galloway Council Archives website (https://info.dumgal.gov.uk/historicalindexes).

Some tax rolls, particularly those for hearth and poll tax, have been indexed and published by historical and genealogical societies. An interesting example is the record of the Edinburgh housemails tax, a one-off tax on house rent or 'mail' imposed in Edinburgh in 1634–1636, published as *Edinburgh Housemails Taxation Book 1634–1636* by Aaron Allen and Cathryn Spence (Edinburgh: Scottish History Society, 2014). Entries give the name of the landlord, names of tenants, a description of the property's location, the amount of rent or mail paid by each tenant, and the annuity or tax to be paid.

EXPERT TIP

Tax records may be helpful for identifying the owner of the property where an ancestor lived, even if the ancestor isn't personally named. Knowing the name of the property owner is particularly useful for locating estate records.

Kirk Session and Heritors Records

Kirk session records were kept by the kirk session of each Church of Scotland parish, consisting of the minister and elders, in addition to the old parish registers. They can contain a variety of different types of document, but the most common are minute books recording the meetings of the session, account books detailing income and expenditure, and communion rolls listing the names of parishioners.

Kirk session records can be used to supplement the information found in parish registers and to learn more about an ancestor's life. The kirk session oversaw the moral behaviour of parishioners, and, of particular value to genealogists, minutes often recorded the names of parents of illegitimate children, those who had contracted irregular marriages (which may not be entered in the parish register) and those guilty of 'antenuptial fornication' (usually revealed by the arrival of the couple's first child less than nine months after the wedding).

Account books record fees paid for the proclamation of banns of marriage, fines for immoral behaviour, and payments made for burials, including the hire of the mortcloth, which may not be recorded in the parish register. They may also list the names of those in receipt of poor relief.

Rolls of male heads of families and the more detailed communion rolls were mainly kept from the 1830s onwards. They may provide occupations and places of residence, list family groups, and record movements in and out of a parish, including emigration overseas.

Some kirk session records include details of 'testificates' received from those entering the parish, or granted to those who were leaving. These were testimonials as to a person's good character, which enabled them to join a new church. They can be very useful for tracing a person's movements, and may indicate a place of origin. Details of testificates were often entered into kirk session minutes, but can sometimes be found in separate lists.

Kirk session records are held by the National Records of Scotland (NRS) and in local archives. The majority have been digitized and can be accessed as browsable digital images at the NRS and in some other archives. There have been plans to make kirk session records available online for several years, and this will hopefully happen in the near future.

Some indexes to selected entries from kirk session records are available online. The FamilySearch website (www.familysearch. org/search) includes a collection of 'Scotland Church Records and Kirk Session Records, 1658–1919', while Findmypast has a 'Scotland, Antenuptial Relationship Index 1661–1780' based on data originally compiled by an academic researcher. Some indexes to Dumfriesshire kirk session records are included on the Dumfries and Galloway Council Archives website (https://info.dumgal.gov. uk/historicalindexes).

Many rolls of male heads of families taken from kirk session records have been indexed by Old Scottish Genealogy & Family History and made available through the individual parish pages of their website (www.oldscottish.com/records.html). These rolls can also be searched through the 'Web: Scotland, Rolls of Male Heads of Families, 1834–1845' collection on Ancestry.

Some kirk session material can be found within the old parish registers (OPRs), while details of some pre-1855 births, deaths and marriages are included within kirk session records. Guides on the NRS website provide details of both (www.nrscotland.gov. uk/research/guides/old-parish-registers/list-of-old-parish-registers). *Parish Registers in the Kirk Session Records of the Church of Scotland* by Diane Baptie (*see* Further Reading) is a more detailed listing, including both records of English presbyterian churches held by the NRS and some lists of inhabitants and male heads of families. Some entries of births, deaths and marriages taken from kirk session records have recently been added to the ScotlandsPeople website, where they are indexed as if they were part of the relevant OPR.

Presbyteries and synods were church courts above kirk sessions that heard more serious cases, usually referred to them by the sessions. Their records are also held by the NRS.

Heritors were the landowners within each parish who were liable to pay parish rates for the upkeep of the church and for assisting the poor. Heritors records, also mainly found at the NRS, may include parish valuations or assessments giving details of heritors and the lands they owned, as well as lists of those in receipt of poor relief. There was some overlap between the responsibilities of the kirk session and the heritors, and the records of both are worth searching.

Most presbyterian churches that broke away from the Church of Scotland kept similar records to kirk session records, including minute books recording church business and the transgressions of parishioners. These can be found, along with any registers of baptisms, marriages and burials, at the NRS and in local archives.

EXPERT TIP

Kirk session records include details of many ordinary people who appear in few other records. Even if there is no particular reason to think an ancestor will be included, it is worth skimming through minute books for the period they lived in a parish. You may discover an ancestor was reprimanded for drunkenness or for arguing with a neighbour!

Poor Relief Records

Prior to 1845, poor relief was the joint responsibility of kirk sessions and heritors, whose records are described above. The Poor Law (Scotland) Act 1845 created a new system of parochial boards (replaced by parish councils in 1894) responsible for poor relief in each parish, with a central Board of Supervision in Edinburgh. The change was not immediate everywhere, with some parishes continuing to maintain their poor as previously, and so kirk session and heritors records may still be worth searching for the post-1845 period.

Records of paupers generally become much more detailed from 1845 onwards, and particularly from 1865 when record keeping was standardized. General registers of the poor, children's separate registers, and registers of applications provide details of not only the individual applying, but also their spouse, children and even their parents. The focus was on establishing a pauper's place of settlement (either through birth, marriage or long-term residence) and on identifying any relatives who might be expected to contribute to their upkeep. These might include adult children who had emigrated or the fathers of illegitimate children. Individual paupers may also be mentioned in parochial board minute books, particularly if there was a dispute over their place of settlement, and there may be details found in these minute books that do not appear in the main registers.

A system of 'outdoor relief' whereby the pauper received regular small payments while remaining in their own home was generally favoured in Scotland. However, the 1845 Act allowed parishes to operate poorhouses, and the number of these gradually increased, with some parishes joining together to establish 'combination' poorhouses, and others setting up smaller almshouses or parish homes. These poorhouses kept their own records and registers in addition to those kept by the parochial boards.

Those whose claims for poor relief were rejected by the parochial board could appeal to their local sheriff court, and those who felt they received inadequate assistance could take their case to the Scottish Board of Supervision. Poor Law inspectors could also apply to the sheriff courts for the removal of paupers who were not native to Scotland, or to pursue fathers who abandoned wives and children.

From 1930, poor relief was no longer operated at a parish level but became the responsibility of county and city councils. The Poor Law was abolished in 1948 and replaced by the modern welfare system. Records from this period are generally closed to public access.

Most post-1845 records of poor relief are held in local archives, although some records for Wigtownshire and Midlothian are held by the National Records of Scotland. Survival of records is extremely patchy, with some parishes having extensive collections of poor relief registers, applications and minutes books, and others having no records of any kind. Some poorhouse records can be found in National Health Service (NHS) archives due to the fact they later became NHS hospitals. Records from sheriff courts and the Board of Supervision are held by the National Records of Scotland.

Many general registers of the poor and registers of applications have been indexed by family history societies and local archives.

Some indexes are only available by visiting the archives in person, but a few are online, including those for Stirlingshire (www. stirlingarchives.scot/poor-relief-indexes) and Paisley (https://libcat. renfrewshire.gov.uk/iguana/www.main.cls?surl=poorlaw). Some poor relief records for Highland parishes have been transcribed and published by genealogist Stuart Farrell and can be purchased from the Scottish Genealogy Society. The minute books of the Board of Supervision for the period 1845–1895 have been indexed by Old Scottish Genealogy & Family History and can be searched through the individual parish pages of their website (www.oldscottish.com/ records.html).

EXPERT TIP

The parish responsible for maintaining a pauper depended upon that person's place of settlement. Records may be found not only in the parish where an ancestor resided at the time they applied for assistance, but also in the parish where they had lived previously, if that was deemed to be their place of settlement. Don't stop searching the records of a parish at the date your ancestor left, as they could still appear for several years afterwards.

Health Records

The records kept by hospitals and other medical institutions can be valuable for shedding light on an ancestor's circumstances, and prior to 1855 may record details of deaths not found elsewhere.

The majority of health records are held by National Health Service (NHS) archives, and closure periods apply for modern records (often 100 years, but sometimes less for adult patients). As most poorhouses included an infirmary, and hospitals typically distinguished between paying and pauper patients, there may be some crossover between poor relief and health records.

Relatively few health records are indexed or online, but some patient registers from the Kelso Dispensary have been indexed by Scottish Indexes (www.scottishindexes.co.uk/dispsearch.aspx), and some patients from the Royal Hospital for Sick Children in Glasgow can be identified through the Historic Hospital Admission Records Project (www.hharp.org). The Aberdeen & North-East Scotland Family History Society has published four volumes of deaths recorded at Aberdeen Royal Infirmary in the period 1743–1897, which include details of occupation, residence and place of birth.

Ancestors who spent time in a mental asylum are relatively easy to identify thanks to the 'General Register of Lunatics in Asylum', which was begun in 1858 and covered the whole of Scotland. The register and the associated 'Notices of Admissions by the Superintendent of Mental Institution', which provides details of patients' conditions, are held by the National Records of Scotland. Records up to 1918 have been indexed by Old Scottish Genealogy & Family History (www.oldscottish.com/asylum-patients.html), with some years also indexed by Scottish Indexes (www.scottish-indexes.co.uk/mcsearch.aspx). Further details of mental health patients can be found in the records of the individual asylums, which are mainly held in NHS archives. Asylum records can reveal a lot of family information so are worth searching for all relatives, not just direct ancestors.

EXPERT TIP

Death and burial records are the most likely sources for identifying an ancestor who spent time in a hospital or asylum, but many people spent only a brief time in such an institution and did not necessarily die there. It is worth checking any available indexes for relatives' names, and particularly looking for anyone who was missing from the family home on census night.

Registers of Sasines

The registers of sasines record property transactions. When a person acquired the right to heritable property (land and buildings) in Scotland, by whatever means, they had to go through a legal process in order to take formal possession of, or be *infeft* (invested) in that property. The Scots word *sasine* (pronounced 'say-zin' and related to the word 'seize') refers to the act of giving legal possession of property, but is also used more generally to refer to the documents recording that act.

Originally the transfer of property involved a symbolic ceremony where certain items (typically earth and stone taken from the property) were handed over to the new owner. The first written records of this sasine ceremony date from 1248, but the origins may be even earlier. The document recording this ceremony was known as an 'Instrument of Sasine'.

There were several attempts made in the sixteenth century to start a register to record instruments of sasine. In 1599, a register was begun under the supervision of the Secretary of State, which was known as the Secretary's Register. This did not include property within burghs (towns) and was abolished in 1609. The surviving registers from this period are incomplete.

A new series of general and particular registers of sasines was begun in 1617. The particular registers each covered a county or sheriffdom, or group of sheriffdoms, while the general register was used primarily to record property that crossed county boundaries. There were some changes made to the sasine registers over the years, but they continued until 1981 when they were gradually replaced by a new system of registration of title. Separate sasine registers for property within burghs were formally established in 1681, but some actually pre-date this. They were abolished from 1926 onwards, with the last being closed in 1963.

The majority of sasine registers are held by the National Records of Scotland (NRS), although some burgh registers can be found in local archives. The general and particular registers are fully indexed from 1781. There are indexes for some, but not all, particular registers prior to 1781, and an incomplete index to the general register. Many of the burgh registers are not indexed. The NRS website has a useful research guide on sasines, which includes details of available indexes (www.nrscotland.gov.uk/research/guides/sasines).

The modern organization responsible for land registration in Scotland is the Registers of Scotland (RoS). Most of the RoS's services (such as identifying the current owners of property) are not relevant to those carrying out historical or genealogical research, but their search sheets, first introduced in 1871, provide a summary of the transactions relating to an individual property, and can be a useful shortcut.

Prior to the start of the sasine registers, details of sasines may be found among collections of family and estate papers, and in notarial protocol books – these were the private records kept by the notaries who drew up the instruments of sasine. Many notarial protocol books are held by the NRS, and a small number have been published by historical societies. Other early property records include original charters (found mainly among family and estate records) and Crown grants of land (the Registers of the Great Seal, Quarter Seal, Prince's Seal and Privy Seal).

The registers of sasines are an invaluable source for tracing the history of a property, and for establishing what lands an ancestor owned. They may also provide evidence of family connections, and can therefore be a valuable source for genealogists. However, they can be difficult to decipher, particularly as early records are often written in Latin, and the legal language used can be confusing.

EXPERT TIP

The registers of sasines will only be useful for tracing ancestors who owned property, which was a small minority of people in Scotland. However, don't presume that only wealthy and titled families are included. An ancestor living in a rural area was most likely a tenant, but one living in an urban area may have been able to acquire a modest property. Some individuals with relatively humble occupations, such as craftsmen and labourers, can be found in the registers of sasines.

Services of Heirs (Retours)

As mentioned in the section on wills and testaments, prior to 1868 heritable property (land and buildings) could not be bequeathed in a will in Scotland. Instead the Law of Primogeniture applied, which specified which relative would inherit. This was usually the eldest son of the person who died owning property, but if there was no son, then any daughters would inherit equally, regardless of number or birth order. If the deceased person had no legitimate children then the next relative in line to inherit would be a brother; however, whether this was an elder or younger brother could actually depend upon how the property had originally been acquired. When a person died with no known legal heir then the Crown was deemed to be the *Ultimus Haeres*, or last heir, and the deceased person's heritable and moveable property would be paid to the Exchequer.

Under the feudal system that operated in Scotland, if a person died holding property directly from the Crown, then their heir could not automatically take full possession but had to prove their right to inherit. An inquest was held, in which a jury of fifteen local men heard evidence as to the heir's right to inherit, and then returned or 'retoured' their decision to the Scottish Chancery. The Chancery would then 'serve' the claimant as heir so that they could take full possession of the property. The resulting records are known as 'Retours' or 'Services of Heirs'.

Retours provide valuable genealogical information, as the relationship between the heir and the previous landholder is always specified. There were two main types of retour: a 'special retour' was concerned with a claim to specific lands held by an ancestor and includes details of those lands, while a 'general retour' just established the general right of the claimant to be recognized as the lawful heir, and does not specify any lands or other property held by the ancestor. Retours were written in Latin up to 1847 (with the exception of the period 1652–1659, when they are in Scots) but they are generally quite formulaic and it is therefore possible to glean the main information with little or no knowledge of Latin. The register of retours is held by the National Records of Scotland (NRS) and dates from 1530 (earlier records were largely lost), although sixteenth-century records and those for the period 1611–1614 are incomplete. The register is fully indexed in two main series.

Abridgements or summaries of retours (in Latin) up to 1700 were published in two volumes in 1811, with a third index volume published in 1816. These are entitled *Inquisitionum ad Capellam Domini Regis Retornatarum, quae in Publicis Archivis Scotiae adhuc servantur, Abbreviatio* (or *Inquisitionum Retornatarum Abbreviatio* for short). The three volumes are available online through Google Books (https://books.google.com), and have been published on CD-ROM by the Scottish Genealogy Society as *Retours of Services of Heirs, 1544–1699*. An edited and rearranged version was produced by Dr Bruce Durie in 2012.

Indexes to the register of retours for the period 1700–2001 are in the form of a series of printed volumes entitled *Indexes to the Services of Heirs in Scotland*. These indexes can be found at the NRS and in some reference and genealogical libraries. Those for the period 1700–1859 are published on CD-ROM by the Scottish Genealogy Society as *Decennial Indexes to the Services of Heirs in Scotland, 1700–1859* and can be purchased through the society's website.

The retours record only the jury's decision, not all the evidence presented at the inquest. Inquests were generally held in burgh or sheriff courts, and these courts kept their own records. Not only are records of inquests generally written in Scots or English, rather than in Latin, but they may give information not found in the retour, such as the names of additional family members and statements by witnesses who gave evidence. A small number of services were never retoured to Chancery and so the inquest may be the only record. Records of inquests do not survive in all cases but may be found among the records of the relevant court, either at the NRS or in local archives.

The retours process was used when a person held land directly from the Crown, but could also be used when a person who did not hold land directly wished to be formally recognized or 'served' as heir. However, there was no legal requirement to do this, and so there will not be a retour in all cases. Instead a document known as a 'Precept of Clare Constat' was issued, in which it was acknowledged that it was 'clearly evident' that the person claiming to be the heir was indeed the rightful heir. There was no central register of such documents and most do not survive, although some may be found among family and estate papers, and they may be copied or referenced as part of a sasine.

The retours process gradually fell into disuse after 1868 and began to be formally abolished in 1964. Other records dealing with the inheritance of property in Scotland include the Register of Tailzies (which records entails specifying who could inherit property in future generations), *Ultimus Haeres* records (which deal with the property of those who died without a known legal heir), and registers of deeds.

EXPERT TIP

As with wills, a retour may only have been recorded many years after a person died, perhaps because the heir needed to prove their legal ownership of the property. It is not unusual to discover that a property was passed down through several generations with no records being found. In order to trace what happened to a person's property after their death, it is often necessary to search wills and testaments, sasines, retours and deeds across a wide range of years.

Registers of Deeds

Deeds are any type of legal document registered with a court. A large number of deeds concern debts and the borrowing of money, but those of most use to genealogists include marriage contracts, apprenticeship indentures, tacks (rental agreements), wills and similar documents.

Deeds are an under-used source for tracing Scottish family history, largely due to the difficulties in locating them. First, a legal agreement did not have to be registered as a deed at all, and might only be recorded many years after it was created. Second, it could be registered in many different places. The Court of Session, sheriff courts, commissary courts, burgh courts and some franchise courts (the private courts of major landowners) all kept their own registers of deeds. Finally, there are relatively few indexes to registers of deeds so it is necessary to search through original records, which can be very time consuming.

Deeds often contain valuable genealogical information but can be difficult to locate. This deed was originally written in 1796 but was not registered until 1799. This copy, dated 1859, comes from the author's personal collection.

Most registers of deeds can be found at the National Records of Scotland (NRS), although some are held in local archives. The register of deeds of the Court of Session was based in Edinburgh and also known as the Books of Council and Session. There are yearly indexes from 1770 to the present day, with some years prior to this also indexed (the earliest indexed period is 1554–1595). A complication for unindexed years is that there were actually three separate registers (known as

Dalrymple, Durie and Mackenzie) and these need to be searched individually.

There are some indexes to sheriff court registers of deeds, mainly from 1809, and these are listed in the 'Deeds Research Guide' on the NRS website (www.nrscotland.gov.uk/research/guides/deeds). A small number of indexes to deeds have been published, including those for Kirkcudbright Sheriff Court and Cupar Sheriff Court.

Registers of deeds contain a legal copy of a document. The original documents are known as warrants and may sometimes be found alongside the registers in a separate series. Warrants show the original signatures of the individuals involved and can be searched when the registers do not survive.

While wealthy individuals are more likely to be recorded in deeds than poor ones, a wide range of society is represented. If looking for a specific deed, the best approach is to draw up a list of all the registers of deeds covering the relevant location and time period, and then to search them systematically, starting with any available indexes.

EXPERT TIP

When searching for deeds the term 'probative writ' may be encountered. This has nothing to do with probate (an English term), but rather refers to a document that is similar to a deed, but which does not contain a clause specifying that it should registered. Often deeds and probative writs were recorded together in a single volume, but if there is a separate register of probative writs this should also be searched.

Burgh Records

Scottish burghs were urban settlements that enjoyed trading privileges and control over their own administration, separate from the county in which they were situated. Burghs were first established in Scotland in the twelfth century, although some had existed as settlements long prior to the granting of burgh status. The most important type of burgh was the royal burgh, whose rights were granted or confirmed by the monarch by means of a burgh charter. Burghs of regality and burghs of barony conferred varying trading rights and had lesser status.

The term 'burgh records' encompasses a wide variety of documents relating to the administration of the burgh and its citizens. It is important for a genealogist to know whether the area in which an ancestor lived was a burgh, not only because of the wealth of records this opens up, but also because burghs were typically administered separately from the surrounding area – as, for example, with property within royal burghs being recorded in separate burgh registers of sasines. A burgh was a small, defined area, generally much smaller than the present town or city of the same name. Parishes that contained a burgh often distinguished between the burgh and the landward (rural) parts of the parish; only those areas within a burgh will be recorded in burgh records.

Types of document frequently found within burgh records include burgh court books (which dealt with both civil and criminal matters), burgh registers of deeds, burgh registers of sasines (and the earlier notarial protocol books), accounts books, council minute books, and property tax and voters rolls. Of particular interest to family historians are burgess rolls and the records of merchant and craft guilds (also known as trade incorporations).

Not every man who lived in a burgh was a burgess, but many merchants and craftsmen were, as burgess status afforded particular trading privileges. The right to be a burgess could be passed from father to son, or acquired through marriage to a burgess's daughter, or by completion of an apprenticeship. The records of burgesses therefore often contain genealogical information.

Merchants and craftsmen living within a burgh might also be a member of their occupation's guild or trade incorporation, and membership might be necessary in order to trade within the burgh. Records of crafts and trades often include membership rolls and minute books recording the admission of apprentices and freemen (masters or full members). Many guilds also had a charitable function and records may contain details of payments to elderly members, widows and children, and poor people outside the incorporation. Membership often passed down through families, and again the records may contain genealogical information.

Burgh records are held by the National Records of Scotland and in local archives (in some cases records may be split across several locations). Records of crafts and trades may be found within burgh records or as separate collections. The National Library of

Scotland has a small collection of craft and guild records, and some are still privately held by the relevant organization, although it may be possible to request access.

Some burgess rolls and lists of apprentices taken from burgh records have been published by historical and family history societies, as have a small number of guild records. Some out-of-copyright publications, such as those published by the Scottish Record Society for Edinburgh and Glasgow, can be found online (*see* www.scottishrecordsociety.org.uk/publications).

EXPERT TIP

Apprenticeships may be recorded in burgh records, in the minute books of individual crafts and trades, and in registers of deeds, although most apprenticeship indentures were not formally recorded. Such records are worth seeking out as they often name the boy's father, or his mother or another relative if the father was deceased. Some Scottish apprentices are listed in the British Board of Stamps' Apprenticeship Books covering 1710–1811, which are indexed on both Ancestry and Findmypast.

Court and Criminal Records

There was a wide range of courts in Scotland dealing with both civil and criminal matters, and people at all levels of society had access to some form of redress for a perceived injustice, even if it was just bringing a neighbour before the kirk session for name-calling. Court and criminal records can therefore be particularly valuable for shedding light on the lives of ordinary people who appear in few other records. Generally speaking, however, the higher the court, the easier it is to find records of an ancestor, as records of lower courts do not always survive and are rarely indexed.

The High Court of Justiciary is the supreme criminal court in Scotland, the Court of Session is the highest civil court, and the Admiralty Court had jurisdiction over all maritime matters, civil and criminal, until 1830. Other courts that heard cases from across Scotland included the Privy Council, the Court of Exchequer and the Commissary Court of Edinburgh, which dealt with divorce and marital cases until 1830.

The main local courts were sheriff courts, which had jurisdiction over a county or part of a county, and dealt with both criminal and civil matters. Other local courts that heard both civil and criminal cases included burgh courts, franchise courts (the courts of major landowners, which were mainly abolished in 1747) and justice of the peace courts. Commissary courts were mainly concerned with wills and testaments, but also heard some civil cases. Police courts dealt with minor criminal offences.

Prison registers are a useful source for those accused or found guilty of a crime, and may provide more personal detail than court records, such as age and birthplace. Debtors could also be imprisoned and therefore appear in prison registers. Police records may include details of criminals, and some police forces kept registers of criminals, which provide physical descriptions and in some cases photographs.

The majority of court and criminal records are held by the National Records of Scotland (NRS), although some can be found in local archives. Many court papers and precognitions (evidence gathered before the trial) for cases heard by the High Court of Justiciary can be identified through the NRS online catalogue, and there is a more detailed 'Solemn Database' of criminal cases available in the NRS search room. The Scottish Indexes website includes 'Scotland's Criminal Database' (www.scottishindexes. com/scotlandscriminaldatabase.aspx), with details of over 150,000 Scottish criminal records, and Fife Family History Society (https:// fifefhs.org) has published the *Fife Kalendar of Convicts, 1790– 1880*. For most other cases it is necessary to know when and where a case was heard, and then to search the available records. The NRS research guide on 'Crime and Criminals' (www.nrscotland.gov.uk/ research/guides/crime-and-criminals) includes a list of prison registers, and a small number of these have been indexed.

EXPERT TIP

Newspapers are an excellent source for identifying court cases, and may provide the names of victims and witnesses as well as the accused. They can be used to locate court and criminal records involving an ancestor, or may provide a more detailed account of court proceedings than surviving court records.

Estate Records

Estate records are the private records maintained and held by land-owning families in Scotland. They are also referred to as family and estate papers, and sometimes as muniments (technically documents establishing legal rights such as property ownership). Some estate records are primarily concerned with the landowning family and with legal documents proving property rights, but the most useful also contain records of the running of the estate and of the tenants who lived and worked there.

Estate records do not exist for all property in Scotland, but are particularly useful for tracing ancestors who lived on large rural estates whose owners would have needed to know who was renting what property, how much they paid, whether they were in arrears, and what improvements were needed on the estate. Large estates were managed by a factor or estate manager, who would have kept these records and whose reports to his employer often included personal observations on the tenants. As tenancies often passed down through families, estate records can be important genealogical sources and can be used to link generations, particularly when parish registers were poorly kept or provide little detail. The most useful types of estate records for tracing tenants include rental rolls and lists of tenants, tacks and leases (rental agreements), estate correspondence, and maps and plans.

Estate records can be found at the National Records of Scotland, the National Library of Scotland, in local and university archives, and in some cases are still privately held by the relevant family (although it may be possible to request access). A small number of records have been published, including some particularly useful lists of tenants on the estates of the Duke of Argyll in the late 1700s.

In order to locate estate records for where an ancestor lived, it is first necessary to identify the landowner. Useful sources for doing this include valuations rolls, land tax rolls, sasines, parish and local histories, and *The Statistical Accounts of Scotland* (described below). *A Directory of Land Ownership in Scotland c.1770* by Loretta R. Timperley (Edinburgh: The Scottish Record Society, 1976) is based largely on land tax rolls and is a useful shortcut for identifying landowners in the late 1700s.

EXPERT TIP

Movements from one part of Scotland to another can sometimes be explained by identifying local landowners. An ancestor who was an estate worker or tenant farmer may have moved between estates owned by the same family.

Military Records

Prior to 1707, the main records for tracing soldiers who fought in the Scottish army are muster rolls held by the National Records of Scotland (NRS). Officers are slightly better documented than regular soldiers, with some surviving records of army commissions. After the Acts of Union of 1707, Scottish soldiers fought in the British (rather than the Scottish) army, and the majority of records concerning the military service of Scottish ancestors will be found at The National Archives (TNA) in Kew, London.

Records for tracing soldiers in the British army include service, pension and discharge records, muster rolls and medal rolls. Many of these have now been digitized and indexed and are available through the Ancestry and Findmypast websites. The TNA website (www.nationalarchives.gov.uk/help-with-your-research/research-guides) includes a large number of detailed research guides on military sources.

Most Scottish families include at least one relative who fought in World War I. Unfortunately, around 60 per cent of World War I service records were destroyed by bombing during World War II, and it is usually easier to trace those who were killed in action rather than those who survived. Medal rolls and medal index cards, available online, provide a more or less complete record of all those who saw active service during World War I, but the lack of personal detail (sometimes only a first initial rather than a full name is given) means it can be difficult to identify soldiers with common names. Pension record cards and ledgers are a useful supplementary source for those injured during the war, and for those who were killed and whose dependants applied for a pension.

The Commonwealth War Graves Commission (www.cwgc.org) provides the best starting point for tracing armed forces personnel who were killed during both world wars. Further information on Scots can be found in the roll of honour of the Scottish National

War Memorial (www.snwm.org), and through local war memorials and rolls of honour. Newspapers often recorded those killed in action (and sometimes the names of local men fighting overseas), and many such reports have been indexed by local libraries.

Records of armed forces personnel who served after 1920 are still held by the Ministry of Defence, but copies can be obtained by contacting the relevant department (*see* www.gov.uk/get-copy-military-service-records for guidance). The ScotlandsPeople website includes various military registers of deaths and soldiers' and airmen's wills (1857–1965), as well as surviving records of military service appeals tribunals for the Lothians and Borders for 1916–1918.

In addition to the regular army, various militia and fencible regiments were raised in Scotland, particularly during the period of the Napoleonic Wars. Militia regiments were raised by ballot, and militia records may include all those eligible to serve in a particular parish, as well as the names of those who were balloted and those who actually served (often a substitute who might come from a different area). Payments made to the wives and children of militiamen who were unable to support themselves may also be recorded.

EXPERT TIP

If an ancestor married or had a child while serving in the armed forces, then marriage and birth records may provide details of his regiment and sometimes his service number. It is particularly worthwhile to look at the birth records of any children born during the two world wars, when details of military service may be hard to identify from other sources.

Militia records can be found at the NRS in a variety of collections including the 'Gifts & Deposits' (GD) series and in local archives. Edinburgh City archives hold a series of army attestation registers for the period 1794–1887, which include both regular and militia soldiers from across the British Isles who attested in Edinburgh, and a partial name index is available. *The Defence of Scotland – Militias, Fencibles and Volunteer Corps 1793–1820* by Arnold Morrison (available online at

www.scribd.com/doc/68100606/the-defence-of-scotland-militias
-fencibles-and-volunteer-corps1793-1820) provides a detailed list
of surviving militia records and their locations.

Statistical Accounts of Scotland

The Statistical Accounts of Scotland are one of the best contemporary sources on everyday life in Scotland in the late eighteenth and
early nineteenth centuries. Despite their name, these are not dry
statistical reports but rather descriptive accounts providing a vast
amount of detail of value to family and local historians.

The first or old statistical account was published in twenty-one
volumes between 1791 and 1799. An original set of 160 questions
in four sections was distributed to the parish minister of each of
Scotland's parishes, with an additional six questions sent in a later
appendix. These covered geography and natural history, the population of the parish (number and ages, average number of births,
deaths and marriages, occupations, religion and so on), agricul-
ture and industry, and miscellaneous questions. The accounts were
published as they were received and so are not arranged in any
particular order.

A second or new statistical account was compiled between 1834
and 1845, and a complete edition, organized by county, was published in fifteen volumes in 1845. This second account followed a
similar pattern to the first, but with the addition of county maps
and contributions by doctors, landowners and schoolmasters.

The accounts can be accessed through a dedicated website The
Statistical Accounts of Scotland 1791–1845 (http://stataccscot.
edina.ac.uk). Full access is by subscription, but non-subscribers can
browse each volume and search by parish name and by means of
an interactive map. The website also provides useful background
information on the accounts.

The Statistical Accounts can also be found on Google Books
and the Internet Archive, although the easiest way to locate a particular parish account within these digitized volumes is through the
links on the Electric Scotland website (www.electricscotland.com/
history/books.htm).

EXPERT TIP

The Statistical Accounts not only give a vivid description of life in an ancestor's parish, but also provide information to aid research, including identifying local churches and the numbers who attended each, naming major landowners, and highlighting problems with the parish registers. For example, in the first account for Urr, Kirkcudbrightshire, the minister reported he had baptised only ten children in twenty-two years, due to the large number of dissenters in the parish and the difficulties in bringing newborn babies to the church.

Published Family Histories

Many histories of particular Scottish families have been published over the last few centuries, and landed and titled families are well documented in works such as *The Scots Peerage* and *Burke's Peerage*. These can be found in genealogical and reference libraries, with many out-of-copyright books now digitized and available online through Google Books (https://books.google.co.uk), Internet Archive (https://archive.org) and the digital gallery of the National Library of Scotland (https://digital.nls.uk/gallery/category/family-history).

EXPERT TIP

Finding a published account of a family can save time unnecessarily duplicating research, but, as with information found in online family trees, details should be verified using original records wherever possible. Published histories may contain inaccurate information, few provide detailed source citations, and even generally well-researched accounts may contain errors or omissions.

Further Sources

This chapter has covered the main records used for researching Scottish family history, but there are many additional sources that may be useful for tracing individual ancestors. These include records of particular occupations (from clergymen and doctors to crofters and lighthouse keepers), educational records (schools and universities) and records of emigrants.

The National Records of Scotland (NRS) online research guides provide a good introduction to many Scottish sources, with more detailed explanations of records of particular interest to family historians given in *Tracing Your Scottish Ancestors: The Official Guide* (*see* Further Reading). However, the main focus of both the online and published guides is, unsurprisingly, the records held by the NRS itself, with only brief mentions of records held elsewhere.

The websites and online catalogues of most archives include information on their records, and some local archives, family history societies and individual genealogists have published research guides to the records of particular counties or regions. The research tools section of the Scottish Archive Network website (www.scan.org.uk) includes various record and subject guides, and other useful resources such as a Scots currency converter.

EXPERT TIP

Solving difficult genealogy problems often involves going beyond the basic sources of births, marriages and deaths, censuses and parish registers to look at a wide variety of different records. Familiarizing ourselves with the records available at a national and local level is one of the best first steps to breaking through any genealogy brick wall.

---

2 Scottish Archives and Record Repositories

The records used for tracing Scottish ancestors can be found in archives and record repositories throughout Scotland, and in some cases, in the rest of the UK and further afield. Some of these repositories have been mentioned previously, but this chapter describes the main Scottish archives and their holdings in a little more detail.

In general in Scotland, original documents are held in archives, while published sources such as books are held in libraries, but there is some cross-over between the two. Many libraries hold some manuscript collections of original documents, and most archives have at least a small reference library of relevant books. Archive and library staff are generally not able to carry out detailed genealogical research for enquirers (unless they offer a paid research service), but they can offer advice on records and supply copies of documents.

Although many records of interest to family historians are now available online, these represent only a small fraction of the wealth of information to be found in Scottish archives. Visiting archives and handling original documents (carefully!) is one of the great pleasures of carrying out family history research, and often the only way to solve complex genealogy problems.

National Records of Scotland

Address: HM General Register House, 2 Princes Street, Edinburgh, EH1 3YY

Website: www.nrscotland.gov.uk

The National Records of Scotland is the prime location for researching Scottish family history.

The National Records of Scotland (NRS) is Scotland's principal record repository. It was formed in 2011 by the merger of the General Register Office for Scotland, whose main function was the registration of births, marriages and deaths, and the National Archives of Scotland, which was itself formerly known as the Scottish Record Office. Although these two departments are physically housed within one building complex in central Edinburgh (comprising General Register House and New Register House), because the way of accessing the records is different for each, it makes sense to treat them as two separate repositories: the ScotlandsPeople Centre and the Historical Search Room.

The ScotlandsPeople Centre
The ScotlandsPeople Centre is the official government family history centre, and provides access to statutory records of births, marriages and deaths, census returns, church registers, wills and testaments, valuation rolls and coats of arms. The majority of records are accessed as indexed, digitized images, although a few are only available on microfilm or microfiche, and there is also a small reference library of genealogical publications. Original records are only produced in exceptional circumstances, although it is possible to request rescans of poor quality images of the statutory registers.

The computer system in the ScotlandsPeople Centre is almost identical to the website of the same name (www.scotlandspeople. gov.uk), and can also be accessed through a network of smaller Local Family History Centres throughout Scotland (at present in Alloa, Glasgow, Hawick, Inverness and Kilmarnock). Online access may be easier for those who do not live near one of the centres, but there are advantages to searching onsite. First, images of modern records (births less than 100 years ago, marriages less than seventy-five years and deaths less than fifty years) are not available online for privacy reasons. Second, the centres charge a daily fee, rather than per image, which is nearly always cheaper and is particularly helpful when researching common surnames or looking to identify extended family members (such as identifying all the children born to a particular couple).

To access the records of the ScotlandsPeople Centre, researchers pay for an individual seat (currently £15 per day) in one of the search rooms, which can be booked and paid in advance through the ScotlandsPeople website, or on the day (although seats are limited). There are additional charges for obtaining copies. Each Local Family History Centre operates its own booking systems.

EXPERT TIP

The unrestricted access to records the ScotlandsPeople Centre provides is indispensable when trying to solve family history problems and overcome research brick walls. The majority of professional genealogists in Scotland use the centres rather than researching exclusively online.

The NRS Historical Search Room

The NRS Historical Search Room provides access to original documents dating from the 1100s to the present day, and is used by a range of historical researchers, not just family historians. Although some indexes and finding aids are available, the majority of records are not indexed by personal name, but are catalogued by the title and description of the document. Instead of entering an ancestor's name into a database (as with the ScotlandsPeople Centre), the NRS catalogue is used to identify records in which an individual may be recorded (for example, by searching for the name of the parish in which they lived). The original documents can then be ordered up and searched manually to locate any entries of interest.

The NRS is the main repository for Scottish public and legal records, but also holds many private and local records, making it one of the most diverse collections in the UK. Records of particular interest to family historians include church records (kirk sessions and non-Church of Scotland registers), sasines, services of heirs, court and criminal records, deeds, estate papers and tax records. Some of the most popular records have been digitized and are accessed on computers within the historical search room using the 'Virtual Volumes' system.

There is no charge for searching records in the Historical Search Room, but it is necessary to first obtain a reader's ticket (which requires two forms of identification). Some records are stored offsite and need to be ordered at least twenty-four hours in advance, so it is a good idea to check the location and availability of records prior to visiting. Some, but not all, records can be photographed using a personal camera for which there is no charge (check with staff before taking photographs). There are charges for paper and digital copies, and some copying restrictions apply.

EXPERT TIP

The Historical Search Room may seem a little intimidating on a first visit, and some of the finding aids can be difficult to use, but most of the staff are friendly and helpful, and can explain how to find what you are looking for if you are unsure.

The Court of the Lord Lyon

Address: HM New Register House, Princes Street, Edinburgh, EH1 3YT
Website: www.courtofthelordlyon.scot

Heraldry and the use of coats of arms is tightly regulated in Scotland, and the Court of the Lord Lyon has jurisdiction over all heraldic matters. Anyone who wishes to apply for a personal coat of arms, or who believes they are entitled to the coat of arms of an ancestor, should petition the Lord Lyon.

Of particular interest to genealogists, the Court of the Lord

Lyon has, since 1672, maintained the Public Register of All Arms and Bearings in Scotland. This can be viewed at the court's offices within the National Records of Scotland for a fee, and entries over 100 years old are also available on the ScotlandsPeople website. The court does not undertake genealogical research, but houses a small manuscript collection, mainly relating to families that bore coats of arms, which can be accessed by appointment.

EXPERT TIP

A coat of arms belongs to a single individual or organization, not to a family or to everyone with the same surname. The vast majority of people in Scotland have no right to a coat of arms, but anyone who wishes to demonstrate their association with a clan and allegiance to the clan chief is permitted to wear the chief's crest encircled with a strap and buckle bearing the clan motto.

The National Library of Scotland
Address: Main building: George IV Bridge, Edinburgh, EH1 1EW
Website: www.nls.uk

The National Library of Scotland holds both published and manuscript sources and has a range of online resources.

The National Library of Scotland (NLS) is one of the legal deposit libraries of the UK. Its main function is to collect published materials relating to Scotland and the Scots, and it has particularly strong map and newspaper collections. The Special Collections Department houses rare books and manuscripts, including family and estate papers and other records of interest to genealogists. The NLS is also home to Scotland's Moving Image Archive, with many films available online, and a dedicated moving image centre in Kelvinhall, Glasgow. The NLS is a reference library only, not a lending library.

Published resources held by the NLS for tracing Scottish ancestors include compiled family histories, monumental inscriptions, street and post office directories, newspapers, electoral registers, and indexes and transcripts produced by historical and family history societies. These can be identified in the main catalogue and are accessed in the general reading room. A small number of books are on open shelves, but the majority need to be ordered out of storage, which can be done in advance of a visit using the online catalogue. The NLS website includes useful guides, and some directories can be accessed online via the digital gallery section, as can military lists, rolls of honour, gazetteers, historical society publications and published family histories. The library also subscribes to a variety of databases, such as digitized newspaper collections.

The National Library of Scotland's map collection includes around two million items, making it one of the largest map collections in the world. Many of the NLS's most useful maps are available online through a dedicated website (https://maps.nls.uk), which includes over 150,000 high quality digital images of maps (not all of Scotland). Online images include maps covering the whole of Scotland dating from 1560 to 1947, maps of each historic county, town plans and views, series maps, coastal maps and admiralty charts, military maps and a collection of estate maps. The maps can be browsed by category and some can be explored through geo-referencing, which allows the user to view maps from different periods side by side. A short introductory video on the website provides guidance on searching. Maps are included in the online catalogue, and those not online can be viewed at the Maps Reading Room in Causewayside, Edinburgh.

Manuscript collections are not included in the NLS's main online catalogue. Work is underway to add details from original paper catalogues to the online 'Catalogue of Archives and Manuscripts Collections', but this is currently incomplete. The 'Manuscript catalogues and guides' page of the NLS website (www.nls.uk/catalogues/manuscripts) is a good starting point for identifying records, and library staff can provide additional guidance.

There is no charge for visiting the National Library of Scotland, and the majority of online resources can be accessed freely anywhere in the world. Anyone can visit the visitor centre, which includes an exhibition area, café and shop, but it is necessary to have a library card to access the reading rooms (available to anyone over sixteen with the appropriate forms of identification).

EXPERT TIP

Many of the online databases to which the National Library of Scotland subscribes can be accessed from home by registered readers whose main address is in Scotland. It is worth registering online even if you are unlikely to visit the library in person.

The National Archives (UK)
Address: Kew, Richmond, Surrey, TW9 4DU
Website: www.nationalarchives.gov.uk

The National Archives (TNA) is the official archive of the UK government and holds more than eleven million records. Although it is not the prime location for researching Scottish family history, many Scots can be found among its collections.

The majority of records that were compiled on a UK-wide basis are held at TNA rather than in Scotland, and these include records of Scots who served in the armed forces and the merchant navy, as well as records of emigrants and immigrants, such as ship passenger lists and naturalizations. The wills of some Scots can be found among the records of the Prerogative Court of Canterbury, and the records of Jacobites captured after the 1715 and 1745 Uprisings, who were tried in England, can also be found at TNA.

The National Archives has worked with several commercial organizations to digitize the collections of most interest to family historians, and these can be accessed online, mainly through

Ancestry (www.ancestry.co.uk) and Findmypast (www.findmypast. co.uk). Further records can be identified through TNA's Discovery catalogue (http://discovery.nationalarchives.gov.uk), and some can be downloaded directly from the website (usually for a fee). A reader's ticket is needed to access original documents at TNA. Records can be ordered in advance of a visit, after registering online.

EXPERT TIP

TNA's online research guides are a great resource for getting to grips with the archives' collections and understanding the content of records commonly used by family historians. They include links to online collections and brief details of records held elsewhere.

Historic Environment Scotland

Address: John Sinclair House, 16 Bernard Terrace, Edinburgh, EH8 9NX
Website: www.historicenvironment.scot

Historic Environment Scotland (formed in 2015 from Historic Scotland and the Royal Commission on the Ancient and Historical Monuments of Scotland) is the public body responsible for Scotland's historic environment. Its diverse responsibilities include maintaining the National Record of the Historic Environment, an archive of over five million items relating to Scotland's archaeological sites, buildings, industry and maritime heritage.

Historic Environment Scotland's collections can be accessed in the search room in Edinburgh by appointment, as well as through a number of specific projects that are listed on its website (www.historicenvironment.scot/archives-and-research/archives-and-collections). The easiest way to identify material of interest is through the Canmore database, which includes information on around 300,000 places in Scotland. The organization also maintains Scran (www.scran.ac.uk), an online learning service containing over 480,000 images and media from museums, galleries and archives throughout Scotland. The collection can be searched by keyword as well as through a geographical search. Access is by subscription only, although many Scottish libraries subscribe with free access for library members.

EXPERT TIP

The collections of Historic Environment Scotland are focused on buildings rather than people, but they may include records of places where an ancestor lived or worked, which can help to bring a family history to life.

Local and Council Archives

In addition to the national record repositories, there are a number of smaller local archives situated throughout Scotland. Many of these began life as facilities to house local government records and are therefore known as council archives or city archives, but their remit has been extended to include all kinds of records relating to their local areas. Due to various administrative boundary changes that occurred in the twentieth century, the areas covered by these local archives are not the same as the historic counties, and records may not always be found in the expected location. Some local archives are physically housed within libraries, although their function is quite distinct.

Sources frequently found in local archives include records of local administration, burgh records, police records, cemetery registers, poor relief records, school registers, and records of local businesses, families and estates. Most local archives have online catalogues or guides to their records as well as some indexes to records of particular interest to family historians. It is worth identifying any archives covering the areas where an ancestor lived and becoming familiar with their holdings and any indexes available online or onsite.

The Scottish Council on Archives website (www.scottisharchives. org.uk) includes a Scottish archives map with links to the websites of local archives throughout Scotland. The website of the Scottish Archives Network (www.scan.org.uk) includes an online catalogue to the holdings of fifty-two Scottish archives, although it is incomplete and has not been updated for some time.

Some local archives recommend that visitors make an appointment, and it is always advisable to contact the archive prior to visiting to check opening hours, if records are held offsite and need to be ordered in advance, and if any identification is required.

EXPERT TIP

Many archivists are experts on the records within their archives and on the history of their local area. They can usually advise on the records they hold relating to a particular subject (which may not always be fully catalogued), and can point researchers towards relevant sources held elsewhere.

University Archives

Most of Scotland's universities contain archives that are accessible to the public. Holdings typically include records of the university and its students, as well as a variety of specialized collections relating to the university's areas of interest. Perhaps due to the fact that universities and their archives often pre-date the creation of local council archives, many also hold records relating to their local areas, including family and estate papers.

Many university archives have online catalogues, and documents can also be identified through the Archives Hub (https://archiveshub.jisc.ac.uk), an online catalogue to the records of over 300 institutions across the UK.

EXPERT TIP

Many university libraries allow members of the public to join on a reference-only basis. This can be a good way of getting access to books that are not available through the local library.

Medical Archives

Historical medical records can be found in a variety of locations, but are most often held in NHS archives. When the National Health Service (NHS) was launched in Scotland in 1948, many existing hospitals and health institutions became part of the NHS, and as a result NHS archives include records not only from the twentieth century but in some cases dating back to the 1700s. Scotland is currently divided into fourteen NHS health board areas. Some have a dedicated NHS archive, while others have chosen to deposit their records in a university or local archive. As these modern health board areas do not correspond to the historic counties, it can be helpful to know which NHS board currently covers the area where an ancestor lived in order to locate any records.

Hospital records typically include admission and discharge registers, patient notes and registers of deaths, as well as staff records. Modern records – those less than 100 years old – may be closed due to privacy restrictions. Some NHS archives have their own online catalogues, or records may be included within the catalogues of other archives (for example the records of NHS Grampian Archives, housed within the University of Aberdeen, can be searched via the university's special collections catalogue). A UK-wide hospital records database is included on the website of The National Archives (www.nationalarchives.gov.uk/hospitalrecords), but it is no longer being updated and information may be out of date.

EXPERT TIP

Many health records are held within local or university archives, but where there is a dedicated NHS archivist, opening hours and access conditions may be different from other collections. Check with the NHS archivist prior to visiting.

Medical practitioners in Scotland had the option of joining the Aberdeen Medico-Chirurgical Society (founded in 1789), the Royal College of Surgeons of Edinburgh (with origins in a craft guild formed in 1505), the Royal College of Physicians of Edinburgh (established in 1681), or the Royal College of Physicians and Surgeons of Glasgow (founded in 1599). All four organizations maintain their own archives in Aberdeen, Edinburgh and Glasgow respectively, and details are given on their websites.

These archives will mainly be of interest if an ancestor worked in the medical profession, but the collections do include some patient records. The Royal College of Physicians of Edinburgh has digitized and transcribed the consultation letters of Dr William Cullen (1710–1790), which include patient names and are fully searchable by name or other keyword (www.cullenproject.ac.uk). The Royal College of Physicians and Surgeons of Glasgow has digitized a series of vaccination records for the city, which can be browsed through their website (https://heritage.rcpsg.ac.uk/collections/show/6), with a name index available on Findmypast as 'Scotland, Glasgow Smallpox Vaccination Registers 1801–1854'.

Specialist Archives and Museums

In addition to the archives described above, there are a number of specialist archives in Scotland that maintain the records of particular groups or organizations. Examples include the Scottish Jewish Archives Centre (www.sjac.org.uk), the Scottish Catholic Archives (www.abdn.ac.uk/special-collections/scottish-catholic-archives-73. php), the Scottish Business Archive (www.gla.ac.uk/myglasgow/ archives/collections/business) and the Royal Bank of Scotland Archives (www.rbs.com/heritage.html). Details can be found on the archives' websites, and access is usually by appointment.

In the Highlands, heritage centres and clan museums are an important resource for family historians. Alongside museum displays, their holdings typically include both published and manuscript sources, and they are particularly valuable for providing access to local knowledge and expertise. Examples include the Timespan Heritage & Arts Centre in Helmsdale, Sutherland (https://timespan.org.uk), and the Museum of the Isles (Clan Donald Centre) on the Isle of Skye (www.armadalecastle.com/ explore/library-archives).

Other museums may also hold documents of interest to family historians. These may relate to their collections of objects, to the museum's benefactors, or simply have been donated over the years. Some such documents can be identified in the catalogues described below.

Local Studies Libraries

Many larger libraries throughout Scotland hold collections relating to their local areas in dedicated local studies or local history departments. These mainly consist of published material, although often some miscellaneous manuscript collections are held that relate to local administration or have been donated.

As well as books relating to local history, industries, places and people, most local studies libraries have microfilm copies of the old parish registers and census records for their areas, and subscribe to various genealogy and newspaper websites. Printed sources such as newspapers, directories and electoral registers are typically found in local studies libraries rather than in archives.

Details of local studies libraries can be found in the libraries and archives sections of local council websites. Most collections are

Local libraries, such as Edinburgh's Central Library, hold a wealth of resources for tracing Scottish family history.

reference only, and it is not necessary to be a member of the library to access them.

EXPERT TIP

Although a lot of the material held by local studies libraries can be identified in the library's online catalogue, some older books, as well as manuscript and microfilm collections, may not be fully catalogued. It is worth checking for information on the library's website, which may highlight any particular treasures, as well as asking staff about what they hold.

Scottish Genealogy Society Library
Address: 15 Victoria Terrace, Edinburgh, EH1 2JL
Website: www.scotsgenealogy.com

The Scottish Genealogy Society was founded in 1953 and is the principal and oldest genealogy society in Scotland, as well as the *de facto* family history society for the City of Edinburgh. The society runs a programme of talks and classes, produces a

The library and family history centre of the Scottish Genealogy Society in Edinburgh holds records relating to families across Scotland.

quarterly journal, *The Scottish Genealogist*, and publishes indexes to Scottish records, with a particular focus on the Edinburgh area.

The society's library and family history centre holds over 4,000 books and CDs, as well as microfilm copies of the old parish registers and censuses for the whole of Scotland, and a large collection of compiled family histories. The library collects journals and publications from all major Scottish family history societies, and has the largest collection of monumental inscriptions (published and unpublished) in Scotland. It also provides access to a number of subscription genealogy websites.

Access is free for members of the society (UK membership is currently £20 a year), and there is a small charge for non-members. Further details are given on the society's website, which also has some useful resources, including an index of articles published in *The Scottish Genealogist*, and an online shop that sells over 2,000 publications relating to Scottish genealogy and history.

EXPERT TIP

The Scottish Genealogy Society's 'Black Book', which can be downloaded for free from the society's website, is a detailed list of churchyards, monumental inscriptions and burials records for every parish in Scotland. It's a great way of checking what records exist for the parish where an ancestor lived.

Scottish Family History Societies

In addition to the Scottish Genealogy Society, there are currently around twenty-five local family history societies throughout Scotland, most focused on a particular county or region. They vary in size, but the majority organize talks and meetings for members, and produce journals and publications relating to their areas of interest. Some keep small libraries of genealogical resources, and both the Aberdeen & North-East Scotland Family History Society and the Tay Valley Family History Society have dedicated research centres holding a wide range of material.

The Scottish Association of Family History Societies (SAFHS) is the umbrella organization for Scottish family history societies, and the SAFHS website (www.safhs.org.uk) has links to the websites of individual societies. These websites include details of membership, useful resources, and lists of publications that can be purchased from the societies.

EXPERT TIP

Several Scottish family history societies have a reciprocal arrangement whereby members of one society can use the library of another society without charge. Check before visiting, and remember to take your membership card!

Family History Library and Family History Centres

Address: 35 North West Temple Street, Salt Lake City, Utah, 84150, USA

Website: www.familysearch.org/ask/locations/saltlakecity-library

The Family History Library (FHL) in Salt Lake City, Utah, USA is the largest genealogical library in the world, and its holdings include microfilmed and digitized records as well as published sources from countries worldwide. The library is open to everyone, without charge, and there is no need to get a reader's ticket.

Since the 1930s, the Genealogical Society of Utah (GSU) – the genealogical branch of The Church of Jesus Christ of Latter-day Saints – now known as FamilySearch, has been microfilming records from around the world in order to preserve them and make them more widely available. These records were accessible on microfilm at the FHL and, through loan, at over 4,500 associated Family History Centres worldwide.

The FamilySearch website (www.familysearch.org) was launched in 1999 by the GSU to provide access to indexes to some of the records held in the Family History Library, and digitized images of FHL microfilms began to be added in 2004. In 2017 the decision was made by the FHL to cease loaning out microfilms, and instead to digitize all films and make the images available through the FamilySearch website. This process is not expected to be completed until 2020. Due to copyright restrictions (imposed by the original owners of the records rather than the FHL), many digitized images can only be viewed from within the FHL or at an associated Family History Centre (FHC) or FamilySearch Affiliate Library (which can be located through a map at www.familysearch.org/locations).

Some records held by the National Records of Scotland, local archives and private organizations within Scotland, have been microfilmed by FamilySearch. These are only a small proportion of the records held by those repositories, but include statutory records, church registers, wills and testaments, sasines, poor relief records and estate records.

The 'Search Historical Records' section of the FamilySearch website provides access to records that have been indexed (discussed in more detail in the next chapter), but only a small proportion of the FHL's holdings are available that way. Instead, to locate all records search the FamilySearch catalogue (www.familysearch.org/catalog/search) by place, subject or keyword. Catalogue entries indicate whether records have been digitized (indicated by a camera icon) and if those records are only available at a centre or affiliate library (indicated by a key over the camera icon). Images accessed via the catalogue can be browsed but not searched by name, although a magnifying glass icon in the catalogue indicates records that have been indexed, and links through to the search page.

EXPERT TIP

The digitization of the Family History Library's microfilmed records means that anyone seeking Scottish ancestors should become familiar with the library's holdings. Even researchers living in Scotland may find that some Scottish records can be more easily accessed at home or through an FHC, rather than by visiting the relevant archive.

Private Archives

A wealth of Scottish records, particularly family and estate papers, have not been deposited in any public archive but are still privately held. The National Register of Archives for Scotland (NRAS) has been locating and cataloguing these records since 1946, and many can be identified through the NRAS Online Register (http://catalogue.nrscotland.gov.uk/nrasregister). Some collections have been catalogued in detail, while in other cases only a general summary is given online, although more information may be held by NRAS.

It is possible to formally request access to collections surveyed by NRAS, but permission is not always granted, and not all owners of records are sympathetic to genealogical researchers. In some cases records can be made available in the National Records of Scotland historic search room, but it is often necessary to travel to wherever the records are held. An initial approach should be made by email to the NRAS, who can advise on collections and liaise with the owner, although this process may take some time.

The National Register of Archives (NRA) is a similar organization to the NRAS but with a UK-wide remit. It can be worth checking both the NRAS and the NRA for Scottish material, as records may have ended up in other parts of the UK, particularly if a family owned property in more than one country. The NRA has now been integrated into The National Archives' Discovery catalogue (http://discovery.nationalarchives.gov.uk).

Some larger private archives employ their own archivist and are keen to make their collections more widely accessible. Examples include the archives of Traquair House, Peeblesshire, home of the Stuarts of Traquair (www.traquair.co.uk/traquair-archives), and Glamis Castle, Angus, ancestral seat of the Earls of Strathmore and Kinghorne (www.glamis-castle.co.uk/the-castle/archives). Initial enquiries should be made to the archivist, and charges may apply.

An exciting ongoing project is 'Friends of the Argyll Papers' (www.friendsoftheargyllpapers.org.uk), which supports the development of the archive of the Campbell family, dukes of Argyll, recognized as one of the most important private archives in the UK, and their promotion to a wider audience. A collection-level description is available on the website, which it is hoped will develop into a fuller online catalogue in the future, although the most detailed surveys are currently held by the NRAS.

EXPERT TIP

Access to private archives is a privilege, not a right. Following the correct procedures for requesting access, and observing any restrictions, will provide the best chance of viewing these valuable records, not only for us but also for any family historians who come after.

Locating Records

As will be apparent from the above descriptions, the records needed to trace Scottish ancestors can be found in a wide variety of archives, libraries and record repositories, and identifying where a particular record is held is not always easy.

The National Records of Scotland (NRS) online catalogue (http://catalogue.nrscotland.gov.uk/nrsonlinecatalogue) is usually the best place to start, as the NRS holds the largest collection of Scottish records, and its catalogue includes some details of documents held in other archives, some of which can be accessed at the NRS as a digitized or microfilm copy.

For records relating to a particular location, the website or online catalogue of the relevant local archive or local studies library is the next port of call, although be aware that online catalogues may not include all holdings. The Scottish Archives Map (www.scottisharchives.org.uk/map) and associated list of archives is a good starting point for identifying local archives, and a simple online search should lead to the website of any archive, library or other record repository.

If the archive doesn't have its own online catalogue, then the catalogue of the Scottish Archive Network (SCAN) (http://catalogue.nrscotland.gov.uk/scancatalogue) will generally provide a summary of holdings, although again this is incomplete and is no longer being updated. SCAN is useful for identifying records in specialist archives or in unexpected locations. Summaries of manuscript collections held by the National Library of Scotland (NLS), which are not all included in the NLS online catalogues, can also be found through SCAN.

Records from over 2,500 archives and record repositories across the UK, including 268 in Scotland, are included in the Discovery catalogue of The National Archives (TNA) (http://discovery.

nationalarchives.gov.uk). These include the holdings of the National Records of Scotland, and private archives surveyed by the National Register of Archives (NRA). Discovery gives a general summary of collections only, but in many cases a hyperlink is provided to the relevant archive's own catalogue, which will provide a more detailed description. It is particularly useful for identifying collections split across several archives, or Scottish records held in other parts of the UK. As Discovery is regularly updated it has partly superseded the SCAN catalogue as the best way of identifying Scottish records, although the sheer volume of results returned for a simple enquiry can be overwhelming. The TNA website provides guidance on searching Discovery, and search results can be narrowed down using a series of filters.

The FamilySearch catalogue (www.familysearch.org/catalog/search) primarily provides details of the holdings of the Family History Library, but because it can be searched by place as well as subject and keyword, it is a useful way of identifying records relating to a particular Scottish parish or county, which may be accessible in multiple locations. Entering a parish name in the search box will bring up a list of available resources, which will typically include microfilmed or digitized records, indexes and publications relating to the area. The catalogue of the Society of Genealogists (www.sog.org.uk/the-library), whose library includes material relating to Scotland as well as the rest of the UK and further afield, can also be searched online.

As described previously, the holdings of many university and specialist archives are included in the Archives Hub catalogue (https://archiveshub.jisc.ac.uk), as well as in SCAN and Discovery. If none of the above catalogues include the records being sought, then they may be privately held and the National Register of Archives for Scotland Online Register (http://catalogue.nrscotland.gov.uk/nrasregister) should be searched.

Finally, some records held in archives are not included in any online catalogue, or are not catalogued at all, and can only be identified by searching paper catalogues at the relevant repository, or contacting archive staff. It is worth adding that not all records survive (or sometimes records we think should exist may never actually have been created in the first place), and again staff at local archives may be able to give guidance or suggest alternative sources.

EXPERT TIP

Archive catalogues are one of the best tools that family historians have for finding records of our ancestors. It's worth spending some time becoming familiar with the various online catalogues, and trying out a variety of different searches. Occasionally you may get lucky and even find an ancestor named in a catalogue description!

3 Researching Scottish Family History Online

In discussing the records used for tracing Scottish family history and the archives that hold them, a large number of websites have already been mentioned. As the internet is likely to be the place that most of us began our family history research, it makes sense to discuss the main websites used for tracing Scottish ancestors in a little more detail. Websites and their contents change frequently so this list is not comprehensive, and additional records will likely have come online since the time of writing.

ScotlandsPeople

www.scotlandspeople.gov.uk

ScotlandsPeople is the main website for tracing Scottish family history online.

CROWN COPYRIGHT, NATIONAL RECORDS OF SCOTLAND

ScotlandsPeople is the prime website for tracing Scottish family history, and a large number of Scottish records can only be viewed online through this site. The National Records of Scotland has chosen to make its most valuable genealogical records available through ScotlandsPeople, rather than working with one of the major commercial family history websites. This has the advantage that the main Scottish records can all be accessed in one place, although the pay-per-view payment method can be frustrating for those more familiar with the subscription model used by most genealogy websites.

The main records available on ScotlandsPeople are statutory records of births, marriages, deaths and divorces (from 1855), census returns (1841–1911), church registers (the old parish registers of the Church of Scotland, Catholic registers and records of other churches), wills and testaments (1513–1925) and valuation rolls (1855–1935). The site also includes coats of arms from the Public Register of All Arms and Bearings in Scotland (1672–1916), records of World War I military service tribunals, and records of the Highland and Island Emigration Society (1852–1857). For privacy reasons, only indexes are available for modern records (that is, births less than 100 years old, marriages less than seventy-five years, and deaths less than fifty years), rather than images of full documents. Indexes and images are updated at the start of each year. The website includes a range of research guides and an image library.

There is no charge to search the indexes on ScotlandsPeople but it is necessary to first create a free account. In order to view images you use credits (which currently cost £0.25 each and are available in batches of thirty), and the number of credits needed varies according to the type of record. Purchased images are automatically saved to an online account, and can also be printed or downloaded as jpegs or PDFs.

EXPERT TIP

The research guides on the ScotlandsPeople website are an excellent place to look for guidance and further information on Scottish records. They cover not only the records available on the site but also a broad range of genealogy-related topics.

ScotlandsPlaces
https://scotlandsplaces.gov.uk

ScotlandsPlaces brings together resources from three national organizations: the National Records of Scotland, the National Library of Scotland and Historic Environment Scotland. As the name suggests, information is organized around places rather than people, but there are a large number of records and resources of value to family historians, all of which are available for free.

The main records on ScotlandsPlaces that name individuals are tax records. These are mostly for the late 1700s, although land tax rolls from 1645–1831 and two taxes from the late 1600s, the hearth tax and poll tax, are also included. Other useful records include Aberdeen burgh registers (1398–1511), Ordnance Survey name books (helpful for identifying place names and sometimes land-owners), reports of the Land Ownership Commission 1872–1873 (which include the names of a large number of landowners), and county and parish boundaries 1892 (helpful for tracking boundary changes that may have affected an ancestor's home).

ScotlandsPlaces includes a gazetteer of inhabited places in Scotland, past and present, which is useful for identifying which parish a particular settlement was in, and for distinguishing places with the same or a similar name. There is also a range of maps, surveys, plans and drawings, and a collection of photographs.

Digitized records, such as tax rolls, are mainly arranged by county and then parish or burgh. Some, but not all, of the records have been transcribed by volunteers, so it is also possible to search them by a keyword, such as a personal name, but spelling has been kept as in the original, and there are no advanced search options.

All the records on ScotlandsPlaces can be searched using a simple search box, which appears in the top right corner of each page. The search term can be any word, such as a place or per-sonal name, but it is not possible to combine terms. For example, a search for the surname Howatson returns a number of results, including a Jean Howatson who appears on the cart tax roll for the parish of Old Cumnock, Ayrshire in 1785, but searching for 'Howatson Cumnock' gives no results at all. For this reason, unless tracing an unusual surname, it is usually easiest to browse the records by place rather than searching directly for an ancestor.

EXPERT TIP

Due to copyright restrictions, images on ScotlandsPlaces cannot be easily downloaded or printed. Any records of interest should be transcribed, along with the details of which source the ancestor was found in, and a link to the relevant image saved in research notes so the record can be located again.

FamilySearch
www.familysearch.org

The FamilySearch website has been mentioned in a previous chapter in connection with the Family History Library (FHL) and the digitized records that can be accessed via the FamilySearch catalogue. Indexed records can be searched on the 'search historical records' portion of the website (www.familysearch.org/search). These include index-only records, indexes linked to images on the site (some of which are only accessible at the FHL), and indexes linked to images available on other websites (mainly subscription-based commercial websites). All resources on FamilySearch are available without charge, but it is necessary to sign up for a free account to access some of them.

Searches can be restricted to Scottish records by typing 'Scotland' into the country box under location on the main search page, or by going to the Scotland Indexed Historical Records page (www.familysearch.org/search/collection/location/1986318?region=scotland), which can be reached via the 'Research by Location' map on the home page. There are currently twenty-two collections identified as covering Scotland, although many of these are actually UK-wide. The most useful are 'Scotland Births and Baptisms, 1564–1950', 'Scotland Marriages, 1561–1910' and 'Scotland Church Records and Kirk Session Records, 1658–1919'. There are also collections of Scottish census records, but because of the very limited information these provide (such as not showing a whole household) it is far better to search the censuses on other sites.

The Scottish births and marriages collections are both index-only databases, and are primarily compiled from records now available on ScotlandsPeople. They include both statutory and church registers, including some entries from secessionist church records as well as Church of Scotland registers, but are incomplete. The differing search options available on the two sites means it is worth searching on FamilySearch to identify records of an ancestor, particularly if they have not been easily located on ScotlandsPeople.

These collections are most valuable for the period 1855–1874, for which statutory registers of births have been fully indexed to include the child's date of birth and the names of both parents, including the mother's maiden surname. This is far more detailed than the information provided in the ScotlandsPeople index for the same period, and is particularly useful for identifying all children born to a particular couple. Statutory marriage records for 1855–1875 have also been indexed to show the date of marriage, but as they don't include other details, such as the couple's ages or the names of their parents, they are less useful.

The 'Scotland Church Records and Kirk Session Records, 1658–1919' collection has been compiled from records held by the National Records of Scotland. It includes details of some births, marriages and deaths that do not appear in the old parish registers, although coverage is limited.

Entries located through FamilySearch include a microfilm number or a digital folder number. The FamilySearch catalogue can be used to identify the relevant film or digital collection, which may be viewed at the Family History Library, or online, if available. Information in the catalogue may also assist in locating the original records in Scotland. Indexing batch numbers for Scottish records (used by FamilySearch to identify the records from a particular parish) can be identified using the place index on the Archer Software website (www.archersoftware.co.uk/igi/fs-sct.htm), and these numbers can be used to restrict search results using the main search page.

FamilySearch does not only include indexed records and the FHL catalogue: the site also hosts family trees, and has a collection of over 350,000 digitized genealogy publications. Another useful feature is the Family History Research Wiki (www.familysearch. org/wiki). This has a large number of research guides, tools and instructional videos, some specific to Scotland. There is a dedicated page for each parish in Scotland, which lists available records with links to some external websites.

EXPERT TIP

The FamilySearch Wiki is based largely on the resources held by the FHL, and does not always include records in local Scottish archives, but the parish pages are a useful starting point for research, and in particular for identifying non-conformist or secessionist churches within each parish, including those with no known records.

Ancestry

www.ancestry.co.uk

Ancestry is the largest commercial genealogy organization in the world, providing access to a wide range of genealogical and historical records. Scottish record collections can be identified via the Scotland Family History Research page (https://search.ancestry.co.uk/places/europe/united-kingdom/scotland), or through the card catalogue, which can be searched by collection title or keyword. A general search can be restricted to Scottish records by selecting 'Scotland' or 'UK and Ireland' from the 'collection focus' dropdown menu on the main search page (after selecting 'show more options').

The main collections for searching Scottish births and marriages on Ancestry are 'Scotland, Select Births and Baptisms, 1564–1950' and 'Scotland, Select Marriages, 1561–1910', which are index-only collections and copies of the similarly titled collections available on FamilySearch, although the different search options on the two sites can make it worthwhile to search both. There is a number of smaller collections of births, marriages and deaths, some of which are indexes to records available online elsewhere (prefixed by the word 'web'). Scots may also be recorded in UK-wide collections, and a few Scottish births can be found in the 'England & Wales, Non-Conformist and Non-Parochial Registers, 1567–1970' collection.

Some digitized and indexed burial records, particularly for the Dumfries and Galloway area, are included in the 'England & Scotland, Select Cemetery Registers, 1800–2016' collection. The 'Scotland, National Probate Index (Calendar of Confirmations and Inventories), 1876–1936' is an index to Scottish wills and testaments that goes beyond the records currently available on ScotlandsPeople and provides more detail than the ScotlandsPeople index, listing the names of executors and values of estates. It can be helpful for identifying the wills of extended family members, although unfortunately the names of executors are not indexed.

Ancestry has indexes only for the 1841–1901 Scottish censuses. Although the quality of the transcription is variable, the large number of search options means that it is often easier to find someone using the Ancestry index than by searching on ScotlandsPeople and wasting credits looking at the wrong family. For tracing individuals between censuses the collections of digitized electoral registers for Aberdeen, Edinburgh, Fife, Glasgow and Perth (not available online elsewhere) are very useful.

EXPERT TIP

Ancestry has used the original enumeration district numbers to compile its census indexes, while ScotlandsPeople has renumbered some districts, particularly in large towns and cities. This means that reference information may not always match up between the two sites. However, page numbers should be identical, and can help to locate a record on ScotlandsPeople for someone identified through the Ancestry index.

Some of the most valuable collections on Ancestry for tracing Scots are the extensive collections of records of the UK armed forces, including the army and navy, which date from the 1700s to the mid-twentieth century. These can be searched by selecting 'military' from the search dropdown menu or as individual collections, although some original records can only be viewed on the Ancestry-owned Fold3 website (www.fold3.com).

Ancestry's collections of 'UK, Outward Passenger Lists, 1890–1960' and 'UK, Incoming Passenger Lists, 1878–1960' include Scottish ports (and Scots who sailed from other ports), and merchant seamen can be identified in crew lists, including those for Glasgow for 1863–1901. There are also large collections covering those employed by the East India Company and India Office, the railways, the post office and in the medical profession (medical registers, nursing registers and nursing applications). There are some small collections of directories and newspapers, and several digitized collections from Perth & Kinross Council Archive and Fife Archives, which include school registers, asylum and poorhouse records, land tax rolls, and the Perth Burgh Register of Deeds 1566–1811.

EXPERT TIP

Remember that Scots may appear in UK-wide collections on Ancestry as well as in specifically Scottish ones. Restricting a search to Scotland, rather than to UK and Ireland, may not return all records of an ancestor.

In addition to providing access to a large number of genealogical records, Ancestry hosts online family trees (created by users of the site) and sells genealogical DNA tests. A range of learning resources are including in the Ancestry Academy section, and message boards allow family historians to ask for and offer advice on a range of topics.

Ancestry is primarily a subscription website with a range of subscriptions offering varying access to records for a month or longer. There is also a pay-as-you-go option for those who only want to access a small number of records. The site offers a fourteen-day free trial for new subscribers (paid membership automatically starts at the end of the trial unless cancelled), and collections are occasionally made available for free for a limited period for promotional events. Some libraries and genealogy societies have subscriptions to Ancestry, which can be used by members.

Findmypast

www.findmypast.co.uk

Findmypast is a UK-based commercial genealogy website, although it has expanded from its UK origins to include records from Ireland, Australia, New Zealand, the United States and Canada. Scottish records can be searched by selecting Scotland from the 'where' dropdown menu on the main search page, or by going to the Scotland records page (https://search.findmypast.co.uk/search-scotland-records). A list of all collections on the site is given in the 'A–Z of record sets' section, which can be searched by title or narrowed down by country and county.

Like Ancestry, Findmypast includes indexes to Scottish births and marriages taken from FamilySearch, and has some indexes to small collections of birth, marriage and death records from other sources. The collections of digitized Scotland Roman Catholic records (baptisms, marriages, burials and congregational records) are particularly useful, and can be browsed as well as searched (unlike the same records on ScotlandsPeople).

Findmypast has indexes only to Scottish censuses 1841–1901, searchable as joint census collections with England and Wales. The quality of the transcription is generally good, but the lack of reference information given in the index can sometimes make it challenging to locate the same individuals on ScotlandsPeople in order to view the full records.

UK-wide collections on Findmypast that contain large numbers of Scots include military records, merchant navy records, passenger lists, collections relating to the British in India, and trades union membership registers. One of the most useful databases is the British newspaper collection, which includes a large number of Scottish titles and is regularly updated.

Specifically Scottish collections on Findmypast include Scotland post office directories and West Lothian electoral registers. A particular strength of the site is its many small datasets acquired from family history societies and individual genealogists. These include births, marriages and deaths from the Church of Scotland and other churches, monumental inscriptions, pre-1841 censuses and population listings, and a variety of other records, many of which are not available on other sites.

EXPERT TIP

Before purchasing a publication from a family history society it is worth checking if the same data are available on Findmypast. In most cases the society benefits every time one of their records is accessed, so you will still be supporting their work and may avoid buying a book that turns out not to include your ancestors. However, be aware that online data collections may not include all of a society's publications, so it is important to check coverage.

In addition to providing access to genealogical records, Findmypast enables users to create a family tree on the site, and sells genealogical DNA tests in association with the company LivingDNA. The site includes 'how to' guides, videos and articles in the blog section.

Findmypast is primarily a subscription website offering a range of research packages that can be taken out for a month or a year, although there is also a pay-as-you-go option. Many indexes can be searched for free, although it is necessary to subscribe to view the full records. Some libraries and genealogy societies have subscriptions to Findmypast that can be used by members.

British Newspaper Archive
www.britishnewspaperarchive.co.uk

The British Newspaper Archive (BNA) is a collaboration between Findmypast and the British Library to digitize up to forty million newspaper pages from the British Library's collection of original and microfilmed newspapers, and to make them available online. The project launched in 2011, and to date there are over thirty-one million pages available. These include newspapers from all parts of Scotland, although some titles cover only a few years. The pages can be browsed, or searched by keyword and a variety of search options, although as searching is done via optical character recognition (OCR), not all instances of a word will be picked up.

Access to the British Newspaper Archive is via a monthly, three monthly or twelve monthly subscription, and there is also a pay-as-you-go option. The same newspapers are available on Findmypast to subscribers with a 'Pro' subscription, but not with cheaper subscription packages.

EXPERT TIP

The British Newspaper Archive (BNA) can be searched for free, but full articles can only be viewed with a subscription. As the advanced search options on the site are far better than those for searching the same records on Findmypast, if you are a subscriber to Findmypast it is worthwhile using the BNA to carry out searches and then, once an article of interest has been identified, using Findmypast to view the full page.

My Heritage
www.myheritage.com

My Heritage is a commercial genealogy website based in Israel, with records from around the world. The site also hosts family trees and sells genealogical DNA tests.

My Heritage's historical records currently have very limited coverage for Scotland, with the majority of collections being either datasets available on other websites or digitized out-of-copyright books, which can be accessed elsewhere. The 'Scottish Deaths, 1747–1868' collection covers selected parishes in Midlothian, East Lothian and Fife only, and is extracted from Church of Scotland parish records available on ScotlandsPeople, but may give more detail than the ScotlandsPeople indexes to the same records.

EXPERT TIP

My Heritage is not heavily used by family historians in the UK, but has a large number of subscribers in Europe, Israel and elsewhere. It may be helpful to researchers looking to connect with family outside the UK or USA.

Deceased Online
www.deceasedonline.com

Deceased Online is a commercial website providing access to digitized and indexed burial and cremation registers from the UK and Ireland. The majority of registers have been sourced from local council burial and crematoria departments, and were often previously difficult to access. Records are not available for all areas of Scotland but there are good collections for Angus, Aberdeen and Aberdeenshire, a small number of records for private cemeteries in Edinburgh, and a large collection of Scottish gravestone indexes (with some images) produced by the Scottish Monumental Inscriptions company. A basic search can be carried out for free, but it is necessary to purchase a subscription or pay-per-view voucher to carry out an advanced search and view the full records.

EXPERT TIP

Scottish burial registers often list married women with both their maiden and married surnames, and this can cause some confusion for indexers. To locate records of married or widowed women, try searching with each surname in turn. Often the alternative surname will appear as a middle name, indicating that the correct entry has been found.

Scottish Monumental Inscriptions

https://scottish-monumental-inscriptions.com

Scottish Monumental Inscriptions is a Fife-based company that photographs and transcribes gravestones from across Scotland. Records can be purchased as PDF files (indexes only) or on CD (indexes and photographs). Some inscriptions can be searched via other websites including DeceasedOnline and Findmypast, although these may not always provide the full information.

Scottish Indexes

www.scottishindexes.com

Scottish Indexes is the record website of professional genealogists Emma and Graham Maxwell. It includes indexes to a number of lesser-known Scottish records, mostly held by the National Records of Scotland. These include sheriff court paternity decrees, non-OPR baptisms, marriages and burials, pre-1841 censuses and population lists, criminal records, mental health records, Kelso dispensary patient registers, and a small number of deeds and sasines. There are also some census indexes for 1841–1861 covering the south of Scotland. There is no charge to search databases on Scottish Indexes. Full records can be obtained from the company for a small fee, or, as reference information is given, the indexes can be used to locate the original records at the National Records of Scotland. Some publications of transcribed records can also be purchased in printed format via the website's bookshop.

Scottish Indexes is one of many websites that can assist with tracing Scottish ancestors.

EMMA AND GRAHAM MAXWELL

EXPERT TIP

Some of Scottish Indexes' records can also be searched via Ancestry, Findmypast and MyHeritage. Some indexes on Findmypast give additional details, but it's worth searching on the Scottish Indexes website as well. Record sets are regularly updated on the site and may contain more entries than the same collections available on other websites.

Old Scottish Genealogy & Family History

www.oldscottish.com

Old Scottish Genealogy & Family History is the website of professional genealogists Penny Lewis and Fergus Smith. It includes indexes to a number of useful collections of records held by the National Records of Scotland: the General Register of Lunatics in Asylums (1858–1915), the Board of Supervision and poor law appeals (1845–1895), anatomy registers (1842–1949), rolls of male heads of families (1834–1845), records of births with no father named (1855–1874), and sheriff court paternity decrees, school leaving certificate exam results (1908–1913), and some kirk session and secessionist church records.

Some indexes are Scotland-wide and arranged alphabetically, while others are arranged by parish and can be accessed through individual parish pages covering every parish in Scotland. Images and further searches of records can be ordered via the website.

EXPERT TIP

Old Scottish's rolls of male heads of families can also be searched via the 'Web: Scotland, Rolls of Male Heads of Families, 1834–1845' collection on Ancestry. This version of the index provides less detail but has the advantage that multiple parishes can be searched at once, and name variants can be used. Once a record is located on Ancestry it is easy to find the same record on Old Scottish to check if further details are given.

Free UK Genealogy
www.freeukgenealogy.org.uk

Free UK Genealogy is a UK-wide charitable organization that aims to index genealogical records and make them freely available online. The organization oversees three separate projects: FreeBMD (covering birth, marriage and death records for England and Wales only), FreeCEN (for UK censuses) and FreeREG (for UK parish registers, including a small number from Scotland).

FreeCEN (www.freecen.org.uk) has good, but not total, coverage of Scottish censuses for 1841–1871 (information on database coverage is given on the website). Although census indexes are available on several other websites, the quality of these transcriptions is high and all information is available for free.

FreeREG (www.freereg.org.uk) is a newer project with a relatively small number of Scottish records, but it has the advantage that it includes burials that have not been indexed by FamilySearch.

GENUKI
www.genuki.org.uk

GENUKI describes itself as 'a virtual reference library of genealogical information of particular relevance to the UK and Ireland', and in content is similar to the FamilySearch Wiki. There are dedicated pages for Scotland, for particular types of records, and for each county and parish.

EXPERT TIP

GENUKI used to be the 'go-to' resource for information on UK records and places, but has now become somewhat outdated. Some parish pages do provide a lot of details on available records and links to useful resources, but others give only very basic or general information. It is worth looking at pages covering parishes where an ancestor lived, but better information may be available elsewhere.

Scottish Handwriting
www.scottishhandwriting.com

The writing encountered in older Scottish documents can be challenging to read as letters can differ significantly from their modern forms as well as from the writing used in other parts of the UK. Words were often spelt phonetically and may be heavily abbreviated.

The Scottish Handwriting website, maintained by the National Records of Scotland, provides a series of tutorials designed to familiarize researchers with older handwriting, as well as a 'problem solver' for tackling difficult words, and 'palaeography posers' to maintain and test reading skills.

Scottish Handwriting is mainly concerned with records from the 1500s–1700s. For help with handwriting from the eighteenth to the nineteenth centuries there is a useful online guide through the University of Edinburgh (www. dumfriesandgalloway.hss.ed.ac.uk/wp-content/uploads/2016/08/ scottish-handwriting-a-concise-guide.pdf).

EXPERT TIP

Taking part in a transcription project is a good way to hone skills in reading old handwriting, and benefits the genealogy community. A list of some current transcription projects is given on the Scottish Council on Archives website (www.scottisharchives. org.uk/explore/what-are-archives/get-involved-online), and both FamilySearch and Ancestry run volunteer projects to index records available on their sites.

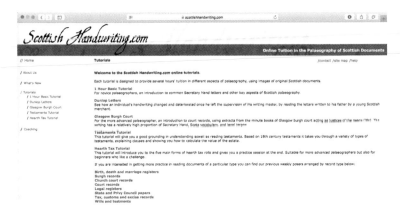

The Scottish Handwriting website includes a range of tutorials that can assist with reading and interpreting the records commonly used in family history research.

CROWN COPYRIGHT, NATIONAL RECORDS OF SCOTLAND

Dictionary of the Scots Language
www.dsl.ac.uk

The Dictionary of the Scots Language is an online dictionary containing over eighty thousand entries for words in use in Scotland from the twelfth century to the present day. It is an indispensable tool for identifying and understanding unusual words encountered in older Scottish documents. There is a quick search box on the home page, but the advanced search options, which include the use of wildcards, are particularly helpful for identifying words with idiosyncratic spellings.

EXPERT TIP

The Dictionary of the Scots Language can be used not only to learn the meaning of words but also to identify hard-to-read words found in older documents. Using the advanced search, put in the letters you can read and replace any uncertain letters with wildcards. The dictionary will provide a list of words that match, and the meaning and context should suggest which is most likely.

Scottish Register of Tartans
www.tartanregister.gov.uk

The Scottish Register of Tartans, launched in 2009, is the official government register of tartans and is maintained by the National Records of Scotland. The register contains information on thousands of tartans, and can be searched by name, category, keywords and colours. The majority of tartans listed are of modern design (although traditional patterns are also included), and they do not necessarily bear much resemblance to those worn by Scots in the past.

Further Websites
This chapter, and the previous one detailing Scotland's record repositories, have covered the main websites for tracing Scottish ancestors, but there are many more sites that may be helpful for tracing particular individuals or families.

There are many websites focusing on particular counties or areas of Scotland as well as on local industries. Am Baile (www.ambaile.org.uk), operated by High Life Highland, is dedicated to the history and culture of the Scottish Highlands and Islands, and includes a newspaper index as well as a large number of photographs and other resources. Our Town Stories (www.ourtownstories.co.uk) is a project by Edinburgh Libraries, which explores the city's history through stories, images and historical maps. Other websites, such as County Sutherland Family History (https://cosuthfamhistory.blogspot.co.uk), the Kirkcudbright County Website (http://kirkcudbright.co) and Mull Genealogy (www.mullgenealogy.co.uk) are the work of local historians and genealogists, and include indexes and transcripts of records and gravestones.

The Scottish Mining Website (www.scottishmining.co.uk) has information on mining and life in mining villages and contains a particularly useful index of accidents and disasters. Shale Oil (www.scottishshale.co.uk) includes digitized employment records and a wealth of information on those who worked in the shale oil industry, while The Bondagers (http://thebondagers.com) highlights the history of female agricultural workers in south-east Scotland.

A general internet search, using the name of the place or industry plus history or genealogy, is often the easiest way to locate such websites. There are also a number of listings websites that provide links to genealogy and local history sites. The largest of these is Cyndi's List (www.cyndislist.com), which describes itself as a virtual card catalogue to the genealogical resources of the internet. The starting point for Scottish resources is the Scotland page (www.cyndislist.com/uk/sct), which links to various categories of records and locations.

A large number of digitized books useful for tracing Scottish family history can be found through Electric Scotland (www. electricscotland.com), Google Books (https://books.google.co.uk) and the Internet Archive (https://archive.org).

EXPERT TIP

Bookmark useful websites you come across during research, or draw up a list of those relating to ancestral homelands. That way they can easily be found again, and when embarking on research into a new branch of the family you will have a useful list of resources to get you started.

---

4 Search Techniques

As discussed in the previous chapters, there is a variety of websites that enable us to access digitized records of our Scottish ancestors, or to locate records that are not available online. To get the most out of these, and to locate the records we need to solve complex genealogy problems, we need to understand how best to search online databases, catalogues and other indexes.

Searching Online Databases

Before beginning a search of any online database, it is worth taking the time to read any background and source information provided, and if possible, determining the coverage. Database titles and date ranges may be misleading or conceal large gaps.

A fundamental approach to searching any genealogical database is that it is best to start off by entering only very basic information, such as a name, and then gradually to add in further details as necessary to get the list of results down to a manageable length. By entering too much information at the start we risk filtering out the correct record because some small detail doesn't match. Once a list of results is down to one or two pages, skimming through them should identify the most likely, and full records can then be examined to determine if they relate to the person being sought.

Most genealogy websites provide a range of search options to overcome the common problems of spelling variations, name variants and indexing errors (discussed in more detail in Chapter 7). Each website has its own search tools, and the range of search options and their differences can be somewhat bewildering (for example, 'fuzzy' versus 'phonetic' matching) but most provide some guidance on searching in their help sections.

Broadly speaking, genealogy websites use a variety of algorithms

Registers of births, marriages and deaths, located within New Register House, part of the National Records of Scotland. It is not possible to search these original registers manually so we rely on indexes and databases to locate the entries we need.

to identify words, primarily names, which are similar to the one entered into the search box (for example, a search for Smith might also return results to the surnames Smyth and Smythe). Some family historians refer to this type of search as a 'soundex' search, although soundex is just one system for identifying variant names

and spellings, and has now been largely superseded by more sophisticated forms of matching. The different search options available on
the major genealogy websites are discussed in more detail below.
All such systems have their limitations – they may return a large
number of unrelated names and yet miss a genuine variant – but
they do make the task of searching for ancestors in a database
much easier. In most cases it is not necessary to consider every possible variant spelling and to repeat the search for each one.

An additional way of overcoming variations in spelling is to
enter part of a name rather than the full one. Some websites include
the option of searching for any name that starts with a particular
letter or string of letters (for example, searching for all surnames
beginning with 'Thom' would return Thom, Thomas, Thompson,
Thomson, Thomsoun, and so on). This may eliminate a large
number of the irrelevant matches returned with a typical variant
spelling search.

A more precise version of this type of search is the use of wildcards. Wildcards are symbols used to replace or represent one or
more letters. The most commonly used wildcards are ? to represent
a single letter, and * to represent one or more letters (sometimes
zero or more). In many cases more than one wildcard can be
used in a single word. For example, a search for Thom*n would
return Thomason, Thompson and Thomson (and eliminate the
forms Thom and Thomas which are likely to be separate surnames) but would not include Thomsoune (although a search for
Thom*n* would).

Another way of searching using only part of a name is to enter
just a surname or just a forename, rather than both. This will typically produce a large number of results, although these can be
reduced by searching a narrow date range and restricting a search
to a particular location. This may be the only way of getting round
very badly transcribed names or unusual variant spellings.

Forenames and surnames can sometimes get indexed in the
wrong order, and swapping the names round in search boxes may
turn up a missing entry. This is also a useful technique for searching digitized newspapers or online transcriptions where the names
may have originally been recorded surname first.

Be particularly wary when searching databases that have
not been indexed manually but instead rely on optical character

recognition (OCR) technology, most commonly newspapers and electoral registers. Depending on the quality of the original print, OCR can easily turn words into an indecipherable string of random characters, and fail to recognize even very common words. Repeating a search using part of a name only, or a place-name instead of a personal one, may identify further records of an ancestor.

EXPERT TIP

Most experienced researchers have their favourite ways of searching databases. It's easy to get into the habit of using the same options for every search, but it's a good idea to try out the various alternatives, particularly as the same search may work differently on different websites. I particularly like to use wildcards, especially multiple wildcards, as this allows a lot of control over the results of a search, but this technique can eliminate variants I hadn't considered. In writing this chapter, I've looked more closely at the search options available on the major genealogy websites (discussed in more detail below) and discovered a few I will be using more frequently in the future.

The ScotlandsPeople website (www.scotlandspeople.gov.uk) provides a wide range of search options for both forenames and surnames. These include exact names only, fuzzy matching (based on a system known as the Levenshtein distance formula), 'names that begin with', name variants (a manually compiled list covering relatively common forenames and surnames only), phonetic matching (based on the Beider-Morse system), and wildcards (* or % can be substituted for zero or more characters, or ? or _ for one character only). The site also allows searches using only a surname or only a forename. Some of these name options will return a large number of results and so are best combined with other search criteria, such as restricting the search to a single parish or district or to a narrow time frame. The default search for surname is 'exact match', while for forename it is 'names that begin with'.

Gender can be selected as male, female or both. It is usually best to keep the gender option on both (if for no other reason than it is easy to forget to change it when beginning a new search and then get no results), but it can be helpful to restrict a search to a single gender if the same or a similar name is used for both sexes. Year range can be a single year, a varying range of years, or left blank to search the whole date range of the database. Searches can be limited geographically to a single county or city, to a single parish or district, or to a selection of parishes or districts. When selecting a single parish or district it is usually best to select the county first so you don't then have to scroll through a long list of districts, although be aware that parishes that were in more than one county will only usually be searchable under one of those counties (not necessarily the one you expect).

Marriages can be searched using the name of one spouse only, or any combination of the names of both spouses (for example, the surname of the groom could be combined with the forename only of the bride). Deaths can be searched using a single surname or a combination of two surnames (mainly useful for searching the deaths of married women), and a mother's maiden surname can be added to the search, although this has not been indexed for all records. Statutory deaths (but not marriages or currently

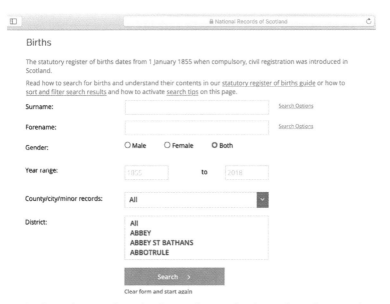

The form for searching births on the ScotlandsPeople website with links to guides to the records and tips on searching.

CROWN COPYRIGHT, NATIONAL RECORDS OF SCOTLAND

church register deaths) can be searched using an age range or a year of birth (which can be plus or minus one, two, three, five or ten years).

Census returns can be searched individually for each census year, or a search can be carried out across multiple census years for the same ancestor, although it is generally better to search a single census at a time unless an ancestor's name is particularly unusual. The census search options include age range but not year of birth. It is possible to search a name in combination with the forename of another person on the same page, but note that this will pick up the second forename appearing in another household on the same page, but not it appearing within the same household recorded across two pages.

Valuation rolls can be searched by name or 'group', which includes public bodies, commercial organizations and multiple individuals, such as heirs or trustees. The status option can be used to search for only owners, or tenants and occupiers. Searches can be restricted by county, parish or burgh/city (selected from a dropdown menu) and place (entered manually), but although house numbers are included in search results, it is not possible to search for a specific number. As properties are often not described exactly as expected, it is generally best to start by entering relatively few details when searching valuation rolls, such as using a single word in the place field.

Wills and testaments can be searched by name, year range and description, and searches can be restricted to a particular court. The description field is useful, but be aware that places of residence are usually as written in the original document, so parish names may be spelled phonetically, and sometimes the name of a farm will be given but not the name of the parish. Restricting a search by court is useful for common names, but the jurisdictions of each court generally did not match county boundaries. In addition, Edinburgh Commissary Court could be used by people from all parts of Scotland as well as to register the testaments of Scots who died outside Scotland. Lists of the relevant commissariat for each parish can be found in *The Scottish Family Tree Detective: Tracing Your Ancestors in Scotland* by Rosemary Bigwood (*see* Further Reading), and knowing these can be useful for identifying additional records.

Search results on ScotlandsPeople can be sorted by clicking on the header at the top of each column, which will then sort the results alphabetically or numerically, based on the contents of that column. This can be useful for making sense of a large number of results, and for avoiding repeating a search with more limited criteria. When searching census returns, searching for all individuals with a particular surname in a particular parish and then sorting by reference number will group those individuals into households (or rather, identify individuals with the same surname recorded on the same or consecutive pages), which can be a useful way of checking that the correct family has been identified before using credits to view the original image. When searching births or baptisms in church registers, sorting by parents' details will group children of the same couple together, although slight variations in either parent's name may result in some children not being listed consecutively.

EXPERT TIP

Help on searching records on ScotlandsPeople can be found by activating the 'search tips' pop-up boxes and through the site's many research guides, some of which are helpfully hyperlinked at the top of each search screen.

On the ScotlandsPeople website it is necessary to search each database individually to use advanced search options, whereas most other commercial genealogy websites allow users either to search individual databases or to search across multiple or all databases at once. There are advantages to both approaches. Searching a single database allows search criteria to be targeted to the type of information recorded in that record set and an ancestor's likely details at the time. Searching across multiple datasets can save time switching between databases, and can identify several records of an ancestor at once, as well as pick up an ancestor in a record set in which they might not be expected to appear.

On the Ancestry website (www.ancestry.co.uk), the search box on the home page gives only basic search options, but advanced options can be found by clicking on 'show more options' or by going to the 'search' page. Starting a search on the home or search page and then filtering results to get to what you need is usually a good approach, but there are times when identifying a particular database through the card catalogue and searching it directly can be more effective or quicker. When searching for Scottish ancestors, selecting the collection focus as 'UK and Ireland' or 'Scotland' will prevent a large number of irrelevant results appearing ('UK and Ireland' is the default option when searching on the UK version of the website).

The default search options on Ancestry search broadly for phonetic and similar matches on name, as well as for individuals whose first name does not match but who match other specified search criteria. Searches can be controlled more precisely by selecting 'match all terms exactly' at the top of the search box. This will then turn every field to an exact search, but further refinements can be made by clicking on the word 'exact' under each search field, which then reveals the further first name options of 'sounds like', similar and initials, the surname options of 'sounds like', similar, or soundex, and year options for plus or minus one, two, five and ten years. Wildcards can also be used instead of letters (? to replace a single letter, or * to replace multiple letters), but a minimum of three letters must be entered. Ancestry's phonetic variations use a variety of algorithms to identify similar sounding names targeted to the specific collection being searched, while 'similar' variations identify common abbreviations, nicknames and variant spellings, and soundex uses the soundex matching system.

An alternative way of searching records on Ancestry is by first creating a family tree on the site. Each person added to the tree will have an individual page that includes a 'search on Ancestry' link underneath the list of Ancestry sources already attached to them. Clicking on this automatically fills in search boxes with the information already known about that person, and will bring up a long list of possible records based on this information (all using a non-exact search). This can be refined in the same way as when starting a search on the main search page. Although this can be a quick way of identifying an ancestor in common records such as censuses, it is usually best to carry out a more targeted search with search criteria selected accordingly.

For each ancestor whose details have been entered on a family tree, Ancestry will produce a list of suggested records described as 'hints'. These are based partly on the records other users have attached to their trees containing same or similarly named individuals. Hints do not include all databases, only the most popular ones (primarily censuses, birth, marriage and death records, and public trees). It is important to note that not every hint will relate to the person it is linked to. In each case the full database entry and original record (if included) should be examined carefully, analysed and compared with what is already known about that person. Only when it is determined that the record most likely does relate to that person should the hint be accepted and the record attached.

EXPERT TIP

Hints are one of the tools available to locate information on the Ancestry website, and can lead to the discovery of new records of an ancestor. However, as with details found in another researcher's family tree, hints should be treated with caution and never accepted indiscriminately.

The Findmypast website (www.findmypast.co.uk) has a simple search box on the home page and more advanced search options available from the 'search' page. Searches can be restricted to Scottish records by selecting 'Scotland' from the 'where' dropdown menu. After carrying out a basic search, it is possible to narrow down the list of results by using the list of categories and sub-categories on the left side of the screen. Results can be further narrowed down by selecting a particular collection from the 'record set' dropdown menu from within the main search box, although this often produces a long and unwieldy list. If searching a particular record set rather than a broader category or sub-category, it is instead better to select the individual collection from the 'A–Z of record sets', which links to a page providing advanced search options designed for that particular collection and giving some background information.

Unlike ScotlandsPeople and Ancestry, Findmypast has only one option for searching variant spellings (a box for 'name variants' can be ticked or unticked for both first names and last names), although the site also allows the use of wildcards (* for zero or more characters and ? for a single character). When searching using a year, the date range can be selected as plus or minus zero, one, two, five, ten, twenty or forty years (two years is the default option).

On the FamilySearch website, the main search screen is found on the 'search historical records' page (www.familysearch.org/search). As the site has such a large number of records covering many countries it is best to begin any search by selecting a country under location in the 'restrict records by' section. There is no option for Britain or the United Kingdom, but choosing Scotland will search UK records identified as covering Scotland, such as military records, as well as specifically Scottish collections.

By default, all search fields on FamilySearch will search for variant spellings, but these can be restricted to an exact search by ticking the box next to that field or by selecting 'match all terms exactly' at the bottom of the search box. Results can be filtered by clicking on the 'collections' tab after carrying out a search and then selecting one or more record sets.

Individual collections can also be searched by typing the name of a collection into the 'find a collection' box on the main search page (starting to type will bring up a list of all matching collections, such as all those beginning with 'Scotland') or by browsing through the list of collections on the 'historical record collections' page (www.familysearch.org/search/collection/list) and then clicking on the name of a collection. However, as the search options do not vary from one collection to another, there is no particular advantage in doing this, other than limiting the number of search results.

EXPERT TIP

A lot of the frustrations in using online databases come from family historians who jump in without taking the time to understand the various search options available, and become quickly disheartened by the thousands of results returned for a simple search. All the major genealogy websites provide search tips as well as detailed guidance on searching their records, but it is necessary to take the time to read these. As the saying goes: if all else fails, read the instructions!

Searching Archive Catalogues

Although the online catalogues of libraries, archives and other record repositories are databases, searching them requires a slightly different set of skills from those needed to search genealogy websites. Many catalogues include some guidance on searching, and it is worth reading this before beginning a search.

A major difference between searching catalogues and genealogy databases is that catalogue search options are generally quite limited, and only exact spellings of names and other words will be returned in most cases. Some alternative spellings of personal and place names have been added to catalogue entries when the spellings used in the original document are particularly unusual, but this is relatively rare. In most cases any word can be used as a keyword, and some catalogues allow searches for specific phrases or using a combination of words (sometimes with 'and' or 'or' options). A date range can usually be specified to limit results, and a catalogue reference can be included where this is known. Many catalogues have both basic and advanced search options, and it is worth exploring these and experimenting with different searches and with a variety of keywords to identify any records of interest.

Another big difference with searching archive catalogues is that rather than searching for a specific ancestor, most of the time a search will be for records of a place where that ancestor may have lived, or an organization they may have belonged to or interacted with. Only a very small number of catalogue descriptions include the names of all the people mentioned in the original document. Although it is always worth putting an ancestor's name into a catalogue, or the name of the farm or community where they lived, to see what comes up (bearing in mind likely spelling variations), this will not find the majority of records in which they are named.

Many archives do not have full online catalogues so it may also be necessary to search paper catalogues and other finding aids. Records in archives are primarily arranged in collections (also called 'fonds') according to the person or organization that created them, and this is reflected in how they are catalogued. Archive staff can assist with identifying records and using catalogues.

EXPERT TIP

As with searching online databases, understanding how archive catalogues work and how best to search them is key to locating records of our ancestors and solving difficult genealogy problems.

Searching Manual Indexes

Not all indexes to genealogical records can be accessed online or through a database – instead, a variety of paper indexes and finding aids, some printed or typed, others handwritten, need to be consulted. Although such genealogical indexes may appear straightforward to use, they may present a number of idiosyncrasies that are not immediately apparent.

Some paper indexes group likely surname variants together under the most common spelling, rather than listing them strictly alphabetically, in recognition of the fact that the same person or family may be recorded under a variety of spellings. This is very helpful for identifying possible surname variants, although some unrelated names may be grouped together and other likely variants may be listed separately, depending on the compiler's interpretation. Unless an index is particularly long, it is often wise to skim through all the names beginning with the first letter of an ancestor's surname to pick up any unusual variant spellings that may not necessarily be listed together.

Some care needs to be taken when searching printed indexes for surnames beginning with 'Mac' or 'Mc', as indexers may handle them in different ways. In some cases 'Mac' and 'Mc' variants will be grouped together as one name (so Macdonalds and McDonalds are all listed under Macdonald), while in other cases they may be listed strictly alphabetically (so Macdonalds and McDonalds appear in different parts of the index, separated by all the other Mac surnames). Mac/Mc surnames may appear in a separate list from other surnames beginning with M, or be intermingled with them. In some older indexes, the Mac prefix was ignored completely and the surname listed under the next letter (so Macdonalds are grouped together under Donald in the section for surnames beginning with D). It's worth taking a moment to figure out which approach the indexer has taken before plunging in and discovering a surname doesn't appear where expected, or completely missing a reference to an ancestor.

Although it may sound obvious, it's a good idea to check whether a book contains a single index or multiple indexes for different sections. For example, the services of heirs are mainly indexed in blocks of ten years, with each published volume covering several decades and containing multiple indexes, including separate supplemental indexes to heirs with different surnames from the deceased person. Books of monumental inscriptions that cover several different burial grounds will usually have a separate index for each location, although multiple burial grounds within a single parish may be indexed together and there may be a cumulative index indicating which parishes a surname can be found in. When searching in a hurry, it's easy to flip to the back of a volume, check the index for an ancestor's name and presume that all entries have been identified when in fact there are several additional indexes that also need to be searched. A quick look at the contents page will usually clarify how a book is arranged, and it is worth reading any introduction, which may provide valuable information on the records themselves as well as identifying any gaps or indexing issues.

Some older handwritten indexes, particularly those compiled at the same time as the records to which they refer, are not fully alphabetized but instead group surnames by the initial letter, with entries arranged chronologically within each letter. These are more time-consuming to search than a full index, but still quicker and easier than beginning with the original records.

Where no indexes exist, minute books can often be used to search records such as registers of sasines and deeds. In this context, a

This entrance to the National Records of Scotland highlights the building's original purpose as a searchroom for legal searchers. Many of the repository's finding aids were not designed with family historians in mind.

minute book is a handwritten volume in which the clerk recorded a brief summary of each transaction, typically giving the date of recording, the names of the main parties involved, the type of document and, in the case of sasines, the name of the property. Entries are arranged chronologically and sometimes only the surnames of the parties, rather than their full names, are given. The advantage of searching a minute book over the full records is that it is quicker to skim down a list of names than to leaf through a whole register. Minute books also usually cover a longer period, so it is only necessary to go through one or two minute books, rather than ten volumes of original records. However, if a minute book only provides surnames rather than full names, and an ancestor had a fairly common name, minute books may only produce a long list of possible entries to check and a large number of registers may still need to be searched. If an approximate date of a record is already known, it may be simpler to go straight to the original volume.

When researching in archives, the term 'calendar' may be found rather than index. Whilst an index usually provides only very brief information, such as a name, date and reference number, a calendar gives a more descriptive summary of a document, noting any pertinent details. The printed indexes to wills and testaments that need to be consulted to identify testaments recorded in the period 1926–1959 (and which can be found on Ancestry for the period 1876–1936) are known as the Calendar of Confirmations and Inventories.

EXPERT TIP

Many older indexes and finding aids were not designed with the needs of the modern genealogist in mind. They were created for the use of clerks who worked in the relevant departments or for legal researchers looking for specific documents. As such they are not always 'user friendly', but are still valuable tools for locating records of our ancestors.

---

5 Interpreting Genealogical Records

Throughout the first few chapters of this book, the terms 'records', 'documents' and 'sources' have been used to describe where the information needed to trace Scottish ancestors and to solve family history problems can be found. This chapter looks at exactly what we mean when we talk about a 'source', and how we can use information given in genealogical sources to draw conclusions and build our family tree.

What is a Source?

In genealogy, a *source* is anything that provides information. It may be a handwritten document, a published book, a digital or microfilm copy of a document, a website, a photograph, a video or audio recording, a physical object (such as a gravestone or an embroidered sampler), or even a person. A *record* refers to a fixed account of an event, often in writing but also by photography or audio or video recording, and a *document* is a written record (handwritten, typed or printed).

When researching Scottish family history we use many different types of sources to trace our ancestors, but these can be divided into three broad categories:

Original records: An original record is usually one created at, or close to the time of the event it describes, which is not based on a previously existing record. When a child was baptised, the entry made in the parish register recording the date of baptism and the name of the child (and hopefully some information about their parents) was an original record. If we are lucky, this original record will still exist and we can use it to learn about our ancestor.

Derivative records: A derivative record is one created from an existing record, either by transcribing the original in full, by editing it in some way, by translating it from one language to another, or by indexing it. When we search an online index to locate an ancestor's baptism record we are using a derivative record.

Authored narratives: An authored narrative is a written record that draws upon many different sources and presents the author's conclusions. The most common authored narratives used in genealogy are family trees (online, published or handwritten) and published family histories. When we input details of our ancestors into family history software or build an online tree on a genealogy website, we are creating an authored narrative.

It is important to understand what type of source we are looking at, as this may affect how reliable the information found within it is. An original record is likely to contain the most accurate information, although it could still contain errors. A derivative record relies on the author's ability to read the original record and to convey its contents; words may have been misread or mistyped and important information omitted. An authored narrative relies not only on the writer's ability to read original records, but also to locate and analyse them; individuals may have been mis-identified and wrong conclusions drawn.

A golden rule of genealogy is that we use original records whenever possible, as they provide the most reliable information on our ancestors. That doesn't mean we shouldn't use derivative records or authored narratives – indeed it would be almost impossible to do family history research without them – but these should be regarded primarily as a means of locating original records, rather than as sufficient in themselves.

Determining what is or isn't an original record is not always straightforward. What about a digital image or a microfilm copy of a document: is that an original or a derivative record? When scanning or photographing original records, information may get cropped off or lost in central margins due to tight binding, or whole pages can get missed out. An image copy is therefore not as reliable as an original document, but very often it will be the only form available to us, as access to fragile and irreplaceable original documents (such as statutory registers, censuses and old parish registers) is often restricted for preservation purposes.

If an image copy is clear and relatively legible, with no obvious cropping, it is conventional to treat it as an original record, although we should always bear in mind the limitations of such copies and keep an eye out for issues such as missing page numbers. If an image copy is unclear or text appears to be missing we should enquire about accessing the original or getting a new copy made. A request can be made for a rescan of a statutory register when researching at the ScotlandsPeople Centre (or accessing the record on the ScotlandsPeople website), and in exceptional cases original census enumeration books can be produced. Original records accessed as digital images in the historic search room of the National Records of Scotland can often be produced when there is a problem with legibility, although this is at the discretion of staff.

Even if we have an actual document in our hands, can we be sure it is an original record of the event? Many of the records we use in family history research are actually contemporary, or near contemporary, copies. Census enumeration books are copies of the original census forms, which were transcribed by the enumerator (the originals were destroyed). The old parish registers may be neat copies of an original register (original registers can sometimes be found among kirk session records, typically described as scroll registers). The majority of wills, testaments and deeds we access are copies transcribed by a clerk into a bound volume, not the originals signed by the parties involved (where originals survive they are usually catalogued as warrants). Gravestones may have been erected many years after the deaths they commemorate, or even replaced when the original became worn.

EXPERT TIP

We may have to make do with copies when these are the only forms of a record that survive, but we should always be aware of the potential errors they may contain, and seek out more original versions where they exist.

What is Information?

Information is what is conveyed when we examine a source. It is what is recorded, rather than what we interpret or conclude something to mean. In genealogy, information is categorized into two main types:

Primary information: This is information concerning an event provided by a participant or eyewitness; it is a first-hand account. When a mother registers the birth of her child she is giving primary information as she was present at the birth.

Secondary information: This is information concerning an event provided by someone who was not a participant or eyewitness, but who has obtained that information from someone else; it is hearsay or a second-hand account. A person registering the death of their parent is providing secondary information as to the parent's age or date of birth as they were not present when that birth occurred.

Not all records have an identifiable informant, and so not all information given in a source can be categorized as primary or secondary. Even when there is a known informant, it is not always possible to gauge that person's knowledge of what they are reporting. A person in Scotland registering the death of their father would be asked to provide the names of their father's parents, but we may not know if they are giving the names of grandparents they grew up with and remember fondly, or of relatives who died long before they were born and whose names they only vaguely recall.

Another complexity surrounds a person's knowledge of their own birth. We were all physically present when we were born, but of course none of us remembers the event, and instead we rely on someone else to tell us when and where it occurred. These days most of us have a copy of our own birth certificate, and we are fairly reliable sources as to the place and date of our birth (if we choose to divulge it!), but it is clear many people in the past did not know exactly when and where they were born. Even after the start of statutory registration, many people probably never saw their own birth record. A person's knowledge as to their own birth is therefore usually considered secondary information, although they are typically more reliable on the subject than other informants.

Categorizing information as primary or secondary is useful because it helps us to determine how much confidence we can place in it. Generally we can give more weight to primary information than secondary information, because someone who was present at an event is likely to be more reliable than someone who has heard the details at second or third hand.

However, it does not always follow that primary information is correct. A person may have misremembered, particularly at an emotional time such as registering the death of a loved one. They may have had good reason to give incorrect information, such as an under-aged teenager overstating his age in order to enlist in the military. Simple vanity may have caused them to be less than honest (this is likely the case with the large number of people who mysteriously aged less than ten years between each decennial census!). It is therefore important to consider an informant's motivation as well as their knowledge.

Logic dictates that the information given on a marriage record as to the names of a person's parents, provided by themselves, should be more reliable than the same information on a death record, usually provided by a relative. However, I have come across several examples, one in my own family, where a marriage record gives slightly incorrect parents' names, while the death record for the same person gives correct ones. In one example this was due to a step-parent's name being recorded in place of a biological parent, in another it was slightly erroneous information given to conceal an illegitimate birth, and in another the only explanation seemed to be clerical error, and the likelihood that the couple were insufficiently literate to notice the mistake. This highlights the importance of not relying on a single record to establish relationships, but looking instead for additional sources to provide corroborating information.

Some readers may be more familiar with the terms primary and secondary *source*, used in the study of history, rather than primary and secondary *information*. The field of genealogy differs from history by considering information separately from the source that contains it. A good reason for this is that genealogical sources frequently contain both primary and secondary information. For example, a census provides primary information as to where a person was residing on census night, but only secondary information as to where they were born. We need to evaluate each piece of information given in the census independently, rather than simply viewing this as an original record and therefore reliable.

EXPERT TIP

Considering whether information is primary or secondary takes a little effort, but it is good to get into the habit of questioning every document we come across, rather than simply accepting what is written at face value. When we do that, new solutions may present themselves to longstanding family history problems.

What is Evidence?

Information becomes evidence when we use it to answer a particular research question. Like sources and information, evidence can be categorized into several different types:

Direct evidence: This is information that directly and unequivocally answers a particular question. If my question is 'Who were Margaret Whyte's parents?', then Margaret's birth record should provide direct evidence of their identity.

Indirect evidence: This is information that may point towards an answer to a research question but is not definitive, and needs to be combined with further information before a conclusion can be reached. If Margaret Whyte was born prior to statutory registration and has no known birth or baptism record, but I locate her in the 1841 census in the household of Thomas and Jean Whyte, this would be indirect evidence that Thomas and Jean were her parents, since relationships between household members were not recorded in this census.

Negative evidence: This is evidence arising from an absence of information, or from a person not being found when and where we might have expected them to have been recorded. For example, if Margaret Whyte was married and living with her husband at the time of the 1851 census but he was recorded as a widower in 1861, this would indicate that Margaret had likely died between 1851 and 1861. If a search of the statutory death registers failed to find her death in 1855–1861, this would be negative evidence pointing to the conclusion that Margaret died in the period 1851–1854.

Direct evidence may seem to be the best way of solving our family history questions, but it may not always exist, and can sometimes be wrong. It needs to be backed up by additional sources and evidence, whether direct, indirect or negative.

When beginning our family history research in the twentieth or twenty-first centuries we usually have a wealth of direct evidence on which to base our conclusions and to build our family tree. Scottish statutory registers of births, marriages and deaths provide clear evidence of parentage, and additional sources, such as censuses, confirm family relationships and places or origin. However, as we get back to the mid-1800s and to the pre-registration period, direct evidence starts to become rarer, and instead we need to consider indirect and negative evidence if we are to continue to extend our family lines. A focus on only those sources that provide direct evidence is often the reason we hit a brick wall in our research.

There are several types of indirect evidence that are commonly used in Scottish research. First, naming patterns can be a strong indication of family relationships, as many families followed a traditional pattern when naming their children (*see* Chapter 7 for details of the Scottish naming pattern). Surnames given as middle names are usually significant, although some children were named after relatives by marriage, employers, or the minister who baptised them, rather than a blood relation.

Witnesses to baptisms are not always named but often include family members, and provide further evidence of extended family relationships. If an ancestor lived in a parish where witnesses to baptisms were routinely recorded, it is worth looking not only at the baptism records of all the ancestor's children to see who the witnesses were, but also at the baptisms of other children with the same surname (or whose mother had the same surname) to see if the ancestor is named as a witness. Identifying these extended family networks can help to distinguish between same-named individuals and may provide clues to earlier generations.

Occupations can sometimes be used as indirect evidence of relationships. Some professions were so common that they are not particularly helpful (in a mining village almost everyone was a miner, for example), but skilled trades were often passed down from father to son, and so a shared occupation between two men with the same surname could imply a relationship. Occupations are also evidence of social status and can disprove a potential relationship – it is very unlikely that an agricultural labourer was the legitimate son of an advocate, for example.

Establishing the location where an ancestor lived is important for finding records in which they may appear, but can also provide indirect evidence of relationships. Ideally, we need to identify not only the parish in which our family lived, but also the exact location within that parish (baptism, marriage, burial and census records may all give a family's place of residence). This may be a village, street, farm, or a small group of farms or cottages (sometimes referred to as a township or fermtoun). Such places were often home to more than one family, but individuals with the same surname are likely to be related. Families – tenants as well as landowners – often lived in the same place for generations, so identifying residents over an extended period can suggest relationships between them. A list of tenants showing a John McKay as the tenant of a particular croft in one year, and a James McKay as the tenant there ten years later, might well suggest that James was the son of John, although, as with all indirect evidence, further records would be needed to support this theory.

Places of burial can also be important indicators of relationships, as many families owned a burial plot or lair where family

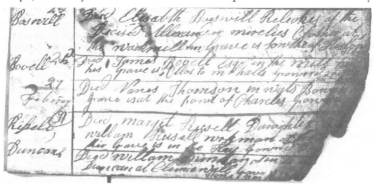

Interpreting genealogical records can be challenging. This burial register suffers from poor handwriting and idiosyncratic spelling and is partly damaged, making it difficult to read.

CROWN COPYRIGHT, NATIONAL RECORDS OF SCOTLAND

members were buried over several generations. Burial registers for the pre-1855 period are sparse, but occasionally lair registers (detailing the owners of lairs and the names of those buried in each plot) survive, and details of lair holders may be given in kirk session records. Burial registers may indicate a place of burial (often as a distance from a particular landmark, rather than in the form of a lair number), and such locations can be used to determine that two people were likely buried in the same or adjacent burial plots.

Gravestones can provide evidence of family relationships as well as dates of death. This stone records three generations of the Mackenzie and Anderson family, including two who died prior to statutory registration, and four who died outside Scotland.

Adjacent gravestones for individuals with the same surname may imply a relationship between them, although if the surname was very common in the parish it could be coincidental. When searching published books of monumental inscriptions it is important to check the plan, as adjacent stones may not always be numbered sequentially, depending on how the burial ground was surveyed.

Finally, not everyone was buried in the parish where they died. If a person was buried in a different parish to the one where they lived and died, this may indicate that their family owned a lair there, and point to their place of origin.

EXPERT TIP

Direct, indirect and negative evidence can be difficult ideas to understand at first, but by applying them to a particular research question we are working on, it is easier to see how these concepts can be used to identify solutions to our family history problems.

Using Evidence

Let's take the fictional Margaret Whyte as an example of how different types of evidence can be used to solve a research problem.

Margaret married her husband, Donald Black, in the mid-1840s, and the parish register states only that she was 'of this parish' with no other identifying information. The 1851 census indicates she was born in the same parish in about 1825, but we are fairly sure there's no record of her birth or baptism (we've checked all the church registers for the area covering a few years either side of her expected year of birth). She died before 1855, so there is no statutory record of her death, which would name her parents. Have we hit the end of the Whyte line, or is there more we can do?

An obvious next step is to search for Margaret in the 1841 census, and we find a Margaret Whyte of about the right age in the same parish in the household of Thomas and Jean Whyte, whose ages suggest they could be her parents (relationships between household members not being recorded in this census). Can we now say that Thomas and Jean are definitely Margaret's parents? Maybe she is their niece rather than their daughter. Perhaps Thomas was married twice and Jean is not Margaret's mother. Maybe Thomas and Jean are not a married couple at all, but a widower and his unmarried sister, who is taking care of the house and children. At this point we need to research Thomas and Jean Whyte further, and to review the records we have concerning Margaret and her family.

We trace Thomas and Jean Whyte through the 1851 and 1861 censuses, and confirm that they are indeed a married couple. We find both their death records in the 1860s, which give Jean's maiden surname as Brown, and name each of their parents. We discover that Jean's mother was also named Margaret, so there's a good chance that the Whytes named their eldest daughter after her, and we locate a record of their marriage, which took place close to the time we think Margaret was born and in the same parish. Is it possible Thomas and Jean did have a daughter named Margaret, but that she was not the Margaret Whyte who married Donald Black? A search of marriage and census records for the parish reveals no evidence of a second Margaret Whyte, and no death is found of a Margaret, daughter of Thomas Whyte and Jean Brown, in the statutory registers, so we can probably discount that possibility.

Looking again at Margaret Whyte's children with Donald

Black, we discover she named her eldest child Jean (she and Donald had only one son, who was named after Donald's father, so it seems likely the family was following the traditional naming pattern, although we can't confirm that Thomas was a family name). Jean Black's birth and baptism were recorded in the old parish register, and we discover the Blacks were then living at the same farm where the Whytes were recorded in 1841, although they had moved to another part of the parish by the time their second child was born.

At this point we still have no direct evidence as to the identity of Margaret Whyte's parents, but we have some strong indirect evidence in the form of naming patterns over two generations, a marriage entry that puts Thomas Whyte and Jean Brown in the right place at the right time, and a baptism entry that places the Whytes and the Blacks on the same farm. We have also considered the possibility of there being two Margaret Whytes, but have found no record indicating that this was the case (negative evidence to support our conclusion).

We can probably be fairly confident that Thomas Whyte and Jean Brown were the parents of Margaret Whyte, although if we are lucky we may find additional evidence by continuing to research the Whyte and Black families. Perhaps Margaret has no gravestone, but we find a burial record indicating that she was buried in the Whyte family burial plot. Perhaps Thomas or Jean left a will and made a bequest to Margaret's children. Perhaps Margaret's daughter Jean Black grew up and married, and we discover her using the middle name of Brown (her grandmother's maiden surname) in later life, even though this name doesn't appear on her baptism record.

In real life we may not discover quite so much indirect evidence as in this fictional example, but it illustrates how indirect and negative evidence can be used to overcome a lack of direct evidence.

Analysing Sources, Information and Evidence

As we carry out research and gather documents relating to our ancestors, we should go through a process of analysis.

We consider our sources: is this an original record? If not, can we obtain an original record of the event? If not, what issues do we need to consider? Could a transcription error have been made? Do we know who created this record and why? What physical condition is it in? Has the page been torn? Has writing faded or ink bled

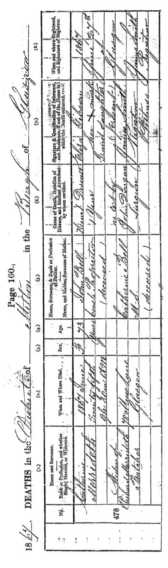

The informant of this elderly widow's death was her granddaughter, who was unable to sign her name. The information provided on the deceased's parents was likely secondary, was incomplete, and may have been incorrect.

CROWN COPYRIGHT, NATIONAL RECORDS OF SCOTLAND

through from one side to the other? Are entries entered neatly in chronological order, or haphazardly and out of sequence? Are there gaps in the registers, which may indicate events that went unrecorded? Does the entry we are interested in appear to have been squeezed in between two others and possibly recorded at a later date, rather than when it occurred? How does the information compare with other entries on the same page? Has information been omitted that appears in other entries?

We consider the information found in those sources: do we know who provided the information? Did they have first-hand knowledge of the event, or were they reporting something heard from someone else (is it primary or secondary information)? Had a significant amount of time elapsed since the event, which might make their recollection hazy? Did they have a reason to provide false or inaccurate information? Are there other examples of them providing inaccurate information, which might cast doubt upon their knowledge or truthfulness?

We consider the evidence found in that information: does it clearly answer our question (direct evidence)? Or does it instead hint at a possible solution and suggest further avenues of research (indirect evidence)? If we haven't found any record of the person we are looking for in this search, can we draw any conclusions from their absence (negative evidence)?

Having gathered information from a variety of sources, we also need to compare the evidence this gives us. Do all sources agree? Or do we have conflicting evidence, which can't all be true? Does all the information come from one individual or source, or do we have independent sources that all match with one another? Have we ignored evidence that doesn't fit with our favourite theory? Is there new information that may shed light on our previous research, or give new significance to a small detail we previously overlooked?

EXPERT TIP

Analysis is something we do subconsciously every time we come across a new record, but it can be helpful to go back and look more critically at records we have found in the past. A fresh look may reveal new information or suggest something we haven't thought of previously.

Dealing with Conflicting Evidence

Conflicting evidence is evidence from different sources (or sometimes a single source) that disagrees, and which cannot all be true. It is something that all family historians will come across eventually, but it can cause confusion and stop us in our tracks. If we don't know which of two versions of events to believe, then we may not know how to proceed. It can be tempting just to dismiss information that disagrees with the majority of the evidence we have, categorizing it as simply 'wrong' – but it is important to take the time to consider all versions of events.

If we come across conflicting evidence, a first step is to consider if all the records do in fact relate to the same person, or if it is possible that we have confused two individuals of the same or similar name. This is easy to do if a surname is very common in an area. There may well be more than one Alexander Fraser with a wife named Mary in a particular parish, with each couple being of a similar age. Nevertheless, common sense should tell us that if an ancestor died in 1879, then he was clearly not the person of the same name recorded in the 1881 census.

Second, we should consider if there is in fact a conflict, or if we may have two different versions of the same information. This may be particularly the case with place names, where a person may name their parish of birth in one census, and a village within that parish in the next. The ScotlandsPlaces website (www.scotlandsplaces.gov.uk) is helpful in identifying in which parish a settlement was located, and for resolving such apparent conflicts. Boundary changes can also cause confusion, as can instances where a parish was partly in one county and partly in another, or where part of the parish was separated from the rest. Local histories, the Statistical Accounts and ScotlandsPlaces may all provide information on these.

Apparently conflicting evidence can arise when records were created at different times. For example, a man who describes his parents as married to one another when he himself marries may be telling the truth, but it doesn't necessarily follow that they were married at the time of his birth.

If we have genuinely conflicting evidence, then the analysis we have carried out of our sources should help to resolve it, and determine how much weight we should give to any particular piece of information. Generally, an original record carries more weight than a derivative one, and primary information carries more weight than secondary information, but there are no hard and fast rules and we always need to consider the possibility of errors or deliberate misinformation. A second-hand report may be more truthful than primary information because the informant had no reason to lie, while an authored narrative may provide a convincing argument as to why an original record is incorrect.

Direct evidence, which provides us with a clear answer to our question, may seem more compelling than indirect evidence, which gives only a vague or incomplete answer, but sufficient indirect evidence may prove that the direct evidence cannot be true. An exact date of birth recorded for someone as an adult may be easily disproved by finding a record of them living prior to that date, even if the correct date of birth cannot be fully determined.

We shouldn't fall into the trap of weighing up evidence simply by the number of times a particular piece of information is repeated. It may be that the same person is providing the information each time and so each source is not independent. We might have four census records for an ancestor as an adult, each providing the same place of birth, and a single census of them as a child giving a different birthplace. It could be tempting to think that four records created at different times outweigh the evidence of a single document. However, that one record may be correct because the informant was a parent with first-hand knowledge of the birth, and not the person himself who mistakenly believed he was born in the parish where he grew up.

Inconsistent ages are one of the most commonly encountered pieces of conflicting evidence. A person may not have known their true age, or may have chosen not to reveal it. The information could have been provided by someone else, who simply made a best guess. Logic generally dictates that an age recorded for someone as a child is more reliable than that recorded for them as an adult. Someone is unlikely to confuse a two-year-old with a six-year-old, although they might easily mistake a sixty-six-year-old for a sixty-two-year-old. Particular care needs to be taken when calculating a year of birth from an age given in the 1841 census, as ages were typically rounded down to the nearest five years. A woman who was really forty-six but reported her age as forty-four (a fairly minor error), would be recorded in this census as aged forty. Calculating her year of birth as 1801 and searching five years either side of that date would miss her actual birth in 1795.

When evaluating conflicting evidence, we need to bear in mind the social customs of the time and place in which our ancestor lived, and some fundamental principles. Until 1929, the minimum age for marriage in Scotland was twelve for a girl and fourteen for a boy (and very few people married before their late teens), so if we know when a female ancestor married, we can determine that any record putting her date of birth at less than twelve years before that, is likely to be incorrect. A woman was unlikely to give birth before the age of twelve or after the age of forty-nine, so any record that suggests an ancestor gave birth at fifty-five should set alarm bells ringing!

I have records placing the year of birth of one of my ancestors, Hector McNeil, at anywhere between 1823 and 1849, but as I know he married in 1857 and had a child born the following year I can be fairly sure he was not born later than 1843, and was most likely born a few years earlier. The ages recorded for Hector on his marriage record and in the 1861 census consistently put his year of birth at around 1833–1834 and I would give more weight to these than the ages recorded for him in later life. Unfortunately, as Hector was born in Ireland (all sources agree on that at least!), I have no record of him prior to 1857, and have yet to determine exactly when and where he was born. However, by analysing all the sources I have gathered that provide evidence of his birth, and by considering who was the informant in each case, their reliability and level of knowledge, I can conclude he was most likely born in the period 1833–1835.

If, after analysing and comparing all the sources gathered, we are unable to resolve conflicting evidence and to determine which of two versions of events is correct, then it may be necessary to identify further sources, which may answer our question, and to carry out additional research. In some cases it may be impossible to resolve conflicting evidence due to a lack of surviving records.

EXPERT TIP

Dealing with conflicting evidence is a skill that all family historians need to develop. Many conflicts can be easily resolved by analysing sources and the information they contain, and considering the knowledge of the informant in each case.

Reaching a Conclusion

Once we have located records of our ancestor, analysed the sources and the information they contain, drawn up a list of the evidence they provide, and considered any conflicting evidence, we are ready to come to a conclusion.

To reach a conclusion for a research question we need to consider all of the evidence together. In some cases, all evidence will agree and point to an obvious conclusion. If we have birth, marriage and death records for an ancestor all naming the same parents, and census records that verify the relationship, then we don't need to spend long reaching a conclusion as to the identity of that person's parents. However, if the evidence is less clear, which will likely be the case when we enter the pre-statutory registration period, then we need to base our conclusion on sound analysis and reasoning.

Summarizing our conclusion in writing is usually a good idea, even if the research is only for ourselves and our immediate family, but it is particularly important when evidence is indirect or conflicting, and when a conclusion is only reached after detailed analysis. If we put research on a particular family line aside for a while and come back to it sometime later, we may not necessarily remember why we reached a particular conclusion, or chose one possible baptism record over another. A written summary setting out our reasoning will prevent us having to go through the same process again.

A written conclusion does not have to be long or complex. It could be a note attached to a particular person or event in a family history database or online tree, or a typed or handwritten document placed in an ancestor's file stored on a computer or in paper format. It could take the form of a single sentence or a bulleted list, rather than needing to be written in any formal way. The important thing is that it summarizes the evidence we have gathered, and explains why we have reached a particular conclusion.

Where there is insufficient evidence to reach a definitive answer to a research question, we may want to qualify our conclusion with words such as 'probably', 'likely', 'possibly' or 'perhaps'. We can then decide whether to continue research into that family line on the assumption that our conclusion is 'almost certain', whether further research is needed, or whether we have truly reached a brick wall.

EXPERT TIP

As a professional genealogist, writing up the results of research is one of my least favourite parts of the job, but it is often the most useful step in the research process. By going through all the evidence gathered and setting it out logically so a client can easily understand what has been found, I often notice things I missed when I first looked at the records. I can more easily decide if there is enough evidence to reach a conclusion, or if further research is needed. Even if just writing rough notes for your own benefit, it can help to imagine that you are explaining your conclusion to someone else. How would you convince them you are right? What flaws might they spot in your argument?

Genealogical Proof Standard

The concepts presented in this chapter are largely drawn from the Genealogical Proof Standard (GPS). This is a set of research standards compiled by the Board for Certification of Genealogists (BCG), an American organization, between 1997 and 2000, based on the best practices that developed in the field of genealogy over the preceding decades. These standards were originally published by the BCG in *The BCG Genealogical Standards Manual* (2000) and later updated in *Genealogy Standards* (2014). A second revised edition of *Genealogy Standards* was published in 2019 (*see* Further Reading).

These ideas are not universally accepted by all those carrying out genealogical research, but have received an increasing amount of attention and support from genealogists worldwide, who recognize the need to ground their family history in solid research practices, and who have found little guidance elsewhere.

The Genealogical Proof Standard states that to reach a solid conclusion regarding an ancestor we need to go through five steps:

1. Reasonably exhaustive research
2. Complete and accurate source citations
3. Thorough analysis and correlation
4. Resolution of conflicting evidence
5. Soundly written conclusion based on the strongest evidence[1]

This chapter has considered points 3–5 of the GPS. Steps 1–2 will be discussed in the next chapter, including how to plan and carry out research, and what we mean by 'reasonably exhaustive research'.

The word 'proof' in the Genealogical Proof Standard is a slightly confusing one. We can rarely say we have 'proved' what happened in the past, as new evidence can overturn previous conclusions and records that all agree may turn out to be wrong. A man named as the father on a birth record may not actually be the biological father, for example. In this context, 'proof' may refer to a test (as in the proverb 'the proof of the pudding is in the eating'), and by judging our research conclusions against the GPS we are testing out their accuracy and alerting ourselves to potential errors and problems.

Relatively experienced family historians will no doubt recognize a lot of the ideas in this chapter, even if they have not specifically heard of the Genealogical Proof Standard, or are not familiar with the exact terms used. There is a lot that is common sense, or which many genealogists will have figured out for themselves over years of research. The Society of Genealogists (UK) has developed a list of similar 'Principles of Genealogical Research', which can be viewed on their website (www.sog.org.uk/learn/education-sub-page-for-testing-navigation/ hints-tips-six-standards-and-good-practice-in-genealogy).

For others, these concepts may be new or may not seem immediately relevant, but it is worth taking the time to understand them and considering how they may be applied to a particular family history problem. Although originally compiled by professional genealogists, these standards not only apply to those undertaking paid research or who intend to publish their family history, but can help all of us to conduct better research. Many of us embark on family history research simply for fun or to leave a legacy to our descendants, but we will inevitably spend a lot of time and money in the process, and if it is worth doing, then it is surely worth doing well. Following good research standards ensures that our work will be as accurate as possible, and allows us to create a family history we can be proud of.

The further reading list at the end of this book includes a number of publications that discuss the Genealogical Proof Standard and associated concepts in more detail. Further information can be found through the website of the Board for Certification of Genealogists (https://bcgcertification.org), and the websites of genealogist and historical writer Elizabeth Shown Mills: Evidence Explained (www.evidenceexplained.com) and Historic Pathways (www.historicpathways.com).

EXPERT TIP

By following the steps of the GPS, identifying relevant records, analysing and citing our sources, correlating evidence and writing a well-reasoned conclusion, we can ensure that our research is as accurate as possible, and that any new evidence uncovered is likely to support our conclusions rather than overturn them.

---

6 Planning and Recording Research

What is a Research Question?

As discussed in the previous chapter, information found in a genealogical source only becomes evidence when we use it to answer a particular research question. So what is a research question, and how do we choose one?

Some of us may begin family history research because we want to solve a particular family mystery or investigate a family story, but many of us start out only with the vague idea that we want to learn more about our family and where they, and we, came from. As we progress and discover more about our ancestors we will face new mysteries and start to form new questions. We may feel bogged down with the sheer amount of information we have gathered and the number of relatives we have identified, and feel uncertain about where to go next. Eventually we will hit the inevitable 'brick wall'. It is at this point that we need to think about our research question.

A research question is any question we have about our ancestors and their lives that we set out to answer through family history research. In order to plan and carry out research effectively we need to know what it is we are looking for, otherwise it is very easy to waste a lot of time going over the same ground and getting nowhere.

A good research question involves a particular ancestor and is specific and focused. Some examples of typical genealogy research questions include:

When and where was Catharine Jack born?

Who were the parents of Andrew Livingston?

Where was Janet Cameron living at the time of the 1851 census?

Which regiment did James MacGillivray serve in, and how long was he in the army?

When and where did Agnes Stevenson die?

Once we have chosen a research question, we can start to think about what records are available that may answer that question, and where they may be found.

EXPERT TIP

Most of us have a lot of questions about our ancestors, but it's best to focus on one at a time. If a particular question seems impossible to solve then we can switch to a different one, which may prove more productive.

Framing a Research Question

Having chosen a research question, the next step is to consider what we already know about the person or family we will be researching. A basic principle of genealogy research is that we work from the known to the unknown. Evaluating the information we already have will point us towards where to look for the answer to our research question.

We should have at least a rough idea of where and when the person lived. We may also know their occupation and the names of some family members. We may already have some indirect evidence to answer our research question.

EXPERT TIP

If at this point you are thinking that all you know about your ancestor is their name, perhaps gleaned from a child's marriage or death record, then you are probably focusing on the wrong ancestor. Instead, switch to a more recent generation. For example, identifying a child's birth, or likely date and location of birth, will also provide a date and location for the parent.

This is a good time to go back over the records we already have and to analyse them in more detail, looking particularly for any clues we may have missed. If information has come from indexes or from derivative rather than original sources, we should try to locate and obtain a copy of the original.

It can be helpful to transcribe handwritten records, not only so we don't have to keep referring to the originals, but because doing so focuses attention on the details. If there are words that are difficult to read, then try to interpret them. Place and personal names may be particularly important.

The information found so far should be summarized in the way that makes most sense to the researcher. This could be a simple list of facts, or a table setting out the sources found so far and what they contain – for example, all the sources relating to a person's place or date of birth. This allows us to compare the evidence found in different sources easily. Some researchers may find the technique of mind mapping – organizing information visually rather than in a list – to be helpful.

Timelines can be used to track an ancestor's movements, to reveal gaps in their lives and to help untangle same-named individuals. Most family history software allows facts about an ancestor to be plotted in this way, although simply listing facts in date order can also be revealing. Determining where an ancestor lived throughout their life is essential for locating records of them.

EXPERT TIP

Remember that information about an ancestor can come not only from records in which they were a main participant, but also from records of their children, spouses, parents and other family members. Such records may have been created long after the ancestor died, in which case the information will likely be secondary, but can still be valuable.

Planning Research

Having chosen our research question and considered what we already know, we next need to plan our research. This involves drawing up a list of possible sources in which our ancestor may appear, and which may answer our research question. The nature of the research question will partly determine what these sources are, but as we will be looking for indirect evidence as well as direct evidence, this will typically involve researching a person throughout their lifetime, as well as possibly researching other family members.

Any gaps in an ancestor's timeline should be considered. For example, if they are 'missing' from a census that took place during their lifetime, we should try and locate them. If we can't find them, then we should consider other sources that may indicate where they were living at that time. A person may simply have been missed out of the census, but such absences could be due to a temporary migration or a period spent in an institution, such as a hospital, prison, poorhouse or asylum. These events could have resulted in the creation of records providing valuable information. If a family is not recorded in the old parish registers they may have been members of a secessionist or non-conformist church, and alternative church records need to be identified and searched.

An ancestor's personal circumstances should also be taken into account when planning research. For example, did they have an occupation for which records are likely to exist, such as serving in the military? Could they have been a burgess or a member of a trade incorporation, or have served an apprenticeship? Were they landowners or tenants? Did they have an illegitimate child? Was a female ancestor widowed at a young age with children to support so that she needed to apply for poor relief? All of these could lead to the creation of records that provide information not only on the ancestor's life at that moment, but also on their wider circumstances and extended family.

Whatever our research question and whatever an ancestor's circumstances, the most important factor affecting which sources we will use is where the ancestor lived. For this reason it is helpful to compile a locality guide for any places of residence.

Creating a Locality Guide

Creating a locality guide for the parish or parishes in which an ancestor lived is helpful not only for locating relevant records, but also for understanding the areas where our ancestors lived. The parish and county pages of the FamilySearch Wiki and GENUKI (*see* Chapter 3) both provide good starting points but will not necessarily list all the resources available. The following list is not exhaustive but gives an idea of what should be included in a locality guide:

- Name of the parish, any alternative names or common spelling variations, major settlements within the parish (including whether any were burghs), the historic county in which it was located, the current council area, the presbytery and synod the parish was in, any other names used for the area (for example, the name of the island for an island parish, or the name of the valley for one in a mountainous area), any geographic peculiarities (such as a parish partly in one county and partly in another), details of any major boundary changes and when these occurred (ScotlandsPlaces and A Vision of Britain Through Time www.visionofbritain.org.uk are both good sources for this type of information), names of neighbouring parishes
- The local archive or archives (check the archive's website for an online catalogue, finding aids and research guides, and any online indexes or details of indexes available onsite)
- The local studies or local history library (check the library's website for an online catalogue, details of the library's holdings and any available indexes)
- The local family history society (check the society's website for relevant publications, useful information and links, and details of resources available to members)
- Covering dates of the old parish register (OPR) and any significant gaps or issues. The National Records of Scotland guide to the OPRs (www.nrscotland.gov.uk/research/guides/old-parish-registers/list-of-old-parish-registers) includes PDFs giving covering dates for each parish as well as linking to the *Detailed List of the Old Parochial Registers of Scotland*, which provides more detail
- Dates, contents and locations of kirk session and heritors records
- Whether the parish included a *quoad sacra* parish or church in addition to the main Church of Scotland church, and details of any records

- Any non-Church of Scotland churches in the parish and in neighbouring parishes, their surviving records, and where they are held (the FamilySearch Wiki and The Statistical Accounts are both useful for identifying local churches, and online archive catalogues can be used to locate records)

Identifying which church an ancestor attended is crucial for locating records of them and their family.

- Burial grounds within the parish, and the locations of any burial or cemetery records, in addition to those found in the OPR
- Published and unpublished monumental inscriptions, and any websites with transcriptions or photographs of gravestones
- Details of the statistical accounts for the parish, and any relevant information these contain
- Local newspapers, whether these are available online, and any compiled indexes
- Street and trade directories, including any available online
- Details of burgh records, if the parish contained a burgh
- Dates, contents and locations of parochial board and parish council records, including records of poor relief
- Any institutions, such as poorhouses and hospitals, within the parish or in neighbouring parishes, and their records
- Details of schools and school records
- The relevant sheriff and commissary courts, and any other local courts (for example burgh courts, justices of the peace, franchise courts)
- The names of major landowners, any family and estate papers and where these are held, including records held privately
- Relevant websites and online records (in addition to those on ScotlandsPeople)
- Published records and indexes
- Any published research guides covering the area
- Published local histories (the Internet Archive, Google Books, the National Library of Scotland catalogue and local library catalogues are all useful for identifying these)
- Maps of the local area over time (the National Library of Scotland's online maps collection is the best source of these). Pay particular attention to the topography of the area, including roads and other means of transport, barriers to travel (such as mountains) and nearby towns, all of which may suggest migration routes for those who entered or left the parish. Maps can also be used to identify an ancestor's likely church, school or workplace

This mercat cross in Culross, Fife, indicates that the village was originally a royal burgh with the right to hold a market. Burghs created a wealth of records, so it's important to know if an ancestor lived in one.

- Any other records for the parish not covered above (for example, any early censuses or population lists)
- Notes covering any other information we come across, which may be helpful for our research

The locality guide should be as detailed as possible, as we will be using it to identify records that may help to solve our research question. However, it may not be practical to go into as much detail in a guide covering a city or large town as in one covering a rural parish.

EXPERT TIP

As most of us have multiple ancestors and families who lived in the same parish, a locality guide can often be used to assist with more than one research problem. When compiling a guide don't focus just on records dating from the lifetime of the ancestor you are currently researching, but instead look at a wider period. It will save time rewriting the guide when research moves to an earlier generation or a different branch of the family.

Writing a Research Plan

By compiling a locality guide and considering our ancestor's personal circumstances and the records that may have been created as a result, we should have identified a number of sources that may help us to solve our research question. The final stage of planning is to write a research plan listing the sources in the order we will search them, with details of where each source can be accessed, whether online or in a physical repository.

There may be some sources that are more likely than others to contain information that will solve our research question, but the order in which records are searched may be determined by practical considerations. It usually makes sense to search indexed records before unindexed ones, and to search records that we can access online or locally before making a research trip to a distant archive.

A research plan is a dynamic document that will change and develop as research progresses. Information uncovered in one source may suggest new records that we hadn't considered previously. Alternatively, we may decide that we don't need to search all the records we have identified after all. New information may also lead to new research questions, and the focus of our research may shift. We may want to begin a new research plan or adapt the one we already have.

EXPERT TIP

Writing and following a research plan is a good way of keeping research focused on the question at hand and of avoiding getting distracted by other ancestral lines.

Planning a Research Trip

If our research plan involves searching sources held in archives, libraries or other record repositories then we will need to plan a research trip. Planning the trip ensures we can get the most out of our time and is particularly important if the archive is some distance from where we live so we cannot easily visit again. The following checklist may be useful in advance of a research trip:

It's important to plan your research and to prepare in advance of visiting a record repository, such as the Family History Library in Salt Lake City, Utah.

- Do as much preparation as possible. This may involve searching online catalogues, finding aids and research guides, and emailing archive staff for advice
- Draw up a list of records to look at. Include the date ranges to be searched, and the names of the person or people you are looking for, bearing in mind there may be more than one ancestor who might appear in the records
- Check the archive's website for opening hours and access conditions. Many archives have limited opening hours and may close for public holidays or stocktaking. Contact the archive directly to check they will be open the day you plan to visit, especially if travelling from a distance. Some archives recommend making an appointment, and records may be stored offsite and may need to be ordered several days in advance
- Plan your journey in advance, and bear in mind that not all archives are easily accessible by public transport. Some archives close for lunch, and you may need to find somewhere nearby to eat or to bring a packed lunch
- Bring any identification needed in order to get a reader's ticket and to access original records. Proof of address and photographic ID may be required
- Check if photography is allowed and whether there are copying restrictions and charges. Make sure you have cash to pay for copies, as not all archives can take card payments
- Bring some change for using lockers, as you will often not be allowed to bring bags and coats into the search room (most lockers take a £1 coin or are free)
- Bring a pencil, as most archives don't allow the use of pens. Make sure it doesn't have an eraser on the end, as these may be prohibited
- Bring a laptop, tablet computer or notebook to make notes, your research plan or list of records to search, and any other information you may need. It is best not to bring large paper files or folders of notes, especially as they may get lost, but being able to access your family tree on a digital device can be helpful

- Remember that not all archives have Wi-Fi, so you may not be able to access an online family tree or information stored in the cloud. Make sure that any information you may need is downloaded to your laptop or digital device
- Make sure that any laptops, tablets and cameras are fully charged as there may be limited seats with electrical sockets

---

EXPERT TIP

When visiting archives, it's good to have a longer list of records to search than you are likely to be able to cover in a single day. Records may be unavailable, you may be able to search them more quickly than you thought, or it may turn out that they do not contain the type of information you expected. It's very frustrating to find yourself with spare time at the end of the day that you can't use productively because you aren't prepared and don't have the right information with you!

Keeping a Research Journal

When carrying out research, whether online or in a physical repository, it's important that we keep a record not only of the information we find, but also of the sources we search, whether they contain records of our ancestors or not. We may think we will remember what we have looked at, but it's easy to lose track or to forget exactly whom we have searched for in a particular record. Keeping a research journal or log may seem a little tedious, particularly for recording online searches, but it saves time in the long run as it prevents us going back and repeating what we have already done. Noting down searches of records in which our ancestor did not appear is important, not only so that we don't waste time looking at the same records again, but because that ancestor's absence may be significant in itself (*see* 'Negative evidence' in Chapter 5).

A research journal can take the form of a notebook, typed research notes, a word-processed document set out in a table, or a spreadsheet. It should be in a form that makes the most sense to us as a researcher, and that we are most likely to keep. A table or spreadsheet set out in columns with appropriate headings can be useful for reminding us to record all the necessary details, and examples can be found online, including through Cyndi's List (www.cyndislist.com/research-methodology/research-notes/forms).

For sources accessed online through a database, we should record the date of the search, the name and address of the website, the name of the specific database searched, the name of the person or people we searched for (including whether we used spelling variations, soundex or similar options and wildcards), the results of the search, and any comments. Comments could include the content and coverage of the database, the source of the information, or whether records have been poorly transcribed.

For online sources that are not in the form of a database, such as websites that provide background information or where records are simply listed on a page, we should record the date of the search, the name and address of the website, the title of the page (and the web address of the specific page if it may be difficult to find again), who or what we were looking for, the information found and any comments.

For digitized records accessed online but not through a database (such as the browsable records on ScotlandsPlaces or records accessed via the FamilySearch catalogue) we should record the date of the search, the name and address of the website, the title of the collection, the address of the page where the collection can be accessed (if it may be difficult to find again), any source or reference information given, who we were searching for, the date range we searched, the range of page or image numbers we searched, the results of the search, and any comments.

For records accessed on microfilm or microfiche or as digitized images in a physical repository, we should record the date of the search, the name and location of the repository, the title of the records, any reference numbers given, the format we accessed the records in, who we were searching for, the date range we searched, the range of page or image numbers we searched, the results of the search, and any comments (for example, if images are of poor quality or pages have been missed).

For original records accessed in a physical repository, we should record the date of the search, the name and location of the repository, the title of the records and the name of any larger collection they are part of, including the name of the creator (if this can be determined), any reference numbers given, who we were searching for, the date range we searched, the range of page numbers we searched (or if the record is not paginated), the results of the search, and any comments (for example, if the record contains gaps or entries are not in date order).

For published books, we should record the title of the book, the name of the author or authors, the name of the publisher, the place and year of publication, where we accessed it, who or what we searched for, whether we just searched the index or read chapters in full, the results of the search, and any comments.

Some sources may not fit neatly into any of the above categories, but from these descriptions the type of information we need to record in our research journal should be clear. Generally the more information we include, the better, and there should be enough detail that either we or someone else could replicate the search and get the same results. There should also be enough information so we don't later question exactly what or who we searched for, and end up having to repeat the search. For example, we should record whether we copied only the entries for a specific ancestor, or if we noted all entries for the same surname.

EXPERT TIP

Keeping a research journal is a good habit to get into as it focuses our attention on the sources we are using and forces us to think about what we are doing, rather than simply typing an ancestor's name into a database and hoping we will find the information we are looking for.

Citing Sources

A source citation is a note attached to a fact or piece of information that describes where that information came from. A citation could be a footnote or endnote in a written document, or a field in a family history database or online family tree.

A basic rule of genealogical research is that any information that is not common knowledge should have a source citation. If I were describing when and where the Battle of Waterloo took place I wouldn't need a source citation as it is an established fact. However, if I stated that my six-times-great-grandfather, a lowly infantryman, fought in the battle, I would need to include a source citation to prove this was indeed the case.

Source citations are important for several reasons. First, they help us to keep track of where we got information, and if necessary, enable us to find the same information again. Second, they let anyone else looking at our family tree understand where we got information from, and enable them to locate the same sources. They can help us avoid plagiarizing the work of others by giving appropriate credit for ideas that are not our own. Finally, writing source citations (whilst it can be tedious) is a good way for us to better understand and analyse our sources. Often simply the act of locating and recording the information we need to write a source citation gives a better understanding of what that source is, how and why it was created, and of its limitations.

There are plenty of models for writing citations to published sources (Harvard and Chicago are two popular academic referencing systems). However, the kind of original records commonly used in genealogical research are more difficult to cite as they do not necessarily fit into any standard citation model and can be very varied. If we are writing up family history research for publication or as part of an academic course there may be guidance to follow on how to write source citations, but most of the time it is up to us to decide exactly how to cite a source.

Undoubtedly, the most detailed guide to writing genealogical source citations is *Evidence Explained: Citing History Sources from Artifacts to Cyberspace* by Elizabeth Shown Mills (*see* Further Reading). This publication includes detailed discussion of evidence analysis and of the principles of source citation, and provides citation models for a wide variety of historical and genealogical records. However, it is written primarily from an American perspective and includes only a small number of citation models specifically for Scottish records, which in some cases indicate an incomplete understanding of Scottish archives and sources. Although the basic models and general principles can be adapted to suit different types of sources, the length and complexity of *Evidence Explained* may be off putting, particularly to those relatively new to family history.

Those who choose to base their source citations upon *Evidence Explained* may find *Mastering Genealogical Documentation* by

Thomas W. Jones helpful (*see* Further Reading). This book does not provide models for citing sources but rather teaches the principles of citation, breaking citations down into their individual elements. It describes itself as a textbook, rather than a reference book, and is primarily based on American examples.

The genealogical studies department of the University of Strathclyde, Glasgow, has created a referencing guide for course students, which can accessed via the university's website (www.strath.ac.uk/studywithus/centreforlifelonglearning/genealogy/genealogyresources). This guide includes citation models for a variety of commonly used Scottish genealogical records, and guidance on citing non-standard sources. These citation models differ in style from those given in *Evidence Explained* but include much the same information.

Ian G. Macdonald, a tutor on the University of Strathclyde's genealogy course, has published a more detailed guide, *Referencing for Genealogists: Sources and Citation* (*see* Further Reading). This expands upon the citation models given in the Strathclyde referencing guide, and includes discussion of the analysis and classification of genealogical sources. This guide is strongly based on UK sources and includes citation models for many common and less widely used Scottish records. Citations made using this system are typically shorter than those created using the *Evidence Explained* style. However, the meaning of some abbreviations and of elements within the citations may be unclear to those unfamiliar with this particular referencing system.

The above referencing guides provide a good starting point for family historians looking to fully comprehend source citations, or who want a particular model to follow. Personally, having used a variety of different citation styles, I am of the opinion that there is no such thing as the perfect source citation. Rather than worrying too much about the exact order in which details are given, or whether they are separated by a comma, semi-colon or full stop, the most important thing is simply to make sure we record the source of all the information we gather on our families, and that we include all the details that we, or someone else, would need in order to locate the same record again.

The previous section on keeping a research journal includes the basic information we need to record for each source we look at.

As further guidance, the details that should be recorded for some commonly used Scottish record types are given below.

Statutory registers
Registration district name (for example: District of Rutherglen)

County or burgh the registration district was in (for example: County of Lanark or Burgh of Aberdeen)

Registration district number (for example: 654 or 168–1)

Type of event (for example: birth, marriage, death, register of corrected entries)

Year the event was registered

Entry number

Name of the person or people recorded

Access method (for example: medium, database name, website name and address, and date of access – e.g. digital image, 'Statutory Registers: Births', ScotlandsPeople (www.scotlandspeople.gov.uk; accessed 17 October 2018)

Old parish registers (OPRs)
Parish name

County name

OPR number and section (for example: 56/2 or 685–1/81)

Type of event (for example: baptism, banns, marriage, burial)

Page or image number

Name of the person or people recorded

Date the event was recorded or took place

Access method (for example, whether on microfilm or as a digitized image, with details of the physical repository or online database and website)

Census returns
District or parish name

County name

Registration district number

Enumeration district number

Page number

Schedule number (not given in 1841)

Name of the head of household (or main person of interest)

Access method

Wills and testaments

Court name (for example: Dingwall Sheriff Court)
Type of record (for example: inventory, will, settlement, eik)
Archival reference number (for example: SC25/44/27)
Page number(s)
Name of the deceased person (including alternative surnames for
women, if given)
Date of recording
Access method

Records accessed in a physical repository

Creator and/or record collection (for example: Southend Kirk
Session, Argyll)
Title of the record and covering dates (for example: minutes and
accounts, 1799–1839)
Archival reference number (for example: CH2/957/1)
Page number(s) (or if the record is unpaginated)
Name of the person or people recorded
Date the event took place or was recorded
Access method (for example: original record, digital image, micro-
film, photocopy)
Name and location of repository (for example National Records of
Scotland, Edinburgh)

In all cases there may be additional information we want to record in
order better to explain what the record is or how it may be located.
For example, if the record was accessed through a database, and
a name or some other important detail is indexed differently from
how it appears on the original record, we may want to note that
so the record can be easily located again: for example, 'Clementina
[indexed as Elermenten] Howe'.

The reference numbers given on the ScotlandsPeople website are
a little confusing as they string together several different numbers,
which refer to different elements, into one long number. For statutory records, the reference number given by ScotlandsPeople is
registration district number followed by entry number, separated
by a space. For the old parish registers the parish or OPR number is
given first, and the reference number is the section of the OPR followed by the image number. For censuses, the reference number is

in the following form: registration district number, enumeration district number, page number, with each element separated by a space.

When writing source citations to entries found in the OPRs it can be helpful to look at the List of Old Parish Registers on the National Records of Scotland website (www.nrscotland.gov.uk/ research/guides/old-parish-registers/list-of-old-parish-registers). For example, if I were researching a family from the parish of Ardnamurchan, Argyll (OPR 505), which included Acharacle and Strontian or Sunart, this list would tell me that a baptism found in 505/2 took place in Strontian, while one of the same date in 505/3 took place in western Ardnamurchan. If I were researching a death that took place in Glasgow, I would discover that a person recorded in OPR 644–1/67 was buried in the Calton burial ground, whilst one recorded in OPR 644–1/68 was buried in the North Street burial ground. This is something that, in both cases, might not be apparent from accessing the image directly through the ScotlandsPeople website.

For most other records, archive catalogues are the best way of identifying any information needed to create a source citation that isn't apparent from the record itself. The National Records of Scotland (NRS) online catalogue (http://catalogue.nrscotland. gov.uk/nrsonlinecatalogue) can be used to interpret the reference numbers found on ScotlandsPeople for wills and testaments, Roman Catholic and 'other' church registers and valuation rolls, as well as the reference numbers given for digitized tax records on ScotlandsPlaces. It may be necessary to remove any final digits representing page numbers and long strings of zeros to turn the number into a reference the NRS catalogue will recognize.

EXPERT TIP

Even if you obtain a copy of a record it is still important to note down source information, both in a research journal and on the copy itself. Reference numbers and other identifying information can be written in the margin of a paper copy, or saved as part of the file name of a digital image. Often dates and locations will not appear on every page of a record, and when you come to look at the copy again you may have no idea where it came from or why you copied it!

Reasonably Exhaustive Research

The first component of the Genealogical Proof Standard (*see* Chapter 5) is 'reasonably exhaustive research'.[1] This is something we should consider when planning our research, when carrying it out, and when analysing the records we have found and deciding whether we have enough evidence to reach a reliable conclusion.

So what exactly is reasonably exhaustive research, and how do we know if we have achieved it? Exhaustive research would involve examining every record created during an ancestor's lifetime, which covers the area they lived in, whether created on a parish, county, Scotland-wide or UK-wide level. Clearly this would be impractical, and so the word 'reasonably' is included to indicate we need only search those records that are likely to provide evidence to answer our research question.

There is no hard and fast rule as to what constitutes reasonably exhaustive research. Rather it is a concept that recognizes that every situation is different, and that it is up to the individual family historian to use his or her judgement as to when enough research has been carried out and sufficient evidence gathered.

The Board for Certification of Genealogists' publication *Genealogy Standards* lists five elements of reasonably exhaustive research:

- It produces at least two independent sources or information items that agree with a research conclusion, whether directly or indirectly
- It includes sources, and records which a competent researcher would use to research the same question
- It involves searches in at least one original record and does not, where possible, rely only on authored narratives or derivative records
- It includes sources providing some primary information, rather than only secondary or undetermined information
- It uses indexes and databases to identify potentially relevant sources[2]

Put in these terms, reasonably exhaustive research is not as daunting as it might first appear. Some research questions can be solved quite easily, for example using only statutory registers and census returns, and still meet the requirements of reasonably exhaustive research. Others will require a lengthier search, and in some cases may yield insufficient evidence to satisfy the conditions of a reasonably exhaustive search.

EXPERT TIP

None of us has an endless supply of time or money. However, if practical considerations mean that reasonably exhaustive research is not possible, we should be aware that any conclusions we reach may not be reliable, and that new evidence uncovered by ourselves or other researchers in the future could overturn them.

Summary

To solve difficult genealogy problems it is necessary to take a logical approach to research. In this and the previous chapter, we have discussed some of the methods that genealogists have developed to ensure their research is as thorough and accurate as possible, as well as some ways of approaching research. The research process can be summarized as follows:

1. Choose a research question relating to a specific individual or family.
2. Identify what is already known about that individual or family, and any specific gaps in that knowledge.
3. Identify the records that may provide evidence to answer the research question, whether available online or held in a physical repository.
4. Write a research plan, and plan trips to the archives holding the records identified.
5. Search the sources identified, recording the searches in a research journal and obtaining copies of relevant documents.
6. Analyse the information and evidence gathered, resolving any conflicting evidence.
7. Decide if there is sufficient evidence to reach a conclusion (if not, steps 3–6 may need to be repeated).
8. Write up the conclusion, citing the sources used to reach it.
9. Repeat the process to answer any new questions that have arisen.

7 Common Causes of Genealogy Problems

There are many reasons why we may be unable to find records of our ancestors. This chapter looks at some common issues that can affect many different types of source, and which may provide a simple solution to an apparently missing record or 'brick wall' ancestor.

Spelling Variations
Spelling was not consistent in the past, and personal names were particularly subject to spelling variations. Whether our ancestors had common or unusual names, we are likely to find them recorded under a variety of different spellings, sometimes within a single document.

Although we may have grown up spelling our surname a particular way and believing our family to be quite distinct from others who spell their surname slightly differently, our ancestors likely had no such notion. As we trace our family lines further back in time, it really doesn't make sense to think about there being a right or a wrong way to spell a name. In older documents even common names can be found spelled in a variety of ways: for example Andrew as 'Andro', John as 'Jhonne', Margaret as 'Margrat', Brown as 'Broune', and Thomson as 'Thomesoune'.

Often the registrar, enumerator or clerk recording the information would simply write down how they thought a name should be spelled, or what they thought they heard, without bothering to ask the person concerned. If that person had limited literacy skills, then they may have been unable to correct errors or even to read what was written about them. Rare names tend to be subject to more spelling variations than common ones, but even something as simple as a heavy cold could result in a name being misheard and therefore misrecorded.

Particular problems may have arisen when a person moved to an area some distance from where they originated, and where their name and accent were unfamiliar. A branch of my family originating in the north of Ireland had the unusual surname of Freckleton (also recorded as Frackleton or Frickleton). After a long search I eventually found them in the 1851 census in Lanarkshire recorded as Freittleting – which perhaps makes more sense if you imagine it delivered in a strong Northern Irish accent! Most of this family appear to have been unable to write prior to the introduction of compulsory education in 1872, and I have sometimes wondered about the role schoolteachers played in eventually fixing the spelling. Presumably the teacher had to make a best guess and then teach the child how to spell their name. This could explain how first cousins living a short distance apart ended up spelling their surname differently.

There is a common misconception that there is some significance as to whether a 'Mac' surname begins with 'Mac' or 'Mc'. Some believe 'Mac' to be Scottish and 'Mc' to be Irish in origin. In fact they are simply alternative spellings of the same word, meaning 'son of', and any family is likely to be found under both spellings at different times. In older documents, and printed sources such as newspapers, the spelling M' (for example M'Donald) may also be found, or there may be a space between the Mac and the rest of the name (such as Mac Donald, rather than Macdonald). All variations should be considered when searching for ancestors, and we should be aware that transcribers and indexers may handle these variants in different ways. Searching databases using 'M' followed by the wildcard symbol and then the rest of the name (for example M*donald) should pick up most forms.

A surname where 'Mac' is followed by a vowel can lead to particular spelling issues, as the letter 'c' may be duplicated or a 'k' added. For example, McIntosh may be recorded as Mackintosh and McInnes as McKinnes or McCinnes. Conversely, where the Mac is typically followed by a 'c' or 'k', this can be omitted. For example, McCormick may be written as McOrmick, or Mackenzie may become McEnzie. A similar effect can occur when the last letter or sound of a forename is the same as that at the beginning of the surname. For example, the name James Sanderson can easily be heard as James Anderson unless enunciated clearly.

In the past, common forenames were often abbreviated when they were written down, the most common being Alexander as Alexr., Charles as Chas., Donald as Dond., James as Jas., Robert as Robt., Thomas as Thos., William as Wm., Elizabeth as Elizt. or Elizth., and Margaret as Margt. Such spellings do not reflect how the name was pronounced, but were simply a convenient shorthand. Some indexers expand such abbreviations to their full versions, and others transcribe them exactly as they are written, so it may be necessary to search for both forms, particularly in online databases. These abbreviations may also be found in some transcriptions, particularly of monumental inscriptions, when the full name appears in the original.

In older Scottish records, words that now begin with 'w' may be written with 'qu'. This is particularly common with Quhyte or Quheit (and many other variations) for the surname Whyte/White. The archaic letters *thorn* (pronounced 'th' but written similar to a 'y') and *yogh* (pronounced 'yh' but written similar to a 'z' or 'y') can also cause problems. The numerous spellings of the surname and occupation Taylor or tailor, which include a 'z' or second 'y', are attempts to render the *yogh*.

SOLUTIONS

Consider which parts of an ancestor's name are likely to be spelled consistently, and which may be subject to change or variations in pronunciation (vowels can often be used interchangeably, added or omitted). Try saying the name out loud or in different accents. Keep a list of possible spelling variations, and add any unusual ones you come across. This is helpful when searching databases or catalogues that only allow a search by exact spelling.

Forename Variants
As well as being spelled in different ways, many names, both forenames and surnames, were subject to genuine variations, which can cause confusion to the uninitiated. In some cases these may be nicknames that are still in use today, such as Rab for Robert, Billy for

William, Alec or Sandy for Alexander, and Maggie for Margaret. In other cases they are names that we now consider to be totally separate, but which in the past were frequently used for a single person.

When it comes to forenames, for some reason female names were subject to much greater variation than male ones, or at least the variants appear in records far more frequently. For example, the 1911 census includes only four Bills or Billys, but over 70,000 Maggies. For males, the names that were mostly frequently used interchangeably in Scotland were Donald/Daniel and Peter/Patrick (so someone baptised as Patrick might marry as Peter, for example). For females the list is far longer, but the following (where some, but not all, spelling variants are given) are particularly common:

Agnes / Ann(e) / Annie / Nan / Nancy
Alexandra / Alexanderina / Alexandrina / Alexina / Lexina / Lexie
Bridget / Bridie / Biddy
Catharine / Catherine / Katherine / Kate / Katie / Rena
Christian / Christina / Christy / Chirsty / Cirsty / Kirsty
Elizabeth / Elisabeth / Eliza / Lizabeth / Liz / Lizzie / Betty / Betsy /
     Bessie / Bethia / Elspeth / Elspet / Elsie
Euphemia / Eupham / Euphan / Effie / Phemie
Grizzel / Grissel / Grace
Giles / Julia / Egidia
Helen / Ellen / Nellie / Eleanor / Helena / Lena
Isabella / Isobel / Ishbel / Isa / Bella / Tibby
Jane / Jean / Jeanie / Janet / Jenet / Jenny / Jessie
Joan / Joanna / Johan / John Ann / John
Lillias / Lily
Sarah / Sally / Sadie
Williamina / Wilhelmina / Mina / Minnie

Jane and Jean were most frequently used interchangeably, while Jessie was more commonly used for Janet, but some Jeans and Janes also went by Janet. Conversely, some families had surviving daughters named Janet and Jean, so the names clearly weren't always viewed as one. Christian and Grizzel changed to the alternative forms over time, particularly over the course of the 1800s when they appear to have fallen out of fashion. Isabella can occasionally be found as a variant of Elizabeth.

Any male name could be turned into a female one by the addition of '-ina', as in Alexanderina and Williamina above, and other fairly common names such as Thomasina and Georgina, but also Andrewina, Hectorina, Jamesina, Robertina. This led to some fairly unwieldy names, which the recipient might shorten to something more manageable (such as Andrina or Robina, or even Bina), and which were all frequently abbreviated as Ina (pronounced 'eye-na'). The first girl in the family to be given such a name was usually named after a particular male relative, but it might then be passed down to several generations of her female descendants.

Some variants seem to have been particular to individuals or families. For example, I researched an Elsie, probably named after her grandmother Elspeth, who also went by Alice (perhaps she didn't much care for Elsie!). I've also come across a Helen who also went by Alison. The best explanation I could come up with is that Alison was pronounced locally as Elison, which is close to Ellen as an alternative for Helen.

Some names that we now consider male, such as Christian and Nicholas, were originally used for women in Scotland. Surnames were frequently given as both middle names and forenames to both sexes, so Stewart and Bruce might be female and Rose could be a boy. Baptism records may not always specify the sex of the child, and both clerks at the time and modern indexers may have jumped to the wrong conclusion, so it may be best to select the 'both' option under gender when carrying out searches for such names.

Gaelic forenames were frequently transliterated into English or matched with English equivalents. Some common ones are John recorded for Ian/Iain, James for Hamish or Seumas, Hugh/Hew for Ewan, Aeneas for Aonghas/Angus, and Norman for Tormod. The female names Mòr and Mòrag can be found as Marion or Sarah (themselves used interchangeably), and although Marsaili is often equated with Marjory or Margery, I traced one who appeared in some records as Marshall, amongst a host of other variations. The appearance of an unusual forename in a Gaelic-speaking area could well have its origins in an attempt to anglicize a Gaelic name.

Few of the old parish registers are written in Latin, but Catholic registers often were, and Latin forms of names can also be found in older records written in Latin, such as services of heirs and sasines. Some Latin names are similar to the English form, such as Maria and Margareta for Mary and Margaret, while others are distinctly different but quite common, such as Jacobus and Gulielmus for James and William. Some Latin names may be potentially confusing: for example, when encountered in a Scottish document, Nigellus is likely to be the Latin form of the forename Neil, rather than Nigel. As with abbreviations, it shouldn't be supposed that the person ever used this form of their name themselves, it was simply how it was recorded in a particular document. Lists of Latin forms of names can be found online and in the two books by Bruce Durie listed in the Further Reading section, although bear in mind that Latin grammar causes a word's ending to change depending on its place in the sentence, so names may not be written exactly as they appear in a word list.

Middle names were relatively rare in Scotland until the 1800s and their use is often inconsistent. Someone baptised with a middle name might never use it, whereas someone born without a middle name might start using one fairly late in life. Middle names may be recorded in some records but not in others, or given only as an initial. Some people were, and are, commonly known by a middle name, and so a middle name may be recorded in place of a forename. Someone with several middle names might change the order, or drop one completely.

SOLUTIONS

Be creative when searching for an ancestor, and consider what possible forms of their forename might be used. Draw up a list of possible name variants to check for, especially any that are not routinely picked up in online searches, and try the 'name variants' option when searching on ScotlandsPeople. Don't ignore a person or family because the names don't match exactly with what you expect, but consider that perhaps forename variants are being used.

Surname Variants

Like forenames, surnames could be subject to variations that are more than simple changes in spelling, and which may not be picked up in a database by standard search criteria.

Many surnames altered over time. For example, the surname Affleck originating in the south-west of Scotland was originally

Auchinleck (derived from a place of that name), and was sometimes shortened to Fleck. There was often no definitive change from one form of the name to another. Individuals may be recorded under various forms throughout their lifetime, and siblings may be found using different versions of a surname at the same period.

Prefixes, such as Mac or O', and suffixes, such as -son, may have been added or lost over time, or swapped, perhaps when the family moved from a Highland to a Lowland parish. For example, a Williamson family may originally have been called MacWilliam. One of my ancestors used the surname Donaldson throughout his life, but was baptised as William Donald. When researching for a client, I hit a brick wall when tracing a McNiven family until I figured out that originally they went by the name Niven.

In older records, women may be recorded under the variant Nic, Nc or N' meaning 'daughter of' rather than Mac ('son of'), so the daughter of James McNeil would be called Jean NcNeil. Gaelic surnames might be transliterated into English in a variety of ways and so are particularly subject to spelling variation, but could also be exchanged with an English equivalent. MacCombie, a variant of MacThomaidh meaning 'son of Tommy', was anglicized in some parts of Scotland as Thomson.

Hereditary surnames were adopted later in the Highlands than in the Lowlands, and were typically taken from the clan or sept chief, regardless of whether there was a blood relationship. Surnames could be changed to suit the times. For example, some families took the surname Fraser and fought for the Lovat Fraser clan in return for food (including oatmeal), and were subsequently referred to as 'boll of meal' Frasers. The majority of tenants on the island of Ulva used the surname McQuarrie until the McQuarrie landowner was replaced by a McDonald and they gradually became McDonalds, in written records at least. The name MacGregor was famously banned in 1603 and those bearing it had to choose another name, at least temporarily. Such changes have implications for descendants attempting to trace their family lines as well as for DNA surname studies.

Sometimes individuals were recorded with aliases that do not indicate any criminal activity but instead refer to the use of a clan and sept name, a Gaelic and English version of a name, a patronymic, an occupation, or a nickname. Thus it is likely that

Alexander Drysdaill, alias Smyth, a smith in Culross, Perthshire, whose testament was recorded in Dunblane Commissary Court in 1599, derived his alias from his occupation. Whereas Patrick Buchquhannn alias Walterson, whose testament was recorded in the same court in 1543, may well have had a father named Walter.

In some fishing communities, particularly in the north-east of Scotland, the small pool of surnames led to the widespread use of 'tee-names' or nicknames in addition to a surname. Such tee-names might be taken from a personal characteristic, a place of residence, the name of a fishing boat, or the name of a relative. Tee-names were sometimes recorded in censuses and valuation rolls, so can be used to distinguish between same-named individuals, when they are known. Tee-names might be recorded instead of a surname, and occasionally they became hereditary surnames over time. In the fishing community of Fisherrow near Musselburgh, now in East Lothian, married men sometimes added their wife's surname after their own as a way of distinguishing themselves from others of the same name.

Many surnames have their origins in patronymics, whereby a surname was derived from the father's forename, so Robert, son of John, becomes Robert Johnson. In some parts of Scotland a system of non-hereditary patronymics, with the surname changing with each generation, survived into the 1800s, so that a Robert Johnson was actually the son of John, but Robert's son would take the surname Robertson, not Johnson. This system was found in Caithness and Sutherland, where a Gaelic form of patronymic was used (sometimes in addition to a hereditary surname), as well

Surname	Forename	Date	Description	Type	Court	Reference Number
Duncanson	John	28/11/1750	alias Haugh, shoemaker in Cambuswallace, parish of Kilmadock	TD	Dunblane Commissary Court	CC6/5/25
Ferguson	John	25/8/1740	alias Gayloch, in Dykehead of Cardross, parish of Port	TD	Dunblane Commissary Court	CC6/5/24
McArie	John	9/11/1738	alias King, in Callender	TD	Dunblane Commissary Court	CC6/5/24
Murray	John	25/1/1722	alias Greigor McGreigor McGinoig, parish of Callendar	TD	Dunblane Commissary Court	CC6/5/23

The results of a search of the wills and testaments database on the ScotlandsPeople website showing several men who were known by aliases.

CROWN COPYRIGHT, NATIONAL RECORDS OF SCOTLAND

as in the Orkney and Shetland Islands where there was a strong Scandinavian influence. In Orkney and Shetland, women used a form of the surname ending in -daughter or -dochter (such as Marione Magnusdaughter and Agnes Davidsdochter).

Surnames were sometimes changed for legal reasons, such as to benefit from an inheritance. A legal document known as a 'Deed of Tailzie' or 'Entail' might specify that a property could only be inherited by a relative with the same surname as the original owner. If the male line died out and the property went to a woman, her husband or son might change his surname to hers in order to inherit. Such changes might be recorded but did not have to be, and it has always been legal in Scotland to call yourself by whatever name you like, provided it is not for the purposes of fraud.

Illegitimate children in Scotland often took their father's surname, regardless of whether the reputed father admitted paternity, although this did not happen in every case. Such children might alternate between using their father's and mother's names. Stepchildren sometimes took their stepfather's surname, and it is common to find stepchildren listed in censuses under a stepfather's surname (and often appearing as if they were his actual children), even if they kept their own name in other records. This may be the result of a misunderstanding on the part of the census enumerator, rather than indicating that the children were generally known by this name.

The standard reference work on Scottish surnames is *The Surnames of Scotland: Their Origin, Meaning, and History* by George F. Black, originally published in 1946 by the New York Public Library and reprinted in several later editions. A digitized copy of the original edition can be viewed online for free through the Hathi Trust Digital Library (https://catalog.hathitrust.org/record/001598191). *The Surnames of Scotland* is not infallible (most names are covered in a single short paragraph), but it provides a good starting point for researching any Scottish surname, and is particularly helpful for listing early references to a name, and variant spellings recorded over time and in different parts of the country. Local histories can be useful for identifying unusual surname changes found in a particular area, and the use of surnames in the Highlands is discussed in detail in *Genealogy in the Gaidhealtachd* by Graeme M. Mackenzie (*see* Further Reading).

SOLUTIONS

Research family surnames including their origins and possible variants. Consider the different surnames an ancestor may have used, and the naming practices in use in their community. If an ancestor is difficult to find, try searching for them in databases with a forename only, and looking for possible matches. As with forenames, don't ignore people or families whose names are only a partial match, but consider if they could be using a variant surname.

Women's Surnames

In Scotland, women did not traditionally lose their maiden name when they married, but rather gained that of their husband in addition to their own. A single woman described as Agnes Campbell, daughter of David Campbell, became Agnes Campbell, wife of George Ferguson, when she married. When a husband is not specifically named, surnames are usually listed in the order they were acquired, so an Agnes Campbell or Ferguson had the maiden name of Campbell and the married name of Ferguson, and a Sarah McPherson or McTavish or McEwen had the maiden name of McPherson, was married first to Mr McTavish and then to Mr McEwen. When maiden and married surnames are the same they may be given in the form of 'Margaret Morrison or Morrison', but this can sometimes be unclear (for example Margaret Morrison, widow of Peter Morrison). When the word 'alias' is used to separate the different surnames used by a woman this usually refers to maiden and married surnames, rather than to the types of aliases used by men, as described above.

Married women were often recorded under their maiden names. This widow's burial record clearly identifies her husband and gives both her maiden and married surnames, but where only one surname is recorded it can be unclear which is being used.

CROWN COPYRIGHT, NATIONAL RECORDS OF SCOTLAND

Any legal document concerning a married or widowed woman will list all the surnames by which she was known (maiden and married), and baptisms in the old parish registers usually list mothers with their maiden surnames, or not at all. Women were generally recorded on gravestones under their maiden surnames, although this changed around the late 1800s to early 1900s when only a married name may be given. Some early statutory death registers have a woman's maiden surname listed as her main surname. Although the husband's name will usually also be given, I have come across a few early death records where a woman is listed as married or widowed, but with no mention at all of the husband's surname.

As described in Chapter 1, the death record of a married or widowed woman is indexed under all surnames by which she was known, provided they are recorded (sometimes a woman's maiden name or a previous married surname may be unknown to the informant of her death). Burials in the old parish registers may give both surnames, or only one, in which case it may be unclear if a maiden or married name is being used. Other records such as prison registers and poor relief records will usually give both of a woman's surnames, although some records may simply list her as 'Widow Brown', in which case the surname is the married one.

Married women were recorded fairly frequently in the 1841 and 1851 censuses under their maiden names. This is helpful for confirming that the right family has been identified, although potentially confusing when searching an index. This is less common for married women after 1851, although widows may still appear under maiden surnames in later censuses. In some cases this seems to have confused census enumerators, as a widow living with a married son and listed under her maiden name may be mistakenly recorded as his mother-in-law, rather than his mother. This can not only conceal the identity of the widow herself, but can also cause a researcher to draw a wrong conclusion concerning the maiden name of the son's wife. Women can sometimes be found in census records listed without a forename, for example as Mrs Adamson, Mrs Andrew Baird, or Widow Cameron, although it is rarer to find men recorded with a title in place of their first name.

Occasionally a woman's maiden name may appear on a census as a middle name or middle initial. Some poor relief registers list both of a woman's surnames without an 'or' between them, so that a maiden name could be mistaken for a middle name, although usually other information will make this clear. I have noticed a slight tendency for Scottish women who died in England to have their maiden surnames listed as middle names on their death certificates. As English death certificates do not give parents' names, and until 1969 had no space to enter a married woman's maiden name, this may reflect the family's attempt to record a name, which in Scotland was viewed as an important part of a woman's identity.

The fact that many Scottish women had surnames as middle names sometimes led to confusion between their middle and maiden names after they married. On my mother's birth record, my grandmother's middle name is mistakenly listed in place of her maiden surname, and I have come across several other examples of this. When starting with a child's birth record, then looking for their parents' marriage, this confusion is usually easily resolved as the parents' date and place of marriage is given and can be used to locate their marriage record. However, when starting with a marriage and then searching for the births of all children born to that couple, it can be easy to miss a birth with a wrong mother's maiden surname appearing in the index. Repeating the search with a woman's middle name in the field for mother's surname may reveal any missing births.

Widows generally remarried under their maiden surnames prior to statutory registration, and sometimes also afterwards. The old parish registers will occasionally name a previous husband, but often there will be no indication at all of an earlier marriage. Statutory marriage records will state if a bride was a widow but may not always record her previous married surname, which can lead to a lengthy search for a previous marriage. This was the case with one of my relatives, Ellen Patterson, who first married in 1863. She married her second husband in 1883 under her maiden name of Ellen Patterson, her third husband in 1905 as Ellen Paterson or Gillespie (her second married surname), and her fourth husband in 1907 as Ellen Patterson again. Her death record lists only her last husband, with no reference to her previous marriages. She may well have had another marriage, which I have yet to discover!

Although ScotlandsPeople deals with the use of maiden and married surnames quite well, other genealogy websites find the use of two surnames by Scottish women harder to handle. Most commonly when both surnames are given in a record, a woman's maiden surname will be indexed as her middle name, but occasionally it may be the other way round. Both possibilities should be considered when carrying out a search.

A slight peculiarity of the indexing of wills and testaments of married women on ScotlandsPeople is that early testaments (recorded in commissary courts) are typically indexed under a woman's maiden surname with her husband's full name given in the description, whereas later ones (recorded in sheriff courts from the 1820s) are more often indexed under her married surname. As women's testaments are indexed under only one surname (not under both, like death records) it is best to search for each surname in turn, although the alternative surname can be entered in the description field to narrow down the number of results.

SOLUTIONS

If a female ancestor can't be found under her married surname, try searching for her under her maiden name. Remember that maiden, married and middle names may be confused or indexed differently from how you expect. Try replacing a woman's forename with 'Mrs' or 'Widow', or even her husband's first name, to see if additional results come up.

Scottish Naming Pattern
When Scottish parents named their children they often followed a traditional naming pattern, which went as follows:

- First son named after his paternal grandfather (his father's father)
- Second son named after his maternal grandfather (his mother's father)
- Third son named after his father
- First daughter named after her maternal grandmother (her mother's mother)
- Second daughter named after her paternal grandmother (her father's mother)
- Third daughter named after her mother

By no means all Scottish families followed this pattern strictly, but it was used widely from around the mid-1700s to the early 1900s. There were some variations on the pattern, such as the order of the paternal and maternal names being switched, or the eldest or second children being named after the parents rather than the third. Younger children might be named after aunts and uncles (particularly helpful if the names were unusual), although children were also named after relatives by marriage, employers or the minister who baptised them, as well as simply being given names their parents liked.

This naming pattern has two great benefits for family historians. First, if we know the names of a couple's children, we can use those names to predict what the couple's parents were likely called. Second, if we know the names of a couple's parents (such as from a statutory marriage record) we can use those names to anticipate what the first three sons and daughters will be named. This is useful for descendant tracing as well as for picking up children who were born and died in between censuses. However, aside from the fact not all families followed a naming pattern, there are some potential issues that need to be considered.

Obviously, in order to use children's names to predict their grandparents' names, we need to be fairly confident that we have identified all of a couple's children and the order in which they were born. Typically, a couple's first child was born fairly shortly after they married, with younger children being born around every two years thereafter until the mother reached her early forties, followed by another one or two children with slightly longer gaps between births. If we have a family with large gaps between the births of identified children this could indicate there were additional children whose births or baptisms were not recorded, and whose names could well be significant. If a couple had only a small number of children, or only children of one sex, it may also be difficult to establish if they were following a naming pattern.

The relatively small pool of forenames used in Scotland could often lead to multiple relatives having the same name. For example, it was not that unusual for a child to have a mother and both grandmothers all with the same name. Although there are examples of the names of living children being repeated in a family in order to follow the naming pattern in these circumstances, particularly in some Highland areas, in most cases a name would only be repeated if the older child died. If we are not aware of the repetition of names within the extended family, it is easy to draw an incorrect conclusion from looking at the children's names. The naming of a younger sibling after one who died was common, and is easy to spot if all the children's names are known. However, a missing birth of a child who died could lead to a significant family name appearing relatively late in the birth order, and the naming pattern being misinterpreted.

When a widow or widower remarried and had a second family, names would not normally be repeated, except when an older child had died. As the old parish registers rarely record the marital status of those getting married, it is easy to miss a previous marriage and to presume that every bride and groom were spinster and bachelor. Where one spouse had been married previously and the other not, or some family names had been used whilst others hadn't, parents following the naming pattern would have had to decide in which order to use remaining family names. If we don't know about a previous marriage we can easily misinterpret the significance of children's names.

I had this problem with one branch of my family. They appeared to be using family names for their children, including giving surnames as middle names, but the order was confusing and it was hard to see a pattern. It was only when I worked out that the husband had been married previously and already had several children that it all fell into place. In this case the name of a child from the first marriage who died young was reused for a child of the second marriage.

Illegitimacy within a family can disrupt the naming pattern in a number of ways. Illegitimate boys were commonly named after their reputed father, while illegitimate girls might be named after their mother, their maternal grandmother (following the naming pattern), or perhaps the paternal grandmother in the hope that the father's family would acknowledge the child. Sometimes illegitimacy seems to have been a reason to abandon family names completely and to give the child a more unusual name. A person born illegitimately may not have named one of their own children after their father, whose identity they may have been only vaguely aware of, and so that name may simply have been missed out of the pattern in the next generation.

There are certainly cases of a person having a surviving legitimate and illegitimate child (or more than one illegitimate child) with the same name, but if the existence of the illegitimate child was sufficiently well known in the community, then the name would likely not be repeated. This was the case with one family I researched, where a man's illegitimate child by one woman was given the same fairly common name as the father of a second woman he later married. This meant that none of the legitimate sons were named after their maternal grandfather, something which could easily have led to the wife's parents being misidentified, had the existence of her husband's illegitimate child not been known.

Although the absence of a family name from the naming pattern can lead to incorrect conclusions regarding the identity of a couple's parents, it can also reveal the existence of a previously unknown child. If a couple appear to have been following the naming pattern but a family name is missing, then we should consider the possibility that there was another child, perhaps born prior to the marriage. After many years of researching one of my ancestral couples I discovered, by chance, that they had a daughter born three years prior to their marriage, who was brought up outside the immediate family. When looking back over my notes I kicked myself for not having realized this sooner. The daughter had the same forename as her mother and both grandmothers, yet I hadn't spotted the absence of this important family name from the couple's known children, or appreciated the significance!

When trying to determine if a couple were following the traditional naming pattern, it is helpful to look at where the parents' own names appear in the birth order of their children. If the third son and third daughter were named after their parents, then the family was likely following the pattern. If a parent's name appears earlier in the birth order, this could indicate multiple relatives with the same name, or that the family was using a variation on the pattern. If a parent's name appears late in the birth order, this may indicate that the family was not following a strict pattern, although family names may still have been used. If a parent's name wasn't given to any of their known children, this could suggest the existence of children born outside of marriage or with a previous spouse. However, if a couple had only a small number of children, then no firm conclusions can be drawn.

The traditional Scottish naming pattern is a valuable tool for the genealogist, but there are many factors that may have led to deviation from the pattern, and which we may not always be aware of. The pattern can add weight to a conclusion based on a variety of other evidence, but we should not rely on it too heavily, or dismiss possibilities that don't fit with expected family names.

SOLUTIONS

Use the Scottish naming pattern to identify potential relatives, tracing both backwards and forwards in time, but be aware of its limitations. Look out for family names that are missing from a couple's children, and consider the possibility of children born to previous relationships, both marital and extra-marital.

Place-Name Confusion

There are many places in Scotland with the same or similar names, and this can lead to an ancestor's birthplace or place of residence being misidentified. Searching for a place-name found in a historical record on a modern map may well take us to the wrong location.

Confusion can occur with parishes with the same or very similar names, and when the name of a parish is used elsewhere in the country as the name of a village, district or farm. As one example, Dalry may refer to a parish in Ayrshire (and also a village or small town within that parish), a parish in Kirkcudbrightshire, or a district in the City of Edinburgh. If an ancestor simply reported their birthplace as 'Dalry', a census enumerator may have assumed which one they were referring to, and added in the county name, without bothering to check.

As with personal names, prior to the twentieth century the spelling of place-names was very inconsistent. This was particularly the case with small settlements, which might have no agreed spelling, or when a Gaelic place-name was transliterated into English. Some place-names have disappeared completely over time, whilst others have come to refer to slightly different areas than they originally denoted. Resources such as gazetteers, contemporary maps and the ScotlandsPlaces website are all useful for identifying ancestral homelands. The Ordnance Survey Name Books, found on ScotlandsPlaces, are particularly useful for recording spelling variations alongside the name that was recorded on the relevant Ordnance Survey map.

SOLUTIONS

Don't assume a place-name is unique, or that a place located on a modern map is the same one where an ancestor lived. Pay attention to information given in an index or database as to parish and county, as well as to what is written on the record itself. Use maps, gazetteers and online resources to locate an ancestor's homeland, and learn more about the area.

Incorrect Information

The problem of records that provide incorrect or conflicting information has been touched on in Chapter 5, and is one all family historians have to contend with. Records may contain incorrect information for a variety of reasons. These include:

- Clerical errors or sloppiness on the part of the recorder
- The informant not being aware of the true facts, or making a guess at information of which they were uncertain
- The informant remembering incorrectly events at which they were present, or information they had been told by another person
- The informant providing information they knew to be incorrect for personal gain, or to avoid their own or another person's embarrassment
- The informant misunderstanding the question they were asked
- The name of one relative being mistakenly given in place of another
- Illiteracy or limited literacy meaning the informant did not spot incorrect details being recorded
- Any combination of the above

There are two ways in which incorrect information can create a brick wall. First, we may have correct information about our ancestor (such as their date and place of birth from a birth record), but the record we are looking for contains incorrect information (such as an inaccurate age). Alternatively, we may have incorrect

This old photograph shows the gravestone of the author's great-grandparents. Agnes's details were recorded many years after she died. Her date of death, age at death, and the spelling of her surname are all incorrect.

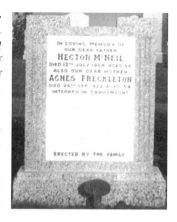

information (such as a wrong place of birth recorded in a census, or incorrect parents' names on a death record) and therefore be searching for our ancestor in the wrong place or at the wrong time, or fail to recognize the correct record when we find it.

The first step in overcoming incorrect information is simply considering the possibility that it may exist. If we focus our search too narrowly, based on what we know or believe to be true, we can easily overlook a record of our ancestor. Reviewing all the information we currently have before beginning a new search is always a good idea. Rather than basing a search for our ancestor's birth on a single record (such as subtracting a recorded age at death from the year of death to get a birth year), we should check all the evidence available. If all records agree, then we can be relatively confident the information is correct, but if not we may need to expand our search beyond the range we had originally considered. Any age that appears to have been rounded up or down (ending in nought or five) is particularly suspect. If we have only a single record that provides evidence of an event and the information is secondary, then we should be especially sceptical.

SOLUTIONS

Don't assume every record will provide correct information. Analyse each document to determine if the information is primary or secondary, and consider if the informant may have had reason to be less than honest. Expand search criteria to take into account the possibility that information may be slightly inaccurate. Don't ignore records that don't match exactly with what you expect to find. Look for corroborating evidence before accepting any piece of information as 'fact'.

Indexing Issues

With the majority of sources used to trace Scottish family history, our first port of call is likely to be an index, rather than an original record. If we can't find the ancestor we are looking for, the problem may not be with the record itself, but instead with the index.

Indexing errors can be caused by the transcriber or indexer misreading the record due to a poor quality image, handwriting that is difficult to read, or lack of familiarity with the names recorded. Unusual names are more likely to be misread than common ones, although bad handwriting can make any name illegible. It can be helpful to consider which letters of an ancestor's name are likely to be clear and read correctly, and which may be easily misinterpreted. For example, a letter 't' in the middle or end of a word could be misread as the letter 'l', particularly if it is not crossed clearly, whereas a letter 'T' at the start of a word may be misread as a 'J' or 'I' (two capital letters that can themselves be easily confused).

Another set of indexing errors may be introduced by typing mistakes, or by a word autocorrecting to another without the typist realizing. These types of error are not uncommon on ScotlandsPeople and likely account for a number of apparently 'missing' records. A few I have come across include the birth of a Jane (female) indexed as John (male), and that of a James (male) indexed as Janet (female), a Lynda indexed as 'Klynda' (probably the typist accidentally hitting two keys next to one another), and the surnames Morris and Morrisey indexed as Morrison (probably the result of an autofill function). Ages on death records may be mistyped, so that an eighteen-year-old is indexed as aged one, or a child of seven months is indexed as seven years. Some statutory records appear to have been indexed under the wrong year or wrong district, which means that no image of the record is attached and attempts to locate the entry by browsing to the given entry number are fruitless.

In some cases, typing mistakes can make a record extremely difficult to find, as search options, such as name variants or phonetic matching, will often not pick up these types of error. If we know fairly precisely when and where an event occurred, then searching using only a surname, or only a forename, and browsing through the possible options, may reveal the missing entry. However, if an event occurred some distance from where we expect (such as a death taking place in a hospital rather than the family home), it may be practically impossible to find. In the case of a Jane indexed as John, it was only when I gave up searching for her birth and decided to look for siblings instead, in the hope of narrowing down where her family was living at the time, that I found her in exactly the year and place I expected. From the index I had presumed the entry related to a brother.

ScotlandsPeople has a 'report an issue' box (found in the top right of the screen after viewing an image), which can be used to report any indexing errors found on the site. They will respond quickly to any messages, and will often refund credits used to view an incorrect record due to an indexing error, although it can take a little time for corrections to appear in the index. Findmypast has options for submitting corrections to transcriptions (through a link below the transcription) and for reporting incorrect or poor quality images. Ancestry has a 'report issue' function, which can be used to report a variety of issues including missing and wrong images, and the site allows users to add alternative information to an index.

One solution to indexing and transcription errors is to search an alternative index to the same records. Indexes to the 1841–1901 Scottish censuses, and to some statutory registers and church records, can be found on several different websites, as discussed in Chapters 1 and 3. Many family history societies have produced census indexes for their areas as well as indexes to deaths and burials found in the old parish registers. These are generally of high quality, due to the indexers' familiarity with local surnames and place names. Indexes to baptisms and marriages in the old parish registers were originally published on microfiche, and these can still be found in some local studies and genealogy libraries, and are occasionally still useful. Unusual spelling variations may be more easily picked up by skimming through a list of names arranged alphabetically, than by searching a database.

The other solution to overcoming transcription and indexing errors is simply to search the original records manually. The ScotlandsPeople website does not have this function, but most records can be browsed at ScotlandsPeople centres, and the majority of digitized records on Ancestry, FamilySearch and Findmypast can be browsed as well as searched. Many local studies and genealogy libraries have the old parish registers and 1841–1901 censuses on microfilm for their local area, and the Scottish Genealogy Society library has a full collection for the whole of Scotland. The Family History Library in Salt Lake City, USA, has microfilm copies of a large number of Scottish records, including some statutory records, the old parish registers, censuses, wills and testaments, and kirk session records, and these are increasingly being digitized and put online. Due to copyright restrictions, many can only be accessed in associated family history centres and libraries around the world. Valuation rolls and wills and testaments can be browsed through the virtual volumes system in the historic search room of the National Records of Scotland.

Searching records manually is most practical when a likely location and an approximate date of an event are known. It is an approach that can form part of a reasonably exhaustive search. Even if the ancestor being sought is not found, searching manually can at least satisfy us that the record genuinely isn't there, and that we aren't simply unable to find it due to a transcription or indexing error.

SOLUTIONS

Use any available database search options, such as name variants and wildcards, to overcome indexing errors. Search databases using only a surname or only a forename, rather than a full name. Identify and search alternative indexes to the same records. Search records manually rather than just relying on indexes.

Researchers' Assumptions

Sometimes a brick wall may arise not due to the records themselves, but because of our approach to the problem. This could be the result of a family story that we accept as fact too readily, or a lack of imagination on our part.

We become so focused on one possible solution to a problem that we fail to consider other potential answers. Perhaps everyone in the family knows that great-grandma was from Ireland so we search fruitlessly for her birth there and eventually decide her parents must not have registered it. We fail to consider that she may have been born in Scotland after her Irish parents moved there, or perhaps in England where her family lived for a few years.

We presume a person's only known marriage was their first, and that all their children were the product of that marriage (but perhaps they were married previously, or had a child born outside marriage). We presume a couple married before all their children were born, and in the same place (but they may have met elsewhere). We presume the relative that no one knows anything about must have died long before we were born (but perhaps the family simply lost touch). We presume people in the past lived in the same place all their lives, and that a man always followed the same occupation (but our ancestors often led more interesting lives than we expect).

Sometimes we construct a complicated scenario to explain a missing record when a simpler explanation is more likely. The elderly relative whose death record we cannot find may have emigrated, but it is more likely that information on their death record was recorded or indexed incorrectly. We would do better to expand our search in the area in which we know they lived, before turning to the records of another country.

It is not always easy to recognize when we are making assumptions, but taking a break from research and coming back to it fresh, discussing the problem with a friend, or setting out our thoughts in writing, can all help.

SOLUTIONS

Don't take family stories at face value, but consider if some of the details may have been embellished or remembered incorrectly. When choosing a research question and drawing up a list of known 'facts' about an ancestor, consider if there is evidence to support those facts, or if instead they may be based on potentially inaccurate assumptions. Always keep an open mind, and consider all possible reasons a record or person cannot be found, instead of focusing on just one.

8 Solutions to Scottish Genealogy Problems

This chapter gives suggestions on how to tackle thirteen problems that are commonly encountered when tracing Scottish genealogy, followed by four 'solutions' for dealing with particularly tough research problems and for taking research further.

There is no one solution to any particular problem. In most cases the approach will vary depending upon when the ancestor lived, particularly whether this was before or after the start of statutory registration, as the availability of records varies considerably over time. Factors such as where an ancestor lived and their social status may also affect which records we need to search. We should also consider the historical period in which an ancestor lived, and any national or local events that may have affected their lives.

Often it is necessary to approach a research problem from several different angles until a solution is found, bearing in mind the common issues discussed in the previous chapter. It is important to consider what records may have been created during an ancestor's whole lifetime, rather than focusing a search too narrowly. If a particular record cannot easily be found, it may be best to put that search on hold for a while, and to look for other records of the ancestor or family. Sometimes information found in another source will lead to the record we were originally looking for more quickly than a long, painstaking search.

Before beginning research following the suggestions in this chapter, it may be helpful to review Chapter 6 on planning and recording research, which covers choosing a research question and developing a research plan.

Problem: Missing Birth or Baptism Record

There are six main reasons why we may have difficulty locating an ancestor's birth or baptism record:

- The birth or baptism did not take place when we think it did
- The birth or baptism did not take place where we think it did
- The child's name at birth was not the same as the one they later used
- The parents' names were not recorded as we expect
- The birth or baptism was never recorded, or the record does not survive
- We don't have enough information to identify the correct birth when we find it

The vast majority of births that took place in Scotland from 1855 onwards were recorded in the statutory registers of births, and so it is often a case of working through each of the other possibilities in turn, and extending search parameters accordingly. When an ancestor was born prior to 1855, the chances of there being no record of their birth or baptism are significantly higher, but before concluding this is the case, we should consider all the other possibilities and research the survival of records for the local area.

Common reasons for the names of the child and parents not being recorded as expected are spelling and name variations, errors in later records, illegitimacy and adoption. Illegitimacy and adoption are covered in more detail later in this chapter, and solutions for overcoming the other common issues were discussed in Chapter 7.

If the problem is that we don't have enough information to identify which of several potential birth or baptism records is correct, then we may need to research our ancestor's life more fully, and to look for further records, which may identify their parents and birth. We may also need to research each potential match and their family in turn in order to either eliminate them or find evidence proving they are our ancestor.

Births *after 1911*

If an ancestor was born after 2 April 1911 (the date of the 1911 census), the main sources pointing to when they were born and who their parents were will be their marriage and death records. Information passed down through the family may also be helpful.

Scottish marriage records provide an exact date of birth and place of birth from 1972 (although only a country of birth may be given), and death records give an exact date of birth from 1967. Prior to this only an age at marriage or death was recorded, and in all cases information may be slightly inaccurate.

If an ancestor's place of birth is not known, it may be necessary to search systematically through all the births that took place in the right period until one is found that matches a known date of birth or parents' names. A mother's maiden surname is given in the birth indexes available at ScotlandsPeople centres from 1929 onwards, but not in online indexes. Visiting one of the centres is usually best when searching twentieth- to twenty-first-century records, if at all possible.

A likely place of birth can often be identified by searching first for the parents' marriage and for the births of any known siblings. The birth of an ancestor's sibling with an unusual name may be easier to identify than that of the ancestor him or herself. Other sources that may indicate where the family was likely to have been living at the time of the birth include valuation rolls, street directories and electoral registers, although unless the parents (generally the father) had an unusual name, it may not be easy to identify the family in these records without at least a rough idea of the area.

If a birth is not found in the expected location, consider whether the mother may have given birth in a hospital or nursing home some distance from where she lived. This might be in a different registration district or even in another county. For example, in the period 1941–1964 many women living in the Glasgow area gave birth in the Lennox Castle maternity home in Lennoxtown. This was then in Campsie registration district in Stirlingshire. It was also common in the past for women having their first baby (and sometimes subsequent babies) to return to their parents' home for the birth, where they would have the assistance of family, friends and neighbours.

Up until 1934, when a birth took place in a different registration district to the one where the father normally resided (or the mother if she was unmarried), the birth was usually registered in the district in which it took place, with a copy sent to the parents' home district, where it was also entered into the register. This created two records of the event, cross-referenced in the margin. This is often helpful for identifying births that took place away from home, but this practice ceased when hospital births became more common.

A birth to a Scottish family may not necessarily have taken place in Scotland. The family may have spent a short period outside Scotland for work (common if the father was in the armed forces), or they may have left Scotland but later returned. The birth may have taken place in another part of the UK or in another country. For births in other parts of the UK, the separate birth indexes for England and Wales and Northern Ireland (and Ireland up until 1922) should be searched. For births in other countries, local records may need to be located, although the birth could also have been recorded in Scottish minor records, which include consular and armed forces births where the father was identified as Scottish. Some overseas births may also be found in the UK overseas births indexes, which are available on Ancestry and Findmypast.

Births in 1855–1911

If an ancestor was born between 1855 and 1911, census records can be used in addition to marriage and death records to identify their likely birthplace, their approximate year of birth and their parents' names. Some of the suggestions for identifying a birth after 1911 may also be applicable.

Any discrepancies between records, such as inconsistencies in age and birthplace, should be noted. Generally, information on age and birthplace found in a census taken when a person was a child will be more accurate than in a census taken when they were older, but there are always exceptions.

It may be necessary to identify in which registration district a particular place was located, as a census may list a village or town of birth, rather than the parish or district. For example, the town of Motherwell in Lanarkshire did not become a registration district in its own right until 1968, and prior to that, events that took place there will be found in Dalziel registration district. A list of registration districts with dates can be found on the National Records of Scotland website.

Remember that for the period 1855–1874 a more detailed index to Scottish births, providing the child's full date of birth and the names of both parents including the mother's maiden surname, is available on FamilySearch and several other websites. Once a likely birth has been identified using this index, the full record can be viewed on ScotlandsPeople.

Registration of births was compulsory in Scotland from 1855, but in the early years a small number of births do not appear to have been registered. If a wide-ranging search on date, place and name does not reveal the missing birth, and searches are undertaken to overcome problems such as spelling and indexing errors, then it is possible the birth was genuinely not registered. Details of the child's birth or baptism may be found in church records instead.

Births prior to 1855

If an ancestor was born in Scotland prior to 1855, they will have no birth certificate as such. There may be a church record giving their date of birth, a church record giving their date of baptism only (from which an approximate date of birth can usually be inferred, although not all children were baptised in their first few months), or there may be no surviving record at all of their birth or baptism.

For most families, the first place to look for a birth or baptism prior to 1855 is in the old parish registers of the Church of Scotland. If a birth is not found there, the next place to search is in the indexed registers of other churches available on the ScotlandsPeople website.

If the birth or baptism is not found on ScotlandsPeople, but a likely parish of birth is known, then researching that parish and its records is a good next step. Check the covering dates of the old parish register, and any known issues such as gaps or poor record keeping. Research what other churches existed in the parish and neighbouring parishes at the time, and where any records are now located, including whether any indexes have been published.

Remember that a person's place of birth was not always the same as their place of baptism, and that some people were only baptised at several years old or even as adults. A baptism register may note that the person was an adult or may give an approximate age, but such details will not necessarily appear in an index, and so

Like churches themselves, old parish registers may have been poorly kept,
contain gaps, or may not survive at all.

such baptisms can easily be overlooked. Searching widely on place and date can help to identify them.

If the probable names of the parents of an ancestor are known, look for any records of them, including their marriage, and the births or baptisms of other children born to them. These records will verify that a couple with those names existed at around the right time, and will indicate where the family was then living. Pay particular attention to the name of the minister who performed the marriage or baptism, if it is given, or to any reference to another church (for example relief or burgher, or the parents being described as dissenters). The ancestor's own marriage record, or the marriage record of siblings (particularly sisters, as marriages were usually performed by the bride's minister), may also indicate a family's likely religious affiliation.

If no record can be found of a couple with the names of an ancestor's supposed parents, this may be an indication that one or both names are incorrect, or it could suggest an illegitimate birth. Look for any families with the same surname in the area at the time, and see if the ancestor could potentially fit into one of those.

If parents' names are not known, then it is necessary to identify any potential baptisms at the right period in a likely location, and to research each family, in order to either eliminate them or prove they are correct. Occupations, locations and naming patterns may all suggest which of several potential baptisms is the most likely.

If no birth or baptism can be identified, or all potential baptisms are eliminated, this may mean the birth was not recorded, or that no record survives. This does not necessarily mean it will be impossible to identify the ancestor's parents. Consider what other records may exist for the time and location, which may provide evidence of relationships. These may include gravestones, kirk session records, wills and testaments, sasines and services or heirs, deeds and estate records. Look for evidence of naming patterns, multiple generations recorded at the same location, names of witnesses to baptisms and to legal documents, as well as for direct evidence of relationships.

SOLUTIONS

- Consider the possible reasons an ancestor's birth or baptism may not have been located, and work through each possibility in turn
- Look for additional records of the ancestor, which may provide information as to their place and approximate date of birth, and which may identify their parents (for example marriage, death and census records)
- Look for the parents' marriage, or the births or baptisms of siblings, to narrow down the ancestor's likely date and location of birth, and to verify that the parents' names are correct
- Check in which parish or registration district a recorded birthplace was, if it was not a parish or district in its own right
- Identify any gaps or known issues with the old parish register for the parish where the ancestor was born
- Research other churches in the area, and search their records as well
- Consider if the ancestor could have been born outside marriage, and *see* the section on illegitimacy below
- Look for other records that may identify the ancestor's family, even if no birth or baptism record survives
- *See* the section below on multiple individuals with the same name if more than one potential birth or baptism is identified

---

Problem: Missing Marriage Record

Some of the main reasons we may have difficulty locating an ancestor's marriage record are these:

- The marriage did not take place when we think it did
- The marriage did not take place where we think it did
- The bride was recorded under a different name to the one we expect (such as a previous married surname)
- The marriage was 'irregular' and not recorded in the usual way
- The marriage record does not survive
- The couple were not actually married

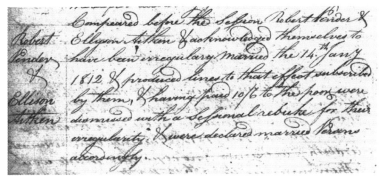

This couple's irregular marriage was noted in the parish register a few months after it occurred, but not all such marriages were recorded.

CROWN COPYRIGHT, NATIONAL RECORDS OF SCOTLAND

For marriages from the mid-1800s onwards, a good way to identify when and where a couple married is to look for the birth records of any children. The date and place of the parents' marriage were recorded on Scottish birth records in 1855 and from 1861 onwards (but not in 1856–1860). Therefore statutory birth records can provide evidence of marriages that occurred prior to 1855 as well as outside Scotland. Such marriage information is, of course, not always correct, but I have found a fairly high level of accuracy, bar minor discrepancies that can be attributed to a lapse in memory, or perhaps to conceal the fact that one or more children were conceived prior to marriage. If a series of birth records relating to the same couple gives widely different dates and places of marriage, then this may be an indication that the couple were not in fact formally married.

If there are no statutory birth records stating the date and place of marriage, identifying the birth or baptism of a couple's eldest child will provide a rough date and probable location, as most couples had a first child born within about a year of their marriage. However, bear in mind that the eldest known child may not necessarily be the couple's first, and it may therefore be necessary to search back a few years. Equally, some couples did not marry until after having one or more children, so it may also be necessary to search forwards in time, although any birth or baptism records are likely to indicate if a child's parents were not married. Remember that children recorded in the census were not always the offspring of the head of the household and his current wife, but could include children born to either from a previous relationship.

As with any database search, when searching for marriages it is generally best to put in as few details as possible. If searching using the full names of both the bride and groom does not produce results, try searching using the name of one spouse only, or using just the couple's surnames and restricting by date range and county as necessary.

Marriages from 1855 onwards

In most cases, identifying a marriage that occurred in Scotland from 1855 onwards is relatively straightforward. Statutory marriage records are available on the ScotlandsPeople website and are indexed by the names of both the bride and groom, which can be cross-referenced or searched individually, and both parties are usually indexed under all surnames that appear on the marriage record (including maiden and married surnames for women who had been married previously).

However, although it might be expected that all marriages that occurred from 1855 onwards would be recorded, in practice this did not always happen. In the case of a regular marriage, a couple had to obtain a marriage schedule prior to their marriage, give it to the officiating minister who completed it at the time of the wedding, and then take it to the registrar, who registered the marriage and kept the schedule. It is clear that in the early days of registration some ministers did not fill in schedules properly, and it appears that some couples did not return the schedule to the registrar, perhaps not understanding the process. If the schedule was not returned, then the marriage would not be officially recorded.

Although there was provision for the recording of irregular marriages (those not conducted by a church minister), these had to be first established by a court of law, typically by obtaining a warrant from a sheriff or sheriff substitute. It is likely some couples were unaware of the procedures for doing this, or simply did not bother. Marriages within gypsy or traveller communities were often not officially recorded, and acceptance by the community was probably more important than a piece of paper.

If a couple's likely religious affiliation is known, then searching church registers may reveal a missing marriage. Some, but not all, marriage records from Roman Catholic and other (non-Church of Scotland) churches from 1855 onwards can be found on ScotlandsPeople in the church registers section. Some post-1854 marriage records from Church of Scotland churches are included in kirk session records (although these are usually banns registers, rather than marriage registers) and records from other churches can be found at the National Records of Scotland, in local archives, or are still held by the churches themselves.

Marriage by cohabitation and habit and repute – that is, living together as married persons and being regarded as such by society, despite not having gone through any form of marriage ceremony – was recognized in Scots Law until 2006. Such relationships could be registered as valid marriages, although this was rare. In this case any marriage record may be found many years later than expected.

Marriages of Scots that took place outside Scotland may be found among minor records (such as consular, foreign and service returns), but need not necessarily have been registered in this way, and it may be necessary to search marriage records from other parts of the British Isles or from other countries. Children's birth records are usually the best way of identifying such marriages, although they may have been reported in local or national Scottish newspapers.

If no record can be found of a couple's marriage, this may indicate that they went through some form of ceremony that they, and their community, considered valid, but which was never officially registered, or they were not in fact married.

Marriages *prior to 1855*

Prior to 1855, the most likely source for identifying a marriage in Scotland is the old parish registers (OPRs) of the Church of Scotland, as the majority of couples had banns of marriage proclaimed in their local parish church, even if they chose to marry elsewhere.

If a marriage cannot be found in the OPRs, then checking the covering dates of the registers for the parish or parishes where the couple is likely to have lived is a sensible step, as a gap in the marriage register can often explain a missing marriage. Kirk session accounts may note payments received for the proclamation of banns and can be an alternative source for marriages (in fact some OPR marriage records have been taken from kirk session accounts), although they may give the name of the groom only, or record only amounts received and not the names of the parties involved.

Any marriage registers from other churches in the area where an ancestor lived should also be searched, particularly when a couple's religious affiliation is known, although relatively few other churches kept marriage registers. Some marriage registers can be found among the records of Roman Catholic and other churches on ScotlandsPeople, and are indexed in the 'Non-OPR Banns/Marriages' collection on the Scottish Indexes website. Other records can be found at the National Records of Scotland, in local archives, or are still held by the relevant church.

Kirk session minutes are a good source for identifying irregular marriages (that is, those that did not take place after the regular proclamation of banns), because when the church became aware of such marriages the couple were often called to appear before the session. Some irregular marriages were subsequently noted in the OPR, although by no means all. Where an OPR marriage is noted as irregular it is always worth checking the kirk session minutes, which may provide further details. In one case I researched, an irregular marriage was recorded in the OPR in 1832, but the associated entry in the kirk session minutes for the parish revealed the couple had actually married two years previously. This explained how they had two earlier children baptised as legitimate in a different parish (where presumably fewer questions were asked!).

Fines paid for irregular marriages may also be noted in kirk session accounts, although such entries typically provide little detail. Couples who were married irregularly could be summoned to appear before a Justice of the Peace or in a burgh, sheriff or commissary court. Any such records are likely to be difficult to find, although kirk session minutes can occasionally make reference to there being a civil case.

Couples guilty of 'ante-nuptial fornication' (pre-marital sex), generally revealed by the arrival of a child less than nine months after their marriage, were also regularly called to appear before the kirk session. Such appearances can provide an approximate date of marriage when no other records survive.

Some details of irregular marriages have been extracted from kirk session and other sources and published, an example being *Irregular Marriages at Portpatrick, Wigtownshire 1759–1826* by Arthur Brack (Dumfries: Dumfries and Galloway Family History Society, 1997). Gretna Green and other towns in the Scottish Borders were particularly famous as the site of irregular marriages, and the National Records of Scotland website has a detailed guide to surviving records (www.nrscotland.gov.uk/research/guides/birth-death-and-marriage-records/irregular-border-marriage-registers). Some Gretna Green marriages are indexed in the 'Gretna Green, Scotland, Marriage Registers, 1794–1895' collection on Ancestry, while Findmypast has the 'Scotland, Irregular & Cross-Border Marriage Index' compiled by the Scottish Genealogy Society from a variety of sources.

Newspapers can be a useful source for marriages prior to 1855, although generally only the marriages of prominent or fairly wealthy people were reported. Some marriage notices have been indexed by local libraries or published by family history societies.

Some wealthier families, particularly those who owned heritable property, had marriage contracts, and these can be found among family papers or in registers of deeds. Such contracts rarely specify when a couple married, but were often drawn up shortly before marriage, although they could also be written later and thus described as postnuptial. Marriage contracts may be referenced in sasines and wills. When a property owner granted a 'liferent' interest in a property to his wife, which gave her use of the property although not the right to sell or bequeath it, this would also be recorded in a sasine. Although this may not necessarily have happened at the time the couple married, it can provide evidence that a marriage had taken place. Occasionally deeds can be found that merely verify that a couple were legally married, possibly in cases where there may have been some dispute.

Up until 1830, Edinburgh Commissary Court had jurisdiction over marital cases (both constitution and dissolution), and court papers can be identified in the National Records of Scotland online catalogue in reference CC8. Cases to get a marriage legally recognized are usually described as a 'Process of Declarator of Marriage'. After 1830, the Court of Session had jurisdiction over such cases, and records can be identified either through the National Records of Scotland online catalogue, or by using finding aids at the NRS.

SOLUTIONS

- Use children's birth records to identify when, where and if a marriage likely occurred
- Search databases using the name of bride and groom separately as well as together, and consider name variations and any alternative surnames used by the bride
- Search church registers as well as statutory records to identify marriages from 1855
- Search the old parish registers and registers of other churches to identify marriages prior to 1855
- Use kirk session minutes and accounts to identify irregular marriages and fill in gaps in parish registers
- Search published indexes of irregular border marriages, particularly for couples who lived in the south of Scotland
- Look for alternative sources such as newspaper marriage notices, deeds and court cases
- Consider if a couple may not have been married, and whether any children could be illegitimate (*see* section on illegitimacy below)

Problem: Missing Death Record

Some of the main reasons that we may have difficulty locating an ancestor's death record are these:

- The name is a common one, and indexes or original records provide little detail

- The death took place some distance from where the person and their family lived
- Information on the death record is inaccurate so we don't recognize it as relating to the right person
- The death took place prior to 1855 and was not recorded

Not all families could afford to erect a gravestone, and some stones have been damaged or removed, so identifying an ancestor's place of burial can be challenging.

Deaths from 1855 onwards

The vast majority of deaths that occurred in Scotland from 1855 onwards were recorded in the statutory registers of deaths, although a small number of bodies were unidentified and therefore the death was registered without a name. The biggest difficulty in locating a death from 1855 is that death indexes provide only a name, the year and district of registration, and the age at death (which may be inaccurate and is not indexed for all deaths prior to 1866). We may therefore have a large number of possible entries to search through in order to locate the right person. When searching online using the ScotlandsPeople website, it is easy to spend a large number of credits looking at the wrong records, and so visiting a ScotlandsPeople Centre is often the best option, if at all practical.

Census records can be used to narrow down the likely period in which a person died. If an ancestor is recorded in one census but not the next, then they probably died in the intervening decade. When searching for the deaths of a couple, it is usually best to search for the wife's death first, as this should be indexed under both maiden and married surnames and should therefore be easier to find. The wife's death record will state if she was then married or a widow, and so will narrow down the date of her husband's death. However, be aware that if a couple separated, they may have described themselves as widowed when this was not the case, or they (or the informant of their death) may have been uncertain as to whether their spouse was still living. Children's marriage and deaths records may also indicate whether a parent was then living or deceased, although this information is not always given (if a parent isn't specifically stated as deceased it doesn't necessarily mean they were living).

Remember that someone may have died in a different district or a different county to the one in which they normally lived, particularly if they spent their final days in a hospital or other institution. If a death cannot be found locally, then expand the search to a wider area. Deaths abroad, in the armed forces and at sea may be found among minor records, although these are not complete.

Looking for alternative records of a death is a good approach when searching death indexes produces a large number of results or fails to identify the correct entry. Alternative sources include wills and testaments, burial records, newspaper reports and gravestone inscriptions. These can be particularly helpful for identifying deaths that occurred outside the expected area or even outside Scotland. Poor relief records often note the deaths of those in receipt of poor relief as well as recording when the spouse, and occasionally parents, of someone applying for relief had died.

Don't overlook deaths that don't match the expected information, as many death records contain inaccuracies. Ages may have been guessed at, and the names of parents and even spouses may be recorded incorrectly. Details such as addresses and the names of informants may help to prove that a possible death is the correct one, although it may also be necessary to look at some of the alternative records described above.

Deaths *prior to 1855*

Searching for a record of a death that occurred in Scotland prior to 1855 can often be challenging, as a large proportion of deaths were not recorded. It may only be possible to determine a rough period in which a person is likely to have died, rather than a specific date.

The old parish registers (OPRs) of the Church of Scotland are one of the main sources for pre-1855 deaths, but many parishes kept no records of deaths at all, or have death registers that only cover a short period. It is a good idea to check the covering dates of the burial register for the parish where an ancestor lived before beginning a search, and to see if any indexes have been produced by the local family history society, which may be more detailed than those on ScotlandsPeople. Often the date given in an OPR will be a date of burial, rather than a date of death, and the record may list only a name without any identifying information.

Remember that an ancestor may not necessarily have been buried in the parish where they lived or died, but instead in a family burial plot or lair elsewhere. Statutory death records for the period 1855–1860 include a place of burial, and may point to where relatives who died prior to 1855 were probably buried.

In addition to the OPRs, burial and cemetery registers containing details of pre-1855 deaths can be found among the collections of Roman Catholic and other church registers on ScotlandsPeople, on the DeceasedOnline, Ancestry and Scottish Indexes websites, in local archives and in local authority burial departments.

Kirk session accounts often include details of payments received for burials (such as for the hire of the mortcloth), and may also note expenses paid for burying paupers, although it is rare to find more information than a name. Kirk session records sometimes include burial or death registers that are not part of the OPR, and minutes occasionally include references to deaths, particularly of church officials.

Monumental or gravestone inscriptions are a particularly important source for pre-1855 deaths as they include details of many deaths not recorded elsewhere and typically provide more identifying information than burial registers, such as ages and the names of relatives. Many have been recorded and published by family history societies.

Newspapers can also be a useful source of information regarding pre-1855 deaths, although, as with marriages, they tend to record only wealthier or more prominent families unless a death was deemed particularly newsworthy, such as a death by accident or murder. Some newspaper death notices have been indexed by family history societies, and many digitized newspapers are available online.

Wills and testaments sometimes specify when a person died (although this may not always be accurate), or should at least give an indication. Other records that deal with the inheritance of property, such as services of heirs, sasines and deeds, also provide an indication as to when a person died.

Hospitals often kept records of patients who died there, and these are perhaps an under-used source for identifying pre-1855 deaths, although a lengthy search may be required unless an approximate date of death is known. Hospitals typically treated patients from a wide area, and not just those who lived locally. Deaths may be noted in general registers of patients, or recorded in separate death registers. Deaths recorded at Aberdeen Royal Infirmary in the period 1743–1822 and 1838–1897 have been indexed and published by the Aberdeen and North-East Scotland Family History Society.

Records of poor relief, including pre-1855 records, often note the deaths of paupers, and may provide information on the deaths of relatives. Since 1842, registers have been kept of bodies supplied to schools of anatomy in Aberdeen, Dundee, Edinburgh, Glasgow and St Andrews. Many of these were paupers who died in poorhouses, asylums, hospitals and prisons. Records are held by the National Records of Scotland (NRS) and are indexed on the Old Scottish website (www.oldscottish.com/anatomy-registers.html).

Accidental deaths that occurred as a result of industrial employment were not routinely investigated until the Fatal Accidents Inquiry (Scotland) Act 1895, but some pre-1855 records do exist for accidental deaths in mines and on the railways (see the NRS guide at www.nrsscotland.gov.uk/research/guides/fatal-accident-inquiry-records). The names of those killed in mining accidents (including prior to 1855) can be found on the Scottish Mining Website (www.scottishmining.co.uk/5.html).

Estate records occasionally note the deaths of tenants, or deaths may be inferred from a change in tenancy, for example from husband to widow, or father to son. Published family and local histories may include information on an ancestor's death, although such sources should be verified with original records wherever possible.

SOLUTIONS

- Use census returns and the records of family members to determine when and where an ancestor is likely to have died
- Expand a search to a wider geographic area if a death is not found in the expected location
- Remember that death records may contain inaccurate information
- Look for alternative sources for deaths from 1855 if an ancestor cannot easily be identified using the indexes to statutory deaths
- When searching for deaths prior to 1855, use a wide range of sources in addition to the old parish registers. These include burial or cemetery registers, kirk session records, monumental or gravestone inscriptions, newspapers, wills and testaments, legal and property records, hospital and poor relief records, and published sources
- Look at the sections below on wills and burial places for further advice on identifying records relating to deaths

Problem: Missing from the Census

Some of the common reasons we may have difficulty locating an ancestor in the census are these:

- They were not living where we expect (including being temporarily outside Scotland)
- Their name or other identifying information, such as age and birthplace, was recorded incorrectly, or not as we expect
- Their name or other identifying information has been indexed or transcribed incorrectly
- They were not living in a family group so cannot easily be identified, particularly if their name was a common one

- They were living in an enumeration district for which records do not survive
- They were missed out of the census

Before beginning a search of the census, it is worthwhile reviewing any records that may point to an ancestor's likely location and personal circumstances at the time. A child is likely to be recorded with his or her parents, a young adult may be living with an employer rather than relatives, a married person is likely to be recorded with their spouse and children, an elderly widow or widower may be living with adult children or grandchildren. Although it may sound obvious, it is also important to check whether the census actually took place in the ancestor's lifetime. A child born in May 1861 will not be recorded in the 1861 census (which was taken on 7 April 1861) and a person who died in March 1911 will not be found in the 1911 census (which was recorded on 2 April 1911).

Records of any births, marriages or deaths in the family that took place close to the time of the census should provide an address or parish of residence. The birthplaces of children recorded in one census may indicate the family's location at the time of the previous census. Alternative sources of addresses include street directories, electoral registers and valuation rolls, and although these are often less easily searchable than census returns, they may be worth consulting if a family is proving particularly challenging to locate.

Transcription errors are common in census indexes, and a simple solution is to search an alternative index or to vary search options. If a family had a fairly common surname, then searching for the family member with the least common forename may help to distinguish the correct household among other similarly named ones. Conversely, as unusual names are more likely to be transcribed incorrectly, searching for a family member with a common name and combining the name with an age and location may lead more quickly to the right household.

Generally speaking, the ages of children are more accurately recorded than those of adults, so searching for the youngest member of the family with a narrow age range may be easier than searching for the head of household with a broad age range to compensate for a possibly inaccurate age. Where a family is believed to have lived at the same address from one census to the next, the names of neighbours identified in one census year can sometimes be used to locate the family in the next or a previous census.

Remember that information such as ages, birthplaces and even names may be recorded incorrectly. Initials may be given instead of full names, or titles such as Rev., Mrs or Widow instead of a forename. ScotlandsPeople usually leaves the forename blank in these cases, although other sites transcribe a title as it appears. Be wary of ditto marks or the abbreviation 'Do.', used to indicate that a piece of information was the same as that given on a previous line. If an enumerator's eye skipped a line when copying details into the enumeration book it could lead to a whole family being recorded with the wrong birthplace.

There appears to have been a slight tendency in 1841 for people to be recorded as born within the county where they were currently residing, when they were actually born elsewhere. Although this may simply be sloppy record-taking, it has been suggested it relates to the idea of settlement, and a person's fear of being returned to their place of birth, should they find themselves in need of poor relief.

Household composition may not always be as expected. Children may have died or left home, or the head of household may have been temporarily absent for work. Don't ignore families that are not an exact match, but rather look for further evidence that a possible household is, or is not, the correct one.

A lot may have changed within a family in between census years. For example, one spouse may have died and the other remarried. It was common for stepchildren to be recorded under the head of household's surname in a census (even if they did not use that surname in any other records), and to be listed as son or daughter rather than stepchild. If an ancestor cannot be located in a census as a child, it is worth researching their parents to identify if both were still living, or if one had remarried, or perhaps formed a new relationship outside marriage.

Where a likely address is known, searching a census index by address rather than personal name can be an effective way of overcoming transcription errors or mangled names. Both Findmypast and Ancestry allow searches by address or place-name, and the research guides section of the National Records of Scotland website includes some street indexes for larger towns and cities that can be used to identify the registration and enumeration districts within which a street was located.

Census returns cannot be easily browsed online, but this can be done at ScotlandsPeople centres, or by using microfilm copies held by genealogical and local studies libraries (with the exception of the 1911 census, which is not available on microfilm). It can be surprisingly quick to skim through the census returns for a small rural area to check for a particular family or place-name, and this may save time searching indexes, or may confirm that a particular person is definitely not recorded there, and it is not simply an indexing error.

If an ancestor cannot be located in the 1841 census, it is worth checking the list of missing 1841 census records on the National Records of Scotland website (www.nrscotland.gov.uk/research/guides/census-records/1841-census). The majority of these are for parishes in Fife. This list may not be comprehensive, however, as I recently discovered that one enumeration district for the parish of Stracathro, Angus, also appears to be missing. Browsing the census manually can help to identify these kinds of gaps. The above list is also useful for highlighting some civil parishes that did not exist in 1841, and in those cases people should be recorded in the relevant existing district (researching jurisdictions and boundary changes should help to identify these).

Not everyone can be located in every census that took place during their lifetime, and individuals and entire households were missed out, but it is worth considering if there may be a valid reason why an ancestor cannot be located. Consider if an ancestor could have been living outside Scotland at the time of the census, or may perhaps have spent time in some kind of institution. Soldiers and sailors in particular may have been recorded away from home, or not at all if they were outside the country.

Finally, although it is frustrating not to be able to locate an ancestor in a particular census, it rarely creates a true brick wall. There are many other records that may enable their birth and ancestry to be traced, and which may point to where they were living at the time.

SOLUTIONS

- Use birth, marriage, death and other records to determine where an ancestor was likely to have been living at the time of the census
- Try searching an alternative index to the census if the ancestor cannot be found using the index on one particular website
- Don't search too narrowly on age, or only for exact spellings of names, as information may not be recorded as expected
- Search for different members of the family or household, not just the ancestor currently being researched
- Search by address, or browse the census manually to overcome poorly recorded or transcribed names
- Remember that married or widowed women may be recorded under their maiden surnames, rather than married ones, and that surnames might change if they remarried
- Consider any circumstances that may have led to an ancestor not being recorded where expected, or living outside Scotland at the time of the census

Problem: Can't Find a Will

If an ancestor's will or testament cannot be found in the 'wills and testaments' database on ScotlandsPeople (or in later indexes to wills and testaments), the most likely explanation is simply that they didn't have one, as only a minority of Scots had any form of testamentary document. However, there are a few reasons why an existing record may not be found, and a variety of other documents that can shed light on what happened to an ancestor's property after their death.

As with any database, when searching for wills and testaments it is important not to restrict search criteria too narrowly. A testament may have been confirmed many years after a person died, and any description may not be as expected. A place of residence may consist of a farm name only, without the name of the parish, and place and personal names may have been spelled phonetically. Married women were typically recorded under their maiden surnames in earlier records, and should be searched for under all known surnames.

Although ScotlandsPeople is the main way of identifying wills and testaments, the 'Scotland, National Probate Index (Calendar of

Confirmations and Inventories), 1876–1936' collection on Ancestry provides an alternative index for the period 1876–1925, as well as being currently the only online index for the period 1926–1936. The Scottish Record Society published a number of indexes to wills and testaments up to 1800, which are arranged by commissary court (for example, *Commissariot Record of Inverness: Register of Testaments, 1564 to 1800*). These are now out of copyright, and digitized copies can be accessed online for free. The society has a useful list of publications with links to online copies on their website (www.scottishrecordsociety.org.uk/publications). Some spelling variations may be more easily identified through a printed list of names, rather than by searching the database on ScotlandsPeople, although it is necessary to first identify in which court a testament was likely have been recorded. The testaments of married women are helpfully cross-indexed under their husbands' names in these indexes, which makes them easier to locate.

The wills of Scots who died owning property in England may have been proved in an English probate court. Prior to 1858, the most likely English court in which to find a Scottish will is the Prerogative Court of Canterbury, although they can also turn up in smaller courts. There is no single database for English wills, although an increasing number of indexes and original records is available online.

Many wills and similar documents, such as trust dispositions and settlements, were not confirmed in a commissary court at all, but instead recorded as deeds. These may be located in the registers of deeds of the Court of Session, a sheriff court, commissary court, burgh court or franchise court. Most deeds are not indexed, but if an ancestor's date of death is known, it is fairly straightforward to search any likely registers of deeds for that year and a few years afterwards.

Even if a will or testament cannot be found for an ancestor, there could still be some records concerning their estate among commissary and sheriff court papers. When a person died, the first stage of the confirmation process was for relatives to obtain a document known as an edict of executry from the clerk of the commissary court. A copy of this edict was posted on the door of the parish church in the deceased's parish (later at the relevant courthouse) to notify creditors who had claims on the estate to come forward. In some cases the confirmation process was never completed, and so there are edicts of executry for individuals who did not have a confirmed testament. These edicts can be found among the records of commissary and sheriff courts (mainly at the National Records of Scotland (NRS)), and give the name and designation of the deceased, the name or names of the next of kin or executors, and sometimes the date of death. A small number of edicts of executry (mainly from the Commissary Court of the Isles and Haddington Sheriff Court) are individually catalogued in the NRS online catalogue, but the majority are not indexed and need to be searched manually. Some warrants of testaments (original documents that were then copied into court registers) may never have been registered, and these warrants can sometimes be found among the records of the relevant court.

Where a trust was set up to administer a deceased person's estate, records of its administration, sometimes continuing for several decades, may provide further information on the family. These may be described as trustees' sederunt books, and some can be found at the NRS and in local archives. Deceased estate and death duty records are relatively little used in Scotland as they rarely provide more genealogical information than the related testaments, but they can provide details of what happened to an ancestor's estate and complement other sources. Records are held by the NRS in reference IRS.

If a couple had a marriage contract drawn up before or after their marriage, this might specify what was to happen to property after their deaths, and means there was no need for either to write a will or have a testament confirmed. Marriage contracts may have been recorded in a register of deeds, either at the time of the marriage or many years later, such as after the couple's deaths. Some can be found among family papers.

Remember that prior to 1868 heritable property (land and buildings) could not be bequeathed in a will. If an ancestor owned heritable property, then the register of retours (services of heirs) and registers of sasines should be searched, in addition to testaments and deeds (*see* Chapter 1).

If a person died without any known legal heir, then their estate may have gone to the Crown as *Ultimus Haeres* or 'last heir'. It was possible for a more distant relative, or someone with a moral claim, to petition the Exchequer to be granted the estate. Records are held by the National Records of Scotland and can be very detailed.

If there was a dispute over the inheritance of an ancestor's estate, then there could have been a court case. Such cases could be heard in a variety of courts, although the Court of Session is probably the best place to begin a search, as many case papers are indexed in the NRS online catalogue. Interesting cases may have been reported in local and national newspapers.

SOLUTIONS

- Search the index to wills and testaments on ScotlandsPeople well beyond the year of death, and leave the description field blank
- Use the alternative index to wills and testaments on Ancestry for the period 1876–1936 and earlier published indexes
- Search for married or widowed women under both maiden and married surnames
- Remember there may be multiple records for the same person (for example will, inventory and eik), and these will contain different information
- Search indexes to English wills and probate records, particularly if an ancestor may have owned property in England
- If there is no confirmed testament, look for an edict of executry, which may name the next of kin or executor
- Search for a will or similar document registered as a deed, rather than as a testament
- If an ancestor may have owned land and buildings, search the register of retours (services of heirs) and registers of sasines to find out who inherited these
- If an ancestor or relative may have died without a known heir, check *Ultimus Haeres* records

Problem: Unknown Burial Place

Many family historians want to know where an ancestor was buried in order to visit the burial site and pay their respects, but as Scottish death records generally do not specify where an ancestor was buried, identifying a place of burial is not always easy.

Statutory death records for the period 1855–1860 do include a place of burial, but this information was not recorded from 1861 onwards and has never been reinstated (although occasionally an entry in the *Register of Corrected Entries* relating to a death may include a burial place). The death records of any relatives who died in 1855–1860 may point to the existence of a family burial plot and suggest where other relatives may be buried, both prior to 1855 and after 1860, but this is unlikely to be helpful for tracing the burial locations of relatives who died from the later 1800s onwards.

Most non-denominational cemeteries are maintained by local authorities or councils. As a result, burial records from around the mid-1800s onwards are mainly held by council burial and crematoria departments, although some older records may be deposited in local archives, and some private cemeteries maintain their own records. Councils typically charge a fee to carry out searches of their registers, and may only do so when fairly precise information is provided, such as a date of death and the name of the cemetery. Council websites are the best way of identifying what records are held, and their access conditions. Searching within the council website for 'cemeteries' should find the relevant page.

A small number of Scottish burial and crematoria registers can be accessed online through DeceasedOnline (www.deceasedonline.com) and in the 'England & Scotland, Select Cemetery Registers, 1800–2016' collection on Ancestry (www.ancestry.co.uk). Some private cemeteries have their own websites with indexes online, such as the Woodside Cemetery and Crematorium in Paisley, Renfrewshire (http://paisleycemetery.co.uk).

The websites and online catalogues of local archives often give details of any burial registers they hold, and archivists can provide further information. A few indexes are available online, such as those for several burial grounds in Dundee on the Friends of Dundee City Archives website (www.fdca.org.uk/council_graveyards.html).

In addition to chronological burial registers, many cemeteries kept lair registers recording all the burials within a particular plot or lair. If an ancestor's burial record includes a lair number, check to see if there is a lair register, which may identify other relatives buried in the same plot. In some cases there may be no gravestone marking a burial plot, but lair numbers can be used to identify the location on a map of the cemetery.

The Scottish Association of Family History Societies (SAFHS) maintains a list of over 3,500 known burial grounds in Scotland on their website (www.safhs.org.uk/burialgrounds.asp). This is a convenient way of identifying what burial grounds existed in a particular town or parish at the time of an ancestor's death, and includes some details of published monumental inscriptions.

Although most death notices published in newspapers are brief, they may include details of an ancestor's funeral, indicating where the person was to be buried. This can be a quick way of locating the burial ground where an ancestor was buried when burial registers are not indexed.

Don't forget to check family papers for any details of funerals or burials. These may include newspaper clippings, funeral cards, receipts for burial plots or other expenses associated with an ancestor's funeral, and photographs of gravestones.

Monumental or gravestone inscriptions are a major source for identifying Scottish deaths and burials, and many have been indexed and published by family history societies. Although originally the focus was on indexing gravestones with details of pre-1855 deaths, many societies have indexed later records, too.

SOLUTIONS

- Check the SAFHS website to identify the burial grounds within an ancestor's town or parish
- Check local council websites to identify the records they hold and how they can be accessed
- Check local archive websites and catalogues to identify the records they hold and whether any indexes are available
- Search online burial records available through commercial genealogy websites
- Use lair numbers to identify multiple relatives buried in the same plot
- Search newspapers for reports of family funerals, and check family papers for any funeral cards or other information regarding burials
- Search published monumental inscriptions to identify an ancestor's gravestone
- Look at the 'Missing Death Record' section above for further advice on identifying deaths and burials

When searching published inscriptions be sure to note grave numbers and to identify these on any accompanying maps before visiting the graveyard, although be aware that these are often not the same numbers used by the burial ground to identify burial plots.

Problem: Illegitimacy

An ancestor born outside marriage is something most family historians will encounter eventually. Illegitimacy can often be the cause of a change of name or of an apparently missing birth or marriage record, so should be considered when facing a variety of brick walls.

Under Scots Law, a child born to parents who were not married to one another was deemed illegitimate at birth, but that child could be legitimated by the subsequent marriage of his or her parents (provided they were free to marry at the time of the conception; this was current until 1968, when that requirement was removed). It was therefore possible for someone to be born illegitimate, but later to have the rights of a legitimate child. The legal status of illegitimacy was abolished in Scotland in 1986.

The most common problem caused by an illegitimate birth is that of identifying the father, who may not be named on the birth record. Identifying the mother can also be challenging, particularly if the child was raised outside the family, or if records provide little distinguishing information. Illegitimacy can lead to a birth being recorded under a name that is different from the one expected, or to it not being recorded at all. It affected whom a person could

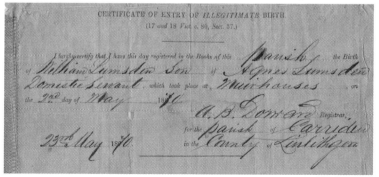

Those born outside marriage carried a stigma for life. There were even special certificates for recording an illegitimate birth, such as this example from the author's personal collection.

inherit from, and who could inherit from them, as well as carrying a social stigma.

From 1855 until 1918 the statutory birth record of an illegitimate child included the word 'illegitimate' in the first column of the birth register, and there were special forms for issuing a certificate relating to an illegitimate birth. The word 'illegitimate' was also included on the death record of an illegitimate person until 1918, although this is less commonly seen, as the informant of a death often omitted to mention that the deceased person's parents were not married to one another.

When the birth of an illegitimate child was registered, the name of the father would only be recorded if he was present at the time of registration to acknowledge paternity. Both parents would then sign as informants, and the birth would be indexed under both surnames. If the father was not present, his name was not recorded, and the child was registered under the mother's surname only, although a father's surname might be given to the child as a middle name. If the mother of an illegitimate child was married or widowed, then an indication would be given that her husband was not the father, either by recording the late husband's date and place of death, which proved he could not have fathered the child, or by the mother's declaration (for example, 'Elizabeth A or B, wife of Alexander B, who she declares is not the father of the child'). The name of the father of an illegitimate person might be recorded on that person's marriage or death record, with the words 'reputed father' written after his name to indicate that the parents were not married, and that the father was not present to acknowledge paternity.

When parents married after the birth of their child, an entry in the Register of Corrected Entries (RCE) could be made to show that the child had been legitimated. However, this did not always happen, as some parents may have been unaware of the procedure, or may simply not have bothered.

It was common in Scotland for illegitimate children to take their father's surname, regardless of whether or not he acknowledged paternity, although this did not happen in every case. Sometimes the child might alternate between using both surnames, or might have used one surname as a child and the other as an adult. When a father did acknowledge paternity, it was not unusual for him or his family to raise the child, although it was more common for an illegitimate child to live with the mother's family.

In the old parish registers (OPRs), a child is often described as 'natural' rather than 'lawful' to indicate that the parents were not married and that the child was illegitimate. Alternatively the child may be recorded as 'born in fornication', or one or both parents described as a fornicator or fornicatrix. Most commonly when an illegitimate child was baptised in the Church of Scotland the register gives the father's name, although occasionally only a mother's name is given. When the church could not identify the father to their satisfaction, an illegitimate child may not have been baptised and no record may appear in the OPR.

Kirk session minutes are one of the main sources for identifying the parents of illegitimate children, including those whose baptisms do not appear in the OPRs. When an unmarried woman was rumoured to be pregnant, or had recently given birth, she would typically be called to appear before the session to confess her sin and name the father of her child. The accused man would then appear before the session and either confess to fathering the child or deny it, although some men refused to appear, or sent a letter rather than appearing in person. If a man denied paternity and the mother continued to accuse him, then witnesses would appear for both parties. In some cases the proceedings might go on for many months until the session felt they had sufficient evidence to come to a decision. If a couple had been seen together, particularly late at night or in a quiet location, it was usually enough to convince the session that the man was indeed the father. From the point of view of family historians, it is often better if the father initially denied the accusation, as more information is likely to then be given about both parents. When a father readily confessed, only the names of the two parents may be given, with no other identifying information.

The child would usually not be baptised until the question of paternity had been resolved and both parents had done penance for their sin, usually publicly in the parish church, and been 'absolved of the scandal'. For this reason kirk session minutes do not name the child, and the sex and date of birth are only rarely recorded. Most kirk session proceedings relating to an illegitimate child took place fairly close to the time of the child's birth, but occasionally records may be found several years afterwards. When parents came from different parishes, or the child was conceived in a different parish to where it was born, or to where the mother usually resided, records concerning an illegitimate birth may be found in the kirk session minutes of more than one parish. Typically it was the parish where 'the guilt was committed' that took precedence.

Kirk session records are a useful source of information on illegitimate births up until around 1900, although this varies from parish to parish. The majority are not indexed, although a few indexes do exist (*see* Chapter 1). Of particular interest for identifying the parents of illegitimate children is the 'Scotland, Antenuptial Relationship Index 1661–1780', available on Findmypast, although this does not cover all parishes.

Most secessionist churches (Presbyterian churches that had broken away from the Church of Scotland) followed similar proceedings to the Church of Scotland for investigating an illegitimate birth. Minute books for such churches are worth searching, in addition to the Church of Scotland kirk session records, in case the parents belonged to a different religious denomination. Non-Presbyterian churches do not seem to have followed the same process, but fathers of illegitimate children may be named in baptism registers. In some cases, mothers of illegitimate children appear to have gone to other churches to have their babies baptised, to avoid the shame of doing public penance in the parish church. In the 1830s–1840s, one Catholic priest in Aberdeenshire regularly baptised the illegitimate children of Protestant parents (including the adulterous child of a Presbyterian parish minister!) on the promise that the child would be brought up in the Catholic faith.

If the church could not get the father of an illegitimate child to admit paternity and support the child financially, another option was for the mother to pursue a civil court case against him. Such cases were usually heard in sheriff courts and are described as 'actions of affiliation and aliment', although they are informally referred to as paternity cases. For illegitimate births from 1855, it is relatively straightforward to identify if such a case exists. If the court found that a man was the father, his name would be added to the birth record either in the margin or, from 1860, in an entry in the Register of Corrected Entries (RCE), giving the name of the court and the date of the action. Obviously, if the court found that an accused man was not the father, no amendment would be made to the birth record, and in a few cases no RCE appears to have been made when one should have been.

An index to sheriff court paternity decrees covering the period 1855–1900 is available on the Old Scottish Genealogy & Family History website (www.oldscottish.com/sheriff-court-paternity-decrees.html), and a small number of cases are individually catalogued in the National Records of Scotland online catalogue (http://catalogue.nrscotland.gov.uk/nrsonlinecatalogue). Generally the mother of the child was the pursuer of the action, and the accused father was the defender, and it is these names that should be searched for in any index, rather than that of the child. Often the date of birth and the sex of the child will be recorded in case papers, but not their name.

For illegitimate births prior to 1855, identifying if an action of affiliation and aliment exists can involve a lengthy search through court papers, although ongoing indexing of these records has made this easier. Records of actions of affiliation and aliment do not survive in all cases (some court records have been 'weeded' and destroyed over the years), but may include processes (bundles of papers relating to the case and describing the evidence presented) and decrees (the official decision of the court). Emma and Graham Maxwell of Scottish Indexes, who have an ongoing project to index these types of cases, estimate that in the 1850s around 15 per cent of illegitimate births resulted in a civil paternity case, although this may have varied over time and by location.[1] The valuable information that such records contain means they are well worth searching out. Scottish Indexes' database of processes and decrees is included on their website as 'Sheriff Court Paternity Decrees' (www.scottishindexes.com/courtsearch.aspx). The website also includes a helpful guide to locating such records (www.scottishindexes.com/learningcourt.aspx).

Poor relief records are another good source for tracing illegitimate children and their parents. Some mothers of illegitimate children had no option but to give birth in the poorhouse, or applied for poor relief after the birth to support themselves and their child. In such cases the poor relief application will usually be in the name of the mother, but may include information on the child and may name the child's father. If an illegitimate person applied for poor relief at any point during their lifetime they may have provided information concerning their birth and parentage.

In the period when most births took place in the family home, mothers of illegitimate children were more likely to give birth in a hospital than married women, and so hospital records are another potentially useful source. These are unlikely to name the father of the child, but may provide more information about the mother than is given on the birth record (such as her age and birthplace). When a birth took place in a hospital or other institution, such as a poorhouse, only a street address may be given on the birth record, rather than the name of the institution. Identifying the address where an illegitimate child was born may therefore open up new avenues of research. Births that took place in a hospital may have been registered by a member of hospital staff, rather than by a relative, and the record may not give the child's forename. I've come across one such birth record where not only was the child's first name not given, but their sex was recorded incorrectly!

Relatively wealthy men often acknowledged and financially supported their illegitimate children, although such arrangements might be made privately. Illegitimate children were sometimes left legacies in wills or deeds, and might be specified as such or referred to more obliquely. In one will I came across, the testator left a bequest to 'a young man.... whose welfare I am interested in'. Other records indicate the young man was almost certainly the testator's illegitimate son.

An illegitimate person could not automatically inherit from either parent (or from grandparents or other relatives), although they could be bequeathed moveable property in a will. Under Scots Law, the property of an illegitimate person could only be inherited by a legitimate child of their body. If they had no legitimate children, their estate would go to the Crown as *Ultimus Haeres*, although a relative could petition the Exchequer to be granted the property. As a result, *Ultimus Haeres* records, held by the National Records of Scotland (NRS), can contain a large amount of genealogical information concerning the families of illegitimate people.

It was possible for a person to be legitimated by the Crown, and some early cases can be found among the records of the Privy Seal (held by NRS in reference PS). Cases concerning legitimation, some of which involved the recognition of an irregular marriage, were heard by the Commissary Court of Edinburgh up until about 1830

(NRS reference CC8), and thereafter by the Court of Session (NRS reference CS). Court papers can be identified either through the NRS online catalogue or by using finding aids onsite.

Genealogical DNA testing can be used to identify or verify the parentage of a child born outside marriage, although it is likely to be most useful when the birth took place in a fairly recent generation. Autosomal DNA tests (which can identify relatives on all family lines) are usually the most useful type of test in these circumstances, although Y-DNA tests (which test the DNA passed from father to son only) may be relevant in some cases. DNA testing is discussed in more detail in a later section.

SOLUTIONS

- When facing a discrepancy in name, or an apparently missing record, consider if illegitimacy could be a possible cause
- Look for a birth under the mother's surname if it cannot be found under the father's surname
- If a statutory birth record indicates that a child was illegitimate, look for additional records that may provide further information, such as a baptism record, a poor relief or hospital record, kirk session minutes, or a civil paternity case (indicated by an RCE)
- Remember that even if a birth record does not name the father of a child, the child's marriage or death record may (sometimes as 'reputed father')
- If a pre-1855 birth or baptism record indicates that a child was illegitimate, or a baptism cannot be found, look for additional records such as kirk session minutes, records of other churches, or a civil paternity case
- Use genealogical DNA testing to identify unknown parentage or to confirm possible paternity
- Look at the next section on adoption if an illegitimate birth led to a child being adopted or raised outside the family

Problem: Adoption and Fostering

Tracing an ancestor who was an adoptee, or raised outside their family, can be particularly challenging as records may be closed to public access or simply not exist.

Adoption was not recognized in Scots Law until 1930, and prior to that date most adoptions were arranged informally and few records exist. From 1930, adoptions were ratified by civil courts, and details of adopted children were entered into the Adopted Children Register. This register includes some children born prior to 1930 and adopted later.

The Adopted Children Register can be consulted on microfiche at the ScotlandsPeople Centre in Edinburgh, but only three full entries can be viewed on a single visit. The entries give the date of birth of the child (and latterly the country of birth but not the specific place), the adopted name, the names and address of the adoptive parents, the date of the adoption order and the name of the relevant court. The original birth name is not given, and there is no information concerning the birth parents. Entries are indexed under the year of birth rather than the year of adoption.

The original birth entry of an adopted child is annotated with the word 'adopted' in the margin, but with no indication as to the date of adoption or the new name of the child. This means that while both records are public, there is nothing to connect the original birth record with the corresponding entry in the Adopted Children Register.

Not all adopted children are adopted out of their birth family. Some children are adopted by stepparents, grandparents or other relatives, and in these circumstances although the child's surname might change, their forenames rarely do. In such cases it can be relatively straightforward to match an original birth record with an entry in the Adopted Children Register.

The majority of court papers relating to adoptions are held by the National Records of Scotland, although some records less than twenty-five years old may still be with the relevant court. All records are closed to public access for 100 years, so none will be publicly accessible until 2030 at the earliest. The adopted person has the right to access their own court records and any adoption agency records once they reach the age of sixteen. Adoptees wishing to access their records or to make contact with birth relatives are recommended to seek advice and counselling before starting a search, and there are a number of organizations that can help with this. Details are given in the National Records of Scotland guide to adoption records (www.nrscotland.gov.uk/research/guides/adoption-records).

The charity Birthlink (www.birthlink.org.uk) maintains the

Adoption Contact Register for Scotland, and adoptees, their families, and birth relatives of an adopted person wishing to make contact can all register with the service. Birthlink offers a range of additional services for people affected by adoption with a Scottish connection. They have also published *Relatively Clear: A Search Guide for Adopted People in Scotland* (Edinburgh: Birthlink, 2009).

Prior to 1930, the biggest challenge in tracing an adopted person is that the person's name could change completely, without any annotation or amendment being made to their original birth record, and with no information given in later records that connects back to their original name and birth. The marriage and death records of an adopted person might specify that the named parents are adoptive, or might simply list them as birth parents, and indeed the adoptee themselves may have been unaware of their true origins. However, in some cases information may be found in the sources described below.

First, it is worth considering if the child may have been brought up within the family. A child born to an unmarried mother or orphaned at a young age may have been brought up by grandparents or other relatives as their own child. It may be helpful to search for the birth of a child with the same forename within the extended family, or to look for a child who seems to disappear from the records.

Some children were 'boarded out' or fostered on an initially temporary basis, with the arrangement gradually becoming permanent over time. In this case information may be found in poor relief records, particularly in children's separate registers and the registers of boarded out children kept by parochial boards, parish councils and later welfare and social work departments. These records can mainly be found in local archives, although any records relating to children are likely to be closed for 100 years. The person concerned may be able to access their own records, or, if that person is deceased, a Freedom of Information request could be made by a close relative to obtain access.

A small number of adoptions prior to 1930 appear to have been privately arranged before the child was born, with the child's birth being registered by the birth mother, with the adoptive parents' surname as a middle name. The birth surname was then dropped once the child was adopted. As with adoptions within the family, searching for the birth of a similarly named child at the right period, but leaving the surname field blank, may reveal a likely birth.

If sufficient information is known about the adopted person, such as an exact date of birth and likely location of birth, it may be possible to search for a possible match without knowing a birth name. In one case I researched involving a pre-1930 adoption, the adoptee's date of birth and birth county were known, and I was able to identify a likely candidate by searching birth registers manually for any births on the right date (luckily the birth took place in a small, rural county), then looking for later records of each possible match in order to eliminate them. Such a search is only possible when searching at a ScotlandsPeople Centre, and will not be practical in all cases.

Some children spent time in a children's home prior to being adopted, and records from the institution may provide information on birth parents and origins as well as on what happened to the child after leaving. For example, the Whinwell Home in Stirling, which opened in the 1890s, arranged adoptions of children sent to the home and case files (held by Stirling Council Archives) are often extremely detailed, recording the progress of children for many years after they left.

The website Children's Homes (http://childrenshomes.org.uk) has information on institutions that housed children across the UK, including Scotland, with some details of where records can be found. Some children's home records are privately held, while others are in local archives, and the National Records of Scotland has a large collection relating to Dr Guthrie's Schools in Edinburgh. Some larger organizations such as Barnardo's (www.barnardos. org.uk/what_we_do/working_with_former_barnardos_children/ family_history_service.htm) and Quarriers (https://quarriers.org. uk/about-us/genealogy) offer research services for those seeking information on relatives, and search fees may apply.

Not all children who spent time in institutions were subsequently adopted. Some were sent overseas to Australia, Canada, New Zealand and South Africa as part of child migration schemes. In recent years there has been increasing recognition of the abuse and injustice that many of these 'home children' suffered. Records may be found in the country where the child was sent, and also among the records of the organizations and institutions in the UK who were involved in the schemes.

Genealogical DNA testing is used extensively by adoptees in countries where adoption records are completely closed, and may also be helpful for identifying birth fathers who are not named in birth or adoption records, for tracing the birth families of pre-1930 adoptees, and for verifying potential or unconfirmed relationships. Autosomal DNA tests (which can identify relatives on all family lines) are likely to be the most useful type of test, although Y-DNA tests (which test the DNA passed from father to son only) may be relevant in some cases. DNA testing is discussed further in a later section.

SOLUTIONS

- Search statutory birth records and the Adopted Children Register to identify if a relative was adopted into or out of the family from 1930 onwards
- Adoptees who were adopted in Scotland can access their own records but may wish to receive advice and counselling before doing so
- Register with the Adoption Contact Register for Scotland to make contact with relatives separated through adoption
- Remember that children may have been adopted within the extended family
- Use known birth dates and locations to identify possible births, and remember that forenames may have been kept after adoption in some cases
- Search poor relief records and records of children's homes and other institutions to trace relatives who were fostered or informally adopted, particularly before 1930
- Use genealogical DNA testing to identify unknown parentage or to confirm possible relationships
- Look at the previous chapter on illegitimacy if an adopted child was born outside marriage

Problem: Divorce and Separation

Not all our ancestors' marriages were happy ones. It can be difficult to identify couples who separated, particularly prior to the mid-1800s, but there are a variety of records that can reveal details of our ancestors' relationships.

It has been possible for a couple to divorce in Scotland since 1560, but divorces were rare prior to the twentieth century. From 1855, statutory marriage records indicate if the marriage ended in divorce, or was found to be bigamous or otherwise invalid, by a note in the margin and an associated entry in the Register of Corrected Entries (an RCE) giving the date the divorce was pronounced. However, this annotation would only happen if the couple both married and divorced in Scotland. Since 1 May 1984, a separate statutory register of divorces has been maintained, which can be searched on the ScotlandsPeople website, and divorce details are no longer entered into an RCE.

From the 1560s to the 1830s divorces, and other cases involving marriage, separation and legitimacy, were heard by the Commissary Court of Edinburgh. The majority of such cases have been individually catalogued in the National Records of Scotland (NRS) online catalogue, and can therefore be easily identified by searching for the names of husband and wife together (although possible spelling variations of names should be borne in mind), and either the reference CC8 or the word 'divorce'. From 1830 to 1984, the court responsible for granting divorces was the Court of Session. Some cases have been individually catalogued in the NRS online catalogue (under reference CS), although manual finding aids may also need to be used. Since 1984, most divorce cases have been heard in sheriff courts, and records may still be held by the relevant court. Further information is given in the NRS research guide to divorce and separation records (www.nrscotland.gov.uk/research/guides/divorce-records).

Divorce papers, consisting of 'processes' and 'decreets' or decrees recording a court's decision, are often extremely detailed and are well worth accessing for any ancestors or close relatives who were involved in a divorce. Under Scots Law, it was possible for a person of limited means to be put temporarily on the poor roll in order to receive financial assistance to pursue a divorce, and so people of all social classes can be found in divorce records. Divorce papers are closed for 100 years under data protection legislation, but close family members of those involved may be able to obtain access through a Freedom of Information request.

A legal separation was an alternative to divorce, and records of separations can be found among the Commissary Court and Court of Session records described above, and were heard in sheriff courts from 1907. If a separation was mutually agreed, then an agreement may have been recorded in a register of deeds, rather than the couple going to court.

A husband who wanted to avoid liability for his wife's debts, usually after they had separated, could take out an 'inhibition' against her. This was recorded in one of the registers of inhibitions, either the general register, particular registers for each county, or registers for regalities up to 1748. Records are held by the National Records of Scotland (in reference DI) and are indexed from 1781.

Men who abandoned their wives and children could be taken to court in order to get them to pay maintenance or 'aliment', and such cases can often be found in sheriff court records (although the majority of aliment cases involved the parents of illegitimate children). A small number of such cases have been indexed by Scottish Indexes (www.scottishindexes.com), along with paternity cases. Many abandoned wives applied for poor relief, and such records can provide a lot of details regarding a marriage, although it should be noted that women sometimes claimed to be abandoned in order to receive poor relief when their husbands were out of work or temporarily away seeking employment.

Bigamy and domestic violence could lead to criminal cases, heard in a variety of courts, which can provide a lot of detail regarding a couple's marriage. Many court cases involving bigamy, divorce, separation or some form of marital disagreement were widely reported in newspapers. Newspaper reports are therefore a good way of identifying cases relating to an ancestor, and may provide details not found in court records. Prison registers can be used to identify ancestors convicted by police and burgh courts, for which few records typically survive.

Ancestors who committed adultery, quarrelled with their spouses, or were reported to have committed acts of domestic violence, might all be called to appear before their local kirk session. Kirk session minutes can therefore also shed light on an ancestor's unhappy marriage.

Although there are many different types of record that may have been created when an ancestor was unhappily married or separated from their spouse, often a couple would simply separate without any form of legal process, and in some cases go on to co-habit with a new partner. Census records can enable such couples to be traced, and if a married couple are consistently recorded at different addresses, this may be an indication they had separated. Sometimes a separated person may have chosen to present themselves as widowed, or may not have known whether their spouse was still alive or not, and so a status of widow or widower should be treated with caution.

SOLUTIONS

- Check statutory marriage records, the register of corrected entries, and the statutory register of divorces to identify divorces from 1855 onwards
- Search the National Records of Scotland catalogue for case papers for divorces and legal separations
- Search digitized newspapers for details of any criminal or civil court cases involving an ancestor and their spouse
- Follow up newspaper reports of court cases in court records held by the National Records of Scotland and in local archives
- Search available indexes to aliment cases and registers of deeds to identify separations
- Look at poor relief records to identify wives abandoned by their husbands who applied for financial assistance
- Search kirk session records for any mention of an ancestor and their spouse
- Be alert to any indication that a couple may have separated, and consider what sources may shed further light on their situation

---

Problem: Multiple Individuals with the Same Name

A common brick wall problem, particularly when tracing families prior to the period of statutory registration, is that of more than one person with the same name. If there is more than one potential birth or baptism for an ancestor in the area they lived in, research on that line obviously cannot progress until the correct birth and parents are identified.

The basic approach to this problem is to research all the potential matches and their families as thoroughly as possible, until it can be proved or disproved that a potential birth is that of our ancestor. This will often involve researching people whom we know are not our ancestors, but who share an ancestor's name, in order to establish who their parents were and therefore eliminate that birth as being our ancestor's.

Looking for deaths and burials is usually a good place to start, and can be a quick and easy way of disproving that a potential birth is correct. If an ancestor died prior to statutory registration there may be no record naming their parents, but if some of the potential matches died after 1854 their death records may name their parents and can be used to eliminate those births.

Eliminating potential matches who died prior to 1855 may be more challenging, but burial registers, kirk session accounts and monumental inscriptions are all useful sources, particularly for identifying individuals who died in infancy or early childhood, and whose records may identify their parents.

If deaths and burials cannot satisfactorily eliminate potential births, then we should search for additional records, which may relate to each potential match. If there are several births at a similar time, there may well be several marriages of same-named individuals at a similar time. Research each couple and their children in turn, looking for naming patterns, occupations, places of residence and names of witnesses, which may link back to a potential birth. Additional sources that could help to distinguish same-named individuals and eliminate potential births include poor relief records, property records and wills and testaments.

Researching the parents and siblings of each potential match can also be useful. Sometimes just identifying the births of younger siblings is enough to show that the family left the area, and so the birth is unlikely to be that of our ancestor, who remained there. A younger sibling given the same name is usually an indication that the older child had died, so could eliminate a potential match even when there is no death or burial record.

Almost any type of document relating to the family has the potential to prove or disprove a family connection. An ancestor may turn up as a witness at the baptism of a niece or nephew, or the heir of a sibling who died unmarried, helping to confirm that a proposed relationship is correct. Looking at original records, rather than relying on indexes, is particularly important for locating these kinds of small details.

Although online family trees should always be treated with

caution, they can save time and effort when trying to eliminate potential matches. Look for family trees that include a potential family, and evaluate the information given. Another researcher may have clear evidence linking their ancestor with a particular birth, thereby proving the birth is not that of our ancestor. This may include records that we cannot easily locate or would not think to search, such as records from another country.

SOLUTIONS

- When faced with more than one possible birth for an ancestor, research each potential match and their family, looking for evidence to prove or disprove a possible connection
- Use death and burial records to eliminate potential matches who died in childhood or after 1854
- Research other people sharing an ancestor's name in the same area in order to identify their parents and eliminate them
- Research extended families and other people sharing an ancestor's surname, looking for evidence of family relationships
- Look at research done by others who may have additional records of a potential family

---

Problem: Lack of Parish Registers

The old parish registers (OPRs) of the Church of Scotland are one of the main sources we use to trace ancestors in Scotland prior to 1855. However, some families did not attend the Church of Scotland, and relatively few records survive for other churches, particularly prior to the 1800s. Some parish registers contain gaps, were poorly kept, or may simply not exist for the period we need. In that case, reliably tracing a family line can be very challenging, but there are a variety of other sources that may help.

Provided the family's parish of residence is known, a good first step is to identify what other records exist for that area, and to draw up a locality guide (*see* Chapter 6). The type and number of available records will vary considerably from one place to another, but there are some kinds of record that may be particularly helpful.

Kirk session records are probably the most useful source for filling in gaps in parish registers, as both minutes and accounts may include details of births, marriages and deaths not recorded in the

OPRs. Ancestors, including those who were not members of the church, may have been called to attend the session or may be mentioned as witnesses, and details such as their age, marital status, occupation and place of residence may be recorded. The covering dates of kirk session records will usually be slightly different from those of the OPR.

Heritors records are the other major source created at a parish level, which can supplement the OPRs. Although fewer people are mentioned in heritors records than in kirk session records, they can provide information on landowners, major tenants, and those in receipt of poor relief.

Monumental (gravestone) inscriptions are valuable for identifying pre-1855 deaths, but can also provide evidence of relationships between generations, and of a family's continued residence in a parish or even at a particular farm. It may be possible to draw up a hypothetical family tree based on gravestones alone, even when records of some intervening generations are missing.

Wills and testaments usually provide the names of family members (except when a creditor was appointed as executor), and inventories in particular may list a large number of other people with whom the deceased was associated, including landlords, tenants, business associates and neighbours to whom money was owed, or from whom it was owing. It is therefore worth seeking out not only the testaments of ancestors, but also those of extended family members, and even of anyone living in the same parish, all of which may mention an ancestor.

Tax records name relatively few Scots, but farm-horse tax records in particular may be useful for identifying tenant farmers in the 1790s. The fact that many eighteenth-century tax records are online on the ScotlandsPlaces website and are searchable for free, means it is worth including them when researching ancestors in this period.

Militia records, particularly the lists of those in each parish liable to serve in the militia, are a valuable source for the 1790s and early 1800s. Occasionally relationships may be stated (such as men being identified as 'son of'), but more common are places of residence, from which relationships to other people of the same surname living at the same place may be inferred. Inclusion, or non-inclusion, on militia lists may also provide evidence of approximate age and marital status, so it is important to check the specific rules concerning liability for serving in the militia at the time the list was drawn up. A variety of records exist for men who actually served in the militia and their families, which may provide information on age and birthplace, as well as naming wives and children.

For ancestors who lived in rural areas, estate records are one of the most valuable sources. When creating a locality guide for a parish, it is important to identify the local landowners and to track down the locations of any estate records, including those that are privately held. Lists of tenants are particularly useful for identifying different generations of the same family living at the same property in different years, while rental agreements and estate correspondence may provide more personal information.

For ancestors who lived in royal burghs and had skilled occupations, burgess records and the records of craft incorporations and merchant guilds should be searched. Records of apprenticeship and of entry as a guild member or burgess may provide details of relationships, as membership often passed from father to son or was obtained through marriage.

Families who owned heritable property (land and buildings) can be traced through the registers of sasines and registers of retours (services of heirs). Such records usually provide clear evidence of relationships, but may need to be searched in conjunction with other sources, such as deeds and wills and testaments, in order to get a complete picture of the family.

A variety of court and legal records may provide details of an ancestor and their family. The courts that covered the area where an ancestor lived should be identified, and may include sheriff, commissary, burgh, justice of the peace and franchise courts. An ancestor may also have been recorded in one of the courts that had jurisdiction over the whole of Scotland, such as the Court of Session, the High Court of Justiciary and the Admiralty Court. Registers of deeds, records of civil cases and criminal court records may all contain valuable information providing evidence of relationships and supplementing the OPRs.

Many of the records described above are not indexed, and a painstaking and time-consuming search is likely to be needed. This may lead to little or no new information being discovered, or only a handful of references to individuals sharing an ancestor's surname, with no indication as to how, or if, they were related. However, all these sources could potentially contain information enabling longstanding brick walls to be demolished and family lines to be extended. A systematic approach and a lot of patience are needed, but hard work may be rewarded with a genealogical gem.

SOLUTIONS

- Identify alternative sources to the old parish registers, and create a locality guide for the parish where an ancestor lived
- Consider an ancestor's personal circumstances, such as their occupation and whether they were a landowner or tenant, and if this may have led to the creation of particular records
- Carry out a systematic search of available records. First search indexed sources and those that are most likely to contain records of an ancestor, such as those created on a parish level
- Look for records of individuals sharing an ancestor's surname who lived in the same location, as well as for records of a known ancestor

Problem: Unknown Place of Origin of a Scottish Emigrant

Scotland has a long history of emigration and migration, with many Scots moving to other parts of the UK and to countries worldwide, particularly North America and Australasia. For descendants of the Scots who left Scotland, the biggest hurdle to tracing Scottish ancestry is often identifying the immigrant ancestor's place of origin. The records available will vary depending on where the emigrant settled and the time period during which they emigrated, but some general advice can be given.

When a record indicates an ancestor was born in Scotland, the temptation may be to start looking for them in Scottish records, but before doing so it is always a good idea to gather as much information as possible from the country where they settled. Some possible sources that may provide information on a specific place of origin (parish, town or county), and name family members, include civil marriage and death records, church records, passenger lists, naturalization records, military records, records relating to institutions and poor relief, wills and probate records, newspaper obituaries, gravestone inscriptions, and town and family histories.

Many family historians whose forebears left the UK are keen to find ships' passenger lists for their ancestors. However, passenger lists of ships leaving the UK were not regularly kept until 1890, and generally provide little personal information prior to the twentieth century. Aside from records from a small number of assisted emigration schemes (such as the Highland and Island Emigration Society, 1852–1857) and records of convicts transported to Australia (which could be considered assisted emigration!), any records of an ancestor's emigration prior to 1890 are only likely to be found in the destination country, and may not exist at all.

Ships' passenger lists from 1890 (and a variety of earlier convict transportation records) are held by The National Archives in Kew, London, but have been digitized and indexed and are available on both Ancestry and Findmypast. A few records can be found in local archives – for example Glasgow City Archives has a small number of passenger lists for ships leaving Glasgow, as well as a register of passports issued by the city between 1875 and 1914.

It is often helpful to research an emigrant ancestor's extended family in the country where they settled, and to look for other people in the same area with the same surname, who may have been relatives. Many emigrants arrived in family groups, including parents and siblings, or were part of chain migration, either settling where they already had family, or assisting relatives to join them when they themselves were settled. Researching relatives, and possible relatives, increases the chances of finding a document that provides information on the family's place of origin. It is also likely to be easier to identify a family in Scottish records rather than a single individual, as the names of known siblings can be used to locate the correct baptism of an ancestor. Each of an emigrant ancestor's children should be thoroughly researched, as at some point in their lives they may have provided information on their parent's origins.

It can be helpful to research the history of the area where an ancestor settled, as they may have been part of a larger migration from a particular part of Scotland. It is also worth considering what events were happening in Scotland at the time they left, and if these may point to a place of origin or further records, such as an ancestor who left during the Highland Clearances. If an ancestor followed a particular trade they may have had the same occupation in Scotland, and even been specially recruited, so researching the industry may provide clues to a place of origin. For example, the skills of granite masons from the Aberdeen area were highly sought after, and many went to work for the granite industries in countries such as the USA, Australia and South Africa.

Many Scots living abroad married within their own communities, and continued to follow the traditional Scottish naming pattern. The names of their children may point to the names of relatives back in Scotland, and the origins of a spouse may indicate the ancestor's own origins. Important family surnames might be passed down as middle names, and some Scots who did not use a middle name whilst in Scotland started using their mother's maiden surname as a middle name after leaving – although it should not be presumed that a surname given as a middle name is always the mother's maiden name.

Many Scottish surnames can be found throughout the country, but a relatively unusual name could suggest a particular place of origin. Researching an ancestor's surname may be helpful for suggesting a particular area of Scotland in which to focus a search. Place-names can also be useful, as an emigrant may have named their new home after their place of origin in Scotland.

Turning to Scottish sources, there are many different types of record that may provide details of an ancestor who left Scotland, but most are not online, not indexed, or only indexed at a local level, so without knowing at least a county of origin it can be very difficult to locate them.

The deaths of some Scots who died outside Scotland were reported in Scottish newspapers, particularly local newspapers from their area. Newspapers can occasionally include details of those who were about to emigrate: for example, a tradesman might advertise the sale of his property before emigrating. Some gravestones in Scotland include details of family members who died abroad, although these were often young, single men or temporary migrants, rather than those who had permanently settled elsewhere.

Kirk session records may provide details of parishioners who had left the parish, including some who left Scotland. Communion rolls, which mainly exist for the early to mid-1800s onwards, may note when a communicant left the church and sometimes their destination, such as 'gone to America'. Kirk session minutes may also provide evidence of emigration and migration, for example noting that the reputed father of an illegitimate child had left the parish and gone to Jamaica, or the husband of a woman accused of adultery had not been heard of for many years and was believed to be living in England.

Poor relief records may provide details of a pauper's relatives living outside Scotland, including the adult children of elderly paupers, who might be expected to contribute financially, and husbands who had left their wives and children. Sometimes only a country of residence is given, but information may include specific places of residence, occupations and details of other relatives, such as whether an adult child was married and how many children they had. Poor relief records will sometimes note that a pauper has been struck off the poor roll because they had emigrated, usually going to join relatives who paid their passage.

Court records are often very detailed for convicts who were sentenced to transportation, but may also include details of those accused of a crime who had fled Scotland, including where they were believed to be living. Such cases were often well reported in newspapers, which may provide additional information. The Registers of the Privy Council of Scotland, published for the period 1545–1691, contain names of Scots who had left Scotland for a variety of reasons.

Details of Scots living outside Scotland who owned or inherited property in Scotland can be found in wills and testaments, and in property records such as valuation rolls, registers of sasines and registers of retours (services of heirs). These sources are fairly well indexed, and so are worth searching on the off-chance an emigrant ancestor's name may appear. The names of Scots living in America have been extracted from wills and registers of retours by genealogist David Dobson and published as *Scottish-American Wills, 1650–1900* (Baltimore: Genealogical Publishing Company, 1991) and *Scottish-American Heirs, 1683–1883* (Baltimore: Genealogical Publishing Company, 1990) respectively.

Some Scots who needed someone to manage their property or business affairs in Scotland during their absence had a deed known as a 'factory' drawn up, appointing another person to act as their 'factor' or representative. Often the factor would be a close relative who could be trusted to carry out the emigrant's wishes. If a factory were drawn up shortly before the person emigrated, they might mention that they were about to leave Scotland (although rarely their destination), and give their occupation, place of residence, and sometimes the names of several relatives. Factories can be found in registers of deeds, although they were not always recorded.

Estate records can include details or lists of tenants who emigrated, particularly if the landowner provided assistance, as well as of tenants removed from their property who may subsequently have emigrated. For example, the records of the Sutherland Estate, held by the National Library of Scotland, include lists of emigrants from the 1830s. Records of trade incorporations or craft guilds may also include details of members who emigrated, who may have followed the same occupation in their new country.

There are a large number of publications relating to Scottish emigrants, containing information from records both in Scotland and in the countries where they settled. Many of these have been compiled by David Dobson, although other authors have published records relating to specific countries. Examples include Dobson's *Directory of Scots banished to the American Plantations, 1650–1775* (2nd edition, Baltimore: Clearfield, 2010), *A Dictionary of Scottish Emigrants to Canada before Confederation* by Donald Whyte (Toronto: Ontario Genealogical Society, 1986–2005), *A Dictionary of Scottish Emigrants into England & Wales* (Manchester: Anglo-Scottish Family History Society, 2005) and *Scots in Prussia* (Edinburgh: Scottish Genealogy Society, 2014). These can be found at the National Library of Scotland and in genealogical and reference libraries. Some can also be accessed online through Ancestry and Findmypast.

Genealogical DNA testing can be used to establish the likely origins of an emigrant ancestor, to identify distant cousins in Scotland, and to confirm potential relationships. Autosomal DNA tests can identify relatives on all family lines, and are most useful when the emigrant ancestor was within a fairly recent generation (around four to seven generations back). Y-DNA tests can be used when there is a direct male line descendant of a male emigrant ancestor who can be tested. DNA testing is discussed in a later section.

Unless very precise information can be found regarding an emigrant ancestor, such as a death record specifying their birthplace and naming their parents, it may be necessary to search Scottish birth and baptism records for potential matches. Each possible match can then be researched in turn. Often it is possible to eliminate potential matches fairly easily, by determining that that person was still living in Scotland after the emigrant ancestor is known to have left.

SOLUTIONS

- Gather as much information as possible from the country where the emigrant settled
- Trace an emigrant's extended family and possible relatives sharing the same surname who settled in the same location
- Research the history of the community where the emigrant settled, and consider what events were happening in Scotland at the time they left
- Investigate the origins of the emigrant's surname and identify the areas where it is most commonly found
- Search published directories of Scottish emigrants
- Look for any records the ancestor may have created in Scotland around the time they left
- Remember the emigrant may have created records in Scotland many years after they left, particularly if they owned or inherited property
- Identify potential births or baptisms in Scotland, and research each one in turn (*see* the previous section on multiple individuals with the same name)
- Look for records of relatives in Scotland that may mention the emigrant
- Take a DNA test to connect with relatives in Scotland

Problem: Unknown Place of Origin Outside Scotland

While a large number of Scots emigrated over the centuries, people from many other countries have come to settle here. Family historians with origins in Scotland may discover an ancestor was actually born elsewhere. Common places of origin include England, Ireland, mainland Europe and the British Empire. Determining an exact place of birth can be challenging, as Scottish census records typically only give a country of birth; however, other sources may be available to trace an immigrant's origins. As with most research problems, the best place to start is by gathering as many records as possible of the immigrant ancestor, even if they seem unlikely to solve the problem directly.

Identify the immigrant in all censuses taken during their lifetime, as one census may give more detailed information than another. Most Scottish statutory records of marriages and deaths unfortunately do not provide a place of birth (the exception being 1855 records and marriages from 1972 onwards), but as most birth records provide the parents' place of marriage, they can sometimes be used to identify a family's place of origin. If an ancestor arrived in Scotland as a child, check for any younger siblings born in Scotland. In some cases the names of an immigrant's parents, provided on their marriage or death record, will be sufficient to identify them in their country of origin.

Identifying an immigrant ancestor's religious affiliation, and the church or other religious organization they attended, will often be useful. Religious records may contain more information than statutory ones, including identifying a previous place of residence. For example, some Scottish Catholic marriage records identify the parish and county in Ireland from which a bride and groom originated, and episcopal marriage registers may include places of origin for ancestors from England, Ireland and elsewhere in Europe.

Poor relief records can be very useful for tracing immigrants to Scotland, as detailed information may be provided on birthplaces and family members, both in Scotland and in the country of origin. This was particularly the case if there was uncertainty as to whether the person had obtained a legal settlement in Scotland and was therefore entitled to receive poor relief. In some cases the immigrant could be sent back to their country of birth, although they might return to Scotland at a later date. Some details of Irish paupers sent back to Ireland can be found in House of Commons parliamentary papers (available online via subscription). Poor relief records may state not only the pauper's place of birth but also that of their parents, so any poor relief records relating to an immigrant ancestor's children should also be located.

For Irish-born ancestors living in Scotland when the old age pension was introduced in 1909, and who were eligible to receive a pension, pension claim forms and the accompanying census searches used to verify ages can be a valuable source. For example, a simple search of the census search forms on the National Archives of Ireland website (http://censussearchforms.nationalarchives.ie) reveals 626 individuals whose address was in Edinburgh and 603 living in Glasgow.

Other records that may provide a specific place of birth for an immigrant include military records, hospital registers, police personnel records, prison registers, and court and criminal records. Gravestones may sometimes provide a date and place of birth, and although few Scots had detailed obituaries, it is certainly worth looking for any newspaper report of an immigrant ancestor's death, which may provide additional details not given in statutory records.

Passenger lists of ships arriving in the UK mainly exist from 1890 (with some surviving records for 1878–1888) and are only for ships arriving from ports outside Europe and the Mediterranean, although these can include passengers who joined the ship in Europe. These are held by the The National Archives in Kew, London, and are available online through Ancestry. Passenger lists may also have been created in the port of origin, which was not necessarily in the ancestor's home country. It is important to note that no passenger lists or other immigration records were kept of people travelling between Ireland and Great Britain, which were part of the same country until 1922.

Citizens of other countries living in Scotland were termed 'aliens', and were of particular concern to the authorities during times of war, such as the period of the French Revolutionary and Napoleonic Wars. Many records were kept at UK level and will therefore be found at The National Archives, although a small number of records can be found in Scotland. For example, Edinburgh City Archives holds registers of aliens for the period 1798–1825, and an index is available on the archives' website (www.edinburgh.gov.uk/downloads/file/1276/registers_of_aliens_1798–1825). A variety of records relating to aliens, including those who arrived at Scottish ports, can be found in the 'UK, Aliens Entry Books, 1794–1921' and 'England, Alien Arrivals, 1810–1811, 1826–1869' collections on Ancestry. An index to records of Belgian refugees during World War I, held by Glasgow City Archives, is available on the archives' website (www.glasgowfamilyhistory.org.uk/explorerecords/pages/belgian-refugees.aspx).

From 1914, aliens were required to register with the police. Relatively few records of alien registrations survive, but some may be found among police records, mostly held in local archives. People termed 'enemy aliens' during World Wars I and II could have been interned and may appear in prison registers (held at the National Records of Scotland) and in internment records (held at The National Archives). Some records are available on Findmypast in the 'Britain, Enemy Aliens and Internees, First and Second World Wars' collection.

Foreigners living in the UK could apply for naturalization in order to become British citizens, although many did not bother. As naturalization was granted by the Home Office in London, records will be found at The National Archives (TNA). There is a useful guide to these records on the TNA website (www.nationalarchives. gov.uk/help-with-your-research/research-guides/naturalisation-british-citizenship), including links to online indexes. A selection of records is available on Ancestry in the 'UK, Naturalisation Certificates and Declarations, 1870–1916' collection.

Many immigrants arrived in extended family groups or settled where they already had family, so researching any known or possible relatives may lead to an immigrant ancestor's origins. An ancestor may not have left any records stating where they were born, but a sibling or other relative may have done so. Relatives may appear as witnesses to baptisms, informants of deaths, or boarders and neighbours in census records. If a surname is relatively unusual, it is worth researching anyone with the same surname living in the same county (or even across Scotland), particularly if they shared an ancestor's country of birth. Many immigrants married within their own religious and national communities, so the origins of a person's spouse could point to their own origins. Researching the immigrant's occupation, community, migration patterns and what was happening in their country of origin at the time they left, may also prove fruitful.

Once as much information as possible has been gathered from Scottish sources, it is time to look at records in the ancestor's country of birth. Every country is different in terms of what records exist, whether those records are held at a national or regional level, whether or not they are indexed or online, and what privacy restrictions apply. Before jumping in, it is a good idea to do some background reading. It may be necessary to take a research trip, or to hire a local researcher to access records not available online, or that are written in another language.

People living in Scotland who were born in the British Empire or North America were most often the children of Scots who had migrated temporarily, or who served in the armed forces and overseas administration. Some records may be found in the UK, such as in Scottish minor statutory records, and the extensive records of British India held by the British Library, many of which are online. The Families in British India Society (www.fibis.org) has indexed many records of the British in India, and their website also includes a useful research wiki. Family connections are likely to be particularly important in tracing such ancestors – for example, parents may have married in Scotland, or siblings may have been born here.

DNA testing may be useful for identifying the likely ethnic origins of an immigrant ancestor and for connecting to relatives in the country of origin. However, genealogical DNA tests are not available in all countries, and so testing may produce few matches in some cases. DNA tests are discussed in a later section.

SOLUTIONS

- Gather as many records as possible of the immigrant ancestor in Scotland, including religious registers and poor relief records
- Search alien and naturalization records for ancestors originating outside the UK and Ireland
- Research known and possible relatives as thoroughly as the ancestor for any clues as to the family's place of origin
- Consider the ancestor's national and religious community and the migration patterns within that community
- Search records in the country of origin for possible matches, and work to eliminate them or to prove the connection
- Use genealogical DNA testing to establish ethnic origins and to identify relatives in the country of origin

Solution: Researching the Extended Family

Throughout this book I have emphasized the importance of researching an ancestor's extended family – their siblings, cousins, aunts, uncles and so on – as well as the ancestor and their immediate family. Perhaps, like me, you sometimes despair of ever finding the time to properly research all the direct ancestors you have already identified. Why, then, should you spend time researching people who are less closely related to you?

Hopefully the reasons for identifying all of an ancestor's children are fairly obvious. Naming patterns may point to the names of grandparents, but can only be reliably established if all of a couple's children are known. Baptism records of children may provide the family's place of residence, the father's occupation and the names of witnesses who may be relatives, all of which may help to identify the family in additional records and connect them to earlier generations. As most women in the past married at a relatively young age and had large families, a woman's childbearing years can be used to estimate her year of birth (few women gave birth before their mid-teens or after the age of forty-five).

Researching each of an ancestor's children into adulthood is the next step of researching the extended family, and is certainly worth doing any time a brick wall is encountered on the direct family line. This should include identifying each child's marriage, death, and the births of any children they had (our ancestor's grandchildren) and tracing them through censuses. Additional records that may provide valuable information on the family include poor relief records, wills and testaments, and records relating to illegitimate births.

Researching an ancestor's children up until their deaths may show that a child who was not recorded in census records with their parents, and who was presumed to have died in infancy, actually lived a long life. Census records may then reveal that that child spent time in an institution or lived with other relatives. In the case of one family I researched, a daughter who was thought to have died young was identified in the census living with a cousin of her mother's, probably helping to take care of several young children. This revealed that relationships between different branches of the family were being maintained not only across generations, but across distance, as both families had moved away from their place of origin into other counties. Tracing the cousin's family line verified that several generations of the original family had been correctly identified.

Researching extended family members who did not marry or have children can be particularly fruitful as they were more likely to leave wills naming a large number of relatives, and were perhaps more likely to acquire money or property than those with a family to support. The complexities of Scottish inheritance law mean that when someone without legitimate children died, their property, both moveable and heritable, may have been inherited by more distant relatives than we might expect, and any resulting records can reveal a lot of information about the family. These records may include wills and testaments, registers of retours, sasines and *Ultimus Haeres* records, as well as court records in cases where there was a dispute as to who should inherit.

In researching the extended family we may not only uncover new information about our direct ancestors, but also come across familiar names. A previously unknown witness to an ancestor's marriage may turn out to be a cousin or a brother-in-law. A neighbouring household recorded in a census may be a married daughter and her family. That frustrating family with names similar to our ancestor's, which we come across every time we search the census, may turn out to be closely related.

Even if research into the extended family does not solve a research problem, it reveals more about the world in which our ancestors lived, their relationships and community. Family relationships were far more important to our ancestors than they are to most of us today, and were maintained across time and space, even in an age when many people had limited levels of literacy. An ancestor's move to another part of Scotland, or even another country, may be explained by identifying relatives already living there and uncovering family networks. A move from a rural to an urban environment may have strengthened a family's ties, rather than loosened them.

Research into our ancestor's extended family can also be done in order to identify living relatives. Photographs, documents and family stories concerning our ancestors may have been passed down another branch of the family, and making contact with living relatives may be the only way of obtaining these. Many people also find it useful to connect with living relatives in order to collaborate on family history research, and such connections can develop into close friendships.

Another reason for researching the extended family may be to resolve the problem of multiple people in a parish with the same name, and to attempt to sort everyone in a parish with the same surname into family groups. Such research can easily spill over into neighbouring parishes and even further afield. When a surname is an unusual one, this may eventually lead to a one-name study: that is, a study of everyone in the county, country or world bearing the surname, often with the aim of connecting all branches back to their place of origin. It is worth checking whether such a study already exists, and seeking out guidance before embarking on one. The Guild of One-Name Studies (GOONS) (https://one-name.org) and The Surname Society (https://surname-society.org) are two organizations that support those carrying out research into particular surnames, and publish lists of current studies. A guide to carrying out a one-name study, *Seven Pillars of Wisdom: The Art of One-Name Studies*, was published by the GOONS in 2012.

Further discussion of the benefits and methods of researching an ancestor's extended family can be found in *Family History Nuts and Bolts: Problem-solving through Family Reconstitution Techniques* by Andrew Todd (*see* 'Further Reading'). This book is based primarily on English research, but contains much that is relevant to tracing ancestors in Scotland. The greater amount of family information found in Scottish statutory registers as compared to their English equivalent, and the fact that women's maiden names are routinely recorded, means that extended families can often be more reliably traced in Scotland than in England. In addition, the unrestricted access to statutory and other records when researching at a ScotlandsPeople centre means it is often possible to trace family members with common names, or those who left their local area, at relatively little cost. These factors make extended family research, or family reconstitution, a particularly useful technique for solving Scottish genealogy problems.

Solution: Researching the Community

In addition to researching an ancestor's extended family, another approach to solving a complex genealogy problem is to research the people our ancestors were associated with and the community they lived in. This is sometimes referred to as 'cluster research', or, using a term coined by genealogist Elizabeth Shown Mills, as researching an ancestor's FAN club – that is, their friends, associates and neighbours.

There are two main reasons why we may want to research our ancestor's wider community. First, the records created by people associated with our ancestors may contain information about our ancestors. Second, these people may in fact turn out to be related to our ancestors and part of their extended family.

The concept of the FAN club was primarily developed in connection with early American research. Frequently in the USA there are few records of births, marriages and deaths prior to the late nineteenth century, but relatively good collections of land, property and probate records (wills and so on). Women's maiden names are rarely recorded and so female lines are often hard to trace. This is quite different from Scotland, where birth, marriage and death records generally begin earlier, few people owned land or left a will, and women are frequently recorded under their maiden surnames in many types of record. As such, the techniques of FAN club research may not seem immediately applicable, but when faced with a particularly tough research problem it is worth casting our net wide as we look for evidence that may help to solve it.

There is clearly a lot of cross-over between the idea of the FAN club and that of researching the extended family. In fact the 'F' of FAN is sometimes considered to represent family, or friends and family, rather than just friends. The main difference is that rather than starting with a known relative and tracing them forwards, we look for people who may be related to our ancestor and trace them both backwards and forwards in time in order to identify the possible connection. These may include witnesses to baptisms and marriages, executors of wills and witnesses to any legal transactions, boarders and lodgers recorded in the same household in the census (not infrequently relatives or people having the same place of origin), neighbours, and others living in the same small community. Any names that appear more than once, or those who share a surname with a known relative, should be prioritized.

In academic historical studies, the term 'prosopography' is used to describe the study of a group of people sharing common characteristics in order to establish a collective biography. This may be a group of people associated with a prominent individual, or those connected to a particular organization, such as a church or religious group, or the community living in a particular location. Such a study often reveals previously unknown family relationships and the importance of family networks.

In genealogical and local history circles, the term 'one-place study' is used to describe research into a specific geographic location, such as a street, village, parish, or a suburb of a larger community, and the people who lived here. For genealogists, this often develops out of the realization that as we trace our family lines back through time and uncover new branches of our family, we are likely to be related to the majority of the people in the community, often in multiple ways. In order to untangle these relationships and better understand the community, it may be necessary to systematically research all the families and individuals who lived there. There are clear parallels to the idea of carrying out a one-name study, and some researchers undertake both.

The Society for One-Place Studies (www.one-place-studies.org) provides a number of resources and educational opportunities for those wishing to undertake a one-place study, and maintains a list of current studies. A separate One-Place Studies Directory (www.oneplacestudy.org) includes, at the time of writing, thirty-nine registered studies in Scotland. Name & Place (www.nameandplace.co.uk) is a data management and mapping app designed for managing the large amounts of data collected in one-place studies, one-name studies and similar projects, which may not fit conveniently into conventional family history software.

It is worth checking whether there are any one-place studies covering an ancestral homeland, as the researcher may already have gathered information on our ancestors. A good example of a Scottish one-place study is the Coldingham One-Place Study (https://coldinghamoneplacestudy.org), which focuses on a rural Berwickshire parish. The study's website includes transcripts and indexes of records, details of local families and a blog. Similar information may be found on websites dedicated to the history of specific parishes, towns or villages, although they may not necessarily be described as one-place studies.

Whether we describe it as cluster research, researching an ancestor's FAN club, prosopography, a one-place study, local history, or simply being nosey about an ancestor's neighbours, there is value in taking our research beyond our ancestor and their immediate family and placing them in the wider context of their community. In so doing, we may uncover new information about our ancestors, discover new relatives, and gain a better understanding of our ancestors' lives and motivations. We may not all have the time to undertake complex studies, but when faced with a challenging research problem, it may pay to spend time looking at the people with whom our ancestor was associated.

Solution: DNA Testing

DNA testing has become more and more popular over the last two decades, with family historians looking to solve genealogical brick walls and to connect with distant relatives. Since they first became available, genealogical DNA tests have become increasingly sophisticated as well as more affordable, and although they will certainly not solve every brick wall, they are something every genealogist should consider when faced with a tricky research problem.

DNA is the fastest developing area of genealogy, with the tests available, and the companies offering them, changing frequently. In this section I will be giving an extremely basic overview, aimed primarily at those with little knowledge of genealogical DNA testing. There are many resources available for those who want to learn more. *The Family Tree Guide to DNA Testing and Genetic Genealogy* by Blaine Bettinger (*see* Further Reading) and the website and wiki of the International Society of Genetic Genealogy (ISOGG) (https://isogg.org) both provide a wealth of information.

There are basically two components to genealogical DNA test results. The first is an analysis of the person's DNA to determine their ancestors' likely geographic origins and ethnicity, either anciently or within the last few centuries. The second is a comparison of the person's DNA with that of other people who have taken the same test, in order to determine probable genealogical relationships. It is the second component, identifying distant relatives, that is by far the most useful to the majority of family historians. However, there are times when ethnicity results may be helpful, particularly if they reveal something unexpected, and analysis of geographic origins is becoming increasingly sophisticated to the point where it may be possible to determine our ancestors' likely counties of origin, rather than just a country or region.

Identifying distant relatives through DNA can verify that

research carried out using traditional genealogical records is correct. For example, if another researcher and I have both traced our families back to the same pair of great-great-grandparents, and DNA results confirm we are likely third cousins, then we can both be fairly confident that those family lines have been correctly identified – provided, of course, that we do not share additional ancestors on other family lines.

More usefully, DNA testing may enable potential relationships to be verified and family lines to be extended. This could involve confirming a man named as the father of an illegitimate child was indeed the father, or that two people sharing a surname and living in the same village at the same time were related. In each case, descendants of those involved would need to be identified, and their DNA compared to determine if they are related, and how closely. Ideally, multiple descendants through different lines would be tested in each case, in order to get the most accurate results.

It should be stressed that DNA testing is not an alternative to traditional genealogical research, but rather an adjunct to it. It is fairly meaningless to discover that a stranger living on the other side of the world is a probable fourth cousin, unless we can determine on which family line the relationship lies, and who the common ancestor was, and then use that information to assist our research. The term 'genetic genealogy' describes the use of DNA testing alongside traditional genealogical records and techniques.

There are three main types of DNA test used by genealogists: autosomal DNA testing, Y-DNA testing and mitochondrial DNA testing.

Autosomal DNA Testing

Autosomal DNA tests detect DNA inherited from all family lines (technically the DNA inherited through autosomal chromosomes that we receive from both parents). These tests can determine relationships from parent/child and sibling level up to second cousin level with a high degree of accuracy. Due to the somewhat random way in which DNA is inherited, relationships beyond second cousin level may not always be accurately reflected in autosomal DNA, and although these tests can be used to identify more distant cousins, they are rarely useful for identifying relationships beyond fifth cousin level.

Autosomal DNA results generally indicate the amount of DNA shared between two individuals (expressed in centiMorgans, or cM) and their predicted relationship based on that amount. DNA results can be linked to an online family tree, which may allow the shared ancestor to be easily identified. Several companies offer autosomal DNA testing. At the time of writing the main providers are AncestryDNA, Family Tree DNA, Living DNA (sold through Findmypast and their own website), MyHeritage DNA and 23andMe, although the word 'autosomal' may not appear in the name of the test. In some cases it is possible to transfer the results received from one testing company, to compare with the database of another company. This has the advantage of allowing additional relatives to be identified without the expense of paying for a completely new test.

Y-DNA Testing

Y-DNA tests detect DNA on the Y chromosome only. This chromosome is inherited solely by males from their father, and so only men can take the test and only relationships on the direct male line will be detected. Y-DNA testing is of particular interest to genealogists because Y-DNA typically follows the line of an inherited surname. Y-DNA is passed from father to son virtually unchanged with only occasional mutations occurring. It is possible to compare the Y-DNA results of two males to see if they share a common male ancestor within a genealogical timeframe, and to use the number of mutations or differences between them to estimate how far back that common ancestor lived. Y-DNA tests can accurately identify more distant relationships than autosomal DNA testing, but only on the direct paternal line. This can be both an advantage, as it may be easier to identify the common ancestor, and a disadvantage, as it can only provide information on a small number of our many ancestors.

The main company offering Y-DNA testing is Family Tree DNA (www.familytreedna.com). The price of a test varies, depending on how many markers are tested. The more markers that are tested then the more accurately a relationship can be determined (in terms of the likely number of generations to the most recent common ancestor), but it is possible to begin with a cheaper test covering fewer markers and to upgrade at a later date. There are many surname projects organized around Y-DNA (some hosted by Family Tree DNA), which can help those sharing a surname to determine if they are related and, particularly in the case of unusual surnames, to pinpoint the origins of a particular name. These projects are typically run by enthusiastic and knowledgeable volunteers who can assist in the interpretation of results, so are well worth joining.

If a genealogical brick wall lies on the direct paternal line, it is worth taking a Y-DNA test and joining any relevant surname projects. Women cannot themselves take a Y-DNA test but can ask a male relative (such as a brother, father or paternal cousin) to take the test on their behalf. Y-DNA testing can be used to assist with research on any family line as long as the ancestor to whom the brick wall relates was male, he had at least one son, there is a continuous male line of descent down to the present, and a living male descendant can be identified who is willing to take the test.

Mitochondrial DNA Testing

Mitochondrial DNA (or mtDNA) tests detect DNA in the mitochondria only. This DNA is inherited by both males and females but comes exclusively from the mother. MtDNA testing is sometimes believed to be the female equivalent of Y-DNA testing, but this is inaccurate. MtDNA mutates less often than Y-DNA and is therefore far less useful for identifying relationships within a genealogical timeframe. The fact that surnames on the female line typically change with each generation also presents challenges in identifying a most recent common ancestor.

The main company offering mitochondrial DNA tests is Family Tree DNA. MtDNA testing does have some practical applications (for example, it played a significant part in identifying the remains of the English king, Richard III, whose remains were excavated in 2012), but the information obtained from such a test primarily relates to ancient origins and rarely helps to extend family lines. In my case, I have taken a full sequence mtDNA test and have matched with ten other people with identical results (as well as a further twenty-two who are more distantly related), but as none of those I have contacted has traced their maternal origins to Scotland, this is unlikely to help me with my maternal brick wall ancestor, who was born in Scotland in about 1802.

Choosing a DNA Test

When thinking about whether to take a genealogical DNA test, and which type of test to take, it is important to consider what we are hoping to find, and whether DNA is likely to provide an answer. Some people undertake genealogical DNA tests to help solve a particular mystery, but for many people it is simply curiosity about their origins or to see what they will find. DNA and genetic genealogy are very complex subjects, and often the only way to begin to understand them is to take a test and start working with our own results.

When considering which company to test with, the biggest factor is the size of their database, as the larger the database, the greater the chance of identifying and connecting with relatives. However, transferring DNA results from one company to another and uploading results to a third-party website such as GEDmatch (www.gedmatch.com) can enable additional matches to be identified.

As a general principle, it is best to start by testing the oldest generation on the relevant family line, as they will have inherited more DNA from the brick wall ancestor than younger generations, and may not be around for many more years to provide their DNA. It can often be useful to test multiple family members on each line, as each will have inherited slightly different (and different amounts) of DNA from a common ancestor. For example, if you are in the oldest living generation, you may want to ask any siblings and cousins to take tests as well.

A word of warning: DNA testing should not be undertaken lightly. Many people have been shocked to find a previously unknown close family member, such as a half-sibling, through a genealogical DNA test. Others have discovered that someone they believed to be closely related, such as a parent, was not in fact a blood relative. Anyone considering taking a DNA test, or asking a family member to test on their behalf, should make sure that they and the test taker are fully aware of the possible repercussions. Some people may also have concerns, not unreasonably, about the security of their DNA data, how it will be used, and who will have access to it. Again, this should be considered before undertaking a test or uploading results to a third-party website.

Finally, although genealogical DNA testing has the power to

break through longstanding brick walls and to provide information not found in paper records, it rarely provides simple answers. Anyone looking to solve a genealogy problem through DNA should expect to spend a long time getting to grips with the subject, sifting through DNA results and comparing shared matches, researching other people's family trees in order to identify a potential link, and dealing with the frustration of people who do not share information or who, having taken a DNA test, have little interest in their family tree. A lot of patience is needed when working with DNA, but the good news is that, as more and more people test, new discoveries may be just around the corner.

Solution: Seeking Guidance

The aim of this book is to introduce the reader to some different approaches to solving genealogical research problems, and to give a better understanding of the records used to overcome Scottish brick walls. It is, of course, not possible to cover all situations or all sources in a book of this length. When a research problem is proving particularly tough to crack, then it may be time to seek help.

One of the best things we can do to improve our skills and knowledge as family historians is to educate ourselves. This may be by reading genealogy books, magazines, journals and online resources, attending talks and classes, or undertaking a more in-depth course of study. To get the most out of the records we use, we need to understand their background and why they were created. We should also seek to put our ancestors and their lives in context. Reading should not be restricted to resources aimed specifically at family historians, but should also include social history, local history and population studies.

Keeping up with what genealogy records are available online can be difficult, as new records are added almost every week. The major genealogy websites all publish regular newsletters by email, and The GENES Blog (http://britishgenes.blogspot.com), maintained by genealogist Chris Paton, is an excellent way of keeping up with news in the world of family history, in Scotland and beyond.

Family history classes, often aimed at beginners, are run by many libraries, local authorities and adult education providers, as well as by private individuals. More advanced online courses on a variety of specific genealogy-related topics are run by Pharos

Teaching & Tutoring Limited (www.pharostutors.com), which is based in England and has a British focus, and the National Institute for Genealogical Studies (www.genealogicalstudies.com), which is based in Canada and runs courses on research in countries world-wide, as well as on research skills and methodology. Both offer certificate programmes, but these are not accredited.

Two universities offering advanced genealogy courses are the University of Strathclyde in Glasgow (www.strath.ac.uk/studywithus/centreforlifelonglearning/genealogy), which provides short courses (online and on campus) and a postgraduate course leading to a certificate, diploma or MSc, and the University of Dundee (www.dundee.ac.uk/cais/programmes/familylocalhistory), which provides modular courses that can be taken individually or together to gain a certificate, diploma or MSc. Both study programmes are accredited by the universities and are well respected within the genealogical field. The Institute of Heraldic and Genealogical Studies (www.ihgs.ac.uk), based in Kent in England, also offers a recognized qualification in genealogy but with less focus on Scottish records. These courses are particularly relevant to those seeking careers in genealogy, but are also undertaken by many people who simply wish to improve their knowledge and skills in order better to research their own families.

Regular talks on a variety of topics are offered by family and local history societies and at family history fairs and conferences. Webinars (seminars broadcast over the internet) relating to family history are offered by many different organizations connected to genealogy, but the main provider is Legacy Family Tree Webinars (https://familytreewebinars.com). Many archives in Scotland put on occasional talks and events, including the National Records of Scotland (*see* www.nrscotland.gov.uk/research/visit-us/events-talks-and-visits), which also has a regular podcast (https://blog.nrscotland.gov.uk/category/podcast). The National Archives in Kew, London (https://media.nationalarchives.gov.uk) also hosts talks and webinars relating to its records, some of which may be relevant to Scottish researchers.

The main genealogy event that takes place in Scotland is the annual conference and family history fair of the Scottish Association of Family History Societies (www.safhs.org.uk), which is hosted by a different society each year. Genealogy conferences and events in other parts of the UK often include talks on Scottish research and are attended by Scottish family history societies. The Scottish Local History Forum (www.slhf.org) and the Scottish Records Association (www.scottishrecordsassociation.org) both put on annual conferences, which, while not aimed specifically at family historians, often cover topics relevant to genealogy, and highlight lesser known records. Some Scottish universities host occasional conferences that are open to the public and may be relevant to those undertaking genealogical research.

Educational opportunities are one motivation for joining a family history society, but access to the society's library and resources, and the opportunity of meeting like-minded individuals, are also good reasons. Seeking a second opinion is often a good way to tackle a genealogy brick wall, both because in explaining we may realize something we had missed previously, and because someone else will often challenge the assumptions we have made and suggest new ways of looking at a problem. There are numerous family history Facebook groups, online forums and message boards that can be used to seek help on a particular genealogy problem, and these are also good ways of connecting to other family historians researching the same ancestors.

Finally, when a genealogy problem is proving particularly hard to solve, or we are unable to access the records we need, then it may be worth hiring a professional genealogist. Professional researchers not only trace whole family trees for clients, but also undertake problem-solving research and carry out look-ups of records in archives. Research is typically charged on an hourly basis, and additional charges may apply for obtaining copies, accessing archives (mainly the ScotlandsPeople Centre, which charges a daily fee) and travel. Most professional genealogists will carry out an initial

The Association of Scottish Genealogists and Researchers in Archives (ASGRA) is the main accrediting body for professional genealogists working in Scotland.

assessment of a research problem for free, in order to provide a quote for research, but will charge for more in-depth analysis.

The Association of Scottish Genealogists and Researchers in Archives (ASGRA) (www.asgra.co.uk) is the main accrediting body for professional genealogists in Scotland. Members are required to prove their competence by submission of a portfolio of work, and to adhere to a code of practice. The Register of Qualified Genealogists (RQG) (www.qualifiedgenealogists.org), open to those with a recognized qualification in genealogy, and the Association of Professional Genealogists (APG) (www.apgen.org), open to anyone who agrees to the code of ethics and professional practices, are two international organizations with members in Scotland. All organizations maintain a list of members on their websites.

When thinking of hiring a professional genealogist, some of the things to consider are the researcher's location, experience, qualifications, membership of professional bodies and relevant specialist skills (such as an expert knowledge of DNA or the ability to read Latin or old forms of handwriting). It is a good idea to send an initial enquiry to several different genealogists in order to determine their availability and to get a brief assessment and quote for research.

Although not every family history problem can be solved, seeking the help of others is a good way of ensuring that all avenues have been explored, and that we are not overlooking a possible solution to our genealogy brick wall.

Further Reading

Scottish Genealogy Guides

Adolph, Anthony *Tracing Your Scottish Family History* (Collins, London, 2008).

Baptie, Diane *Parish Registers in the Kirk Session Records of the Church of Scotland (with pre-1855 censuses, lists of head of families etc)* (The Scottish Association of Family History Societies, Aberdeen, 2004).

Baptie, Diane *Registers of the Secession Churches in Scotland* (The Scottish Association of Family History Societies, Aberdeen, 2000).

Bigwood, Rosemary *The Scottish Family Tree Detective: Tracing Your Ancestors in Scotland* (Manchester University Press, Manchester, 2006).

Clarke, Tristram *Tracing Your Scottish Ancestors: A Guide to Ancestry Research in the National Records of Scotland and ScotlandsPeople*, 6th edition (Birlinn, Edinburgh, 2011).

Durie, Bruce *Scottish Genealogy*, 4th edition (The History Press, Stroud, 2017).

Durie, Bruce *Understanding Documents for Genealogy & Local History* (The History Press, Stroud, 2013).

Irvine, Sherry *Scottish Ancestry: Research Methods for Family Historians*, 2nd edition (Ancestry Publishing, Provo, 2003).

Mackenzie, Graeme M. *Genealogy in the Gaidhealtachd: Clan and Family History in the Highlands of Scotland* (Highland Family History Society, Inverness, 2013).

Nicoll, Andrew R. *Scottish Catholic Family History: A family historian's guide to Catholic Parish Registers and Cemetery Records for Scotland and the Bishopric of the Forces* (The Aquhorties Press, Edinburgh, 2011).

Nisbet, Kenneth A. M. *The Register of Corrected Entries and its use for family history* (The Scottish Genealogy Society, Edinburgh, 2013).

Paton, Chris *Discover Scottish Church Records*, 2nd edition (Unlock the Past, St Agnes, 2016).

Paton, Chris *Discover Scottish Civil Registration Records* (Unlock the Past, St Agnes, 2013).

Paton, Chris *Discover Scottish Land Records*, 2nd edition (Unlock the Past, St Agnes, 2017).

Paton, Chris *Down and Out in Scotland: Researching Ancestral Crisis* (Unlock the Past, St Agnes, 2015).

Sinclair, Cecil *Jock Tamson's Bairns: A History of the Records of the General Register Office for Scotland* (General Register Office for Scotland, Edinburgh, 2000).

Steel, D. J. *Sources for Scottish Genealogy and Family History* (Phillimore, Chichester, 1970).

Genealogical Methodology and Research Techniques

Bettinger, Blaine T. *The Family Tree Guide to DNA Testing and Genetic Genealogy*, 2nd edition (Family Tree Books, Blue Ash, 2019).

Board for Certification of Genealogists *Genealogy Standards*, 2nd edition (Ancestry, Nashville, 2019).

Jones, Thomas W. *Mastering Genealogical Documentation* (National Genealogical Society, Arlington, 2017).

Jones, Thomas W. *Mastering Genealogical Proof* (National Genealogical Society, Arlington, 2013).

Litton, Pauline M. *Pitfalls and Possibilities in Family History Research* (Swansong Publications, Harrogate, 2010).

Macdonald, Ian G. *Referencing for Genealogists: Sources and Citation* (The History Press, Stroud, 2018).

Merriman, Brenda Dougall *Genealogical Standards of Evidence: A guide for family historians* (Ontario Genealogical Society, Toronto, 2010).

Meyerink, Kory L., Tolman, Tristan L., Gulbrandsen, Linda K. *Becoming an Excellent Genealogist: Essays on professional research skills* (ICAPGEN, Salt Lake City, 2012).

Mills, Elizabeth Shown *Evidence Explained: Citing history sources from artifacts to cyberspace*, 3rd edition (Genealogical Publishing Company, Baltimore, 2017).

Mills, Elizabeth Shown *Professional Genealogy: Preparation, practice & standards*, 2nd edition (Genealogical Publishing Company, Baltimore, 2018).

Morgan, George G., Smith, Drew *Advanced Genealogy Research Techniques* (McGraw-Hill Education, New York, 2014).

Osborn, Helen *Genealogy: Essential Research Methods* (Robert Hale, London, 2012).

Rose, Christine *Genealogical Proof Standard: Building a solid case*, 4th edition (CR Publications, San Jose, 2014).

Todd, Andrew *Family History Nuts and Bolts: Problem-solving through family reconstitution techniques*, 3rd edition (Andrew Todd, Bury, 2015).

Wintrip, John *Tracing Your Pre-Victorian Ancestors: A Guide to Research Methods for Family Historians* (Pen & Sword Family History, Barnsley, 2017).

Notes

Chapter 4
1. Board for Certification of Genealogists, 'Ethics and Standards', *Board for Certification of Genealogists* (https://bcgcertification.org/ethics/ethics-standards : accessed 1 May 2019).

Chapter 5
1. Board for Certification of Genealogists, 'Ethics and Standards', *Board for Certification of Genealogists* (https://bcgcertification.org/ethics/ethics-standards : accessed 1 May 2019).
2. Board for Certification of Genealogists, *Genealogy Standards: 50th Anniversary Edition*, Board for Certification of Genealogists, Washington DC, 2014, pp. 74–75.

Chapter 8
1. Emma and Graham Maxwell, 'Learning Zone – Finding Paternity Cases in Sheriff Court Records', Scottish Indexes (www.scottishindexes.com/learningcourt.aspx#q3 : accessed 1 May 2019).

Index